A GENTLE

Spirit

❧ ❦ ❧

Journal

*P*resented to:

_____

*B*y: _____

_____

_____

*O*n: _____

_____

_____

A GENTLE

Spirit

Journal

BARBOUR
PUBLISHING

Published by Barbour Publishing, Inc., P.O. Box 719, Uhrichsville, Ohio 44683
www.barbourbooks.com

Our mission is to publish and distribute inspirational products offering exceptional value and biblical encouragement to the masses.

ecpa Member of the
Evangelical Christian
Publishers Association

Printed in Belgium.
4 3 2 1

The unfading beauty of a gentle and quiet spirit,
which is of great worth in God's sight.
1 PETER 3:4 NIV

In our lives, God's tender qualities should be growing day by day, week by week, and year after year. When we cultivate a godly, gentle spirit in our own lives, we bring grace and pleasure to those around us.

How do we help that beautiful spirit grow in our lives? First, our spirit must be watered by the Living Water—Jesus Christ and His Word. Daily meditation on the Scriptures, along with the challenging and encouraging insights of other Christians, will create a gentle spirit ready to provide comfort and shelter for those who enter our lives.

This daily devotional journal provides the elements for your growth: helpful Scripture passages and Godly wisdom from dozens of well-known, Spirit-led Christian women, such as

- Joni Eareckson Tada
- Ruth Bell Graham
- Amy Carmichael
- Elisabeth Elliot
- Hannah Whitall Smith
- Corrie ten Boom
- and many more.

Plus, there's ample space for you to record your own spiritual insights, praise notes, and prayer requests.

As you reflect upon the verses, draw encouragement from each devotion, and keep a journal of your experiences, you'll be developing *A Gentle Spirit* of your own.

A Blessed New Year

Mrs. Charles E. Cowman

But the land. . .is a land. . .which the Lord thy God careth for: the eyes of the Lord thy God are always upon it, from the beginning of the year even unto the end of the year.
DEUTERONOMY 11:11–12

Today, dear friends, we stand upon the verge of the unknown. There lies before us the new year and we are going forth to possess it. Who can tell what we shall find? What new experiences, what changes shall come, what new needs shall arise? But here is the cheering, comforting, gladdening message from our Heavenly Father, "The Lord thy God careth for it." "His eyes are upon it away to the ending of the year."

If He be the Source of our mercies, they can never fail us. No heat, no drought can parch that river, "the streams whereof make glad the city of God."

The land is a land of hills and valleys. It is not all smooth nor all downhill. If life were all one dead level, the dull sameness would oppress us; we want the hills and the valleys. The hills collect the rain for a hundred fruitful valleys. Ah, so it is with us! It is the hill difficulty that drives us to the throne of grace and brings down the shower of blessing; the hills, the bleak hills of life that we wonder at and perhaps grumble at, bring down the showers.

We cannot tell what loss and sorrow and trial are doing. Trust only. The Father comes near to take our hand and lead us on our way today. It shall be a good, a blessed new year!

SETTING GOALS FOR THIS YEAR
Cheryl Biehl

Don't Forget Yourself—Often we as Christian women get so involved in meeting the needs of others that we forget to take time to refresh ourselves. If you have flown on a commercial airliner lately, you will recognize the speech that the flight attendants recite just before takeoff. It goes something like this, "In the event of a loss of cabin pressure, an oxygen mask will automatically be lowered. If you are sitting beside a child, first secure your own mask before applying the child's."

Why would they advise you to do that? Are they promoting an "adults over children" philosophy? Hardly. They realize that unless you as the adult are getting the oxygen you need, you'll be of no help to the child, and you will both perish.

Jesus, filled with absolute love and compassion, went to the mountains to spend time with His Father in prayer, to renew His weary body and soul. When the crowd pressed in upon Him, He suggested to the disciples that they all get away from the crowd and go to the mountains alone.

Are you getting enough "oxygen" in your life to be of maximum benefit to those around you? It is not a selfish gesture to set goals allowing you to "refill your cup." Just as an empty teakettle will crack or melt as the heat under it is turned up, so you also will break as the heat of life is turned on "high" when your "cup"—your emotional and spiritual life—is dry.

Wilt thou be made whole?
JOHN 5:6

TOTAL CONSECRATION
Elizabeth Prentiss

Saying, Father, if thou be willing, remove this cup from me: nevertheless not my will, but thine, be done.
LUKE 22:42

If you ask how you may know that you have truly consecrated yourself to Him, I reply, observe every indication of His will concerning you, no matter how trivial, and see whether you at once close in with that will. Lay down this principle as law—God does nothing arbitrarily. If He takes away your health, for instance, it is because He has some reason for doing so; and this is true of everything you value; and if you have real faith in Him, you will not insist on knowing the reason. If you find, in the course of daily events, that your self-consecration revolts at His will—do not be discouraged, but fly to your Savior and stay in His presence till you obtain the spirit in which He cried in His hour of anguish, "Father, if thou be willing, remove this cup from me: nevertheless not my will, but thine, be done" (Luke 22:42). Every time you do this it willl be easier to do it; every such consent to suffer will bring you nearer and nearer to Him; and in this nearness to Him you will find such peace, such blessed, sweet peace as will make your life infinitely happy, no matter what may be its mere outside conditions. Just think of the honor and the joy of having your will one with the Divine will and so becoming changed into Christ's image from glory to glory!

Keeping God's Attention
Joni Eareckson Tada

There's nothing more frustrating than trying to keep someone's attention. I went through that game as an immature teenager, desperately seeking to impress the captain of the football team from our neighboring high school.

I vividly recall those ridiculous mental gymnastics I went through. . .trying to dress right. . .combing my hair just so. . .working so hard to impress. I felt that his fondness for me waxed and waned according to how clever and cool my overtures were.

What a disaster that relationship was! Through it all, however, I learned something that's stayed with me through the years.

I'm reminded of that frenzied high school relationship every time I catch myself trying to keep God's attention.

Oh, please don't make the mistake of supposing God's interest in you waxes and wanes in response to your spiritual temperature. God's love doesn't vacillate according to how many victories you have over sin or how many times you use His name in your prayers. His love for you goes deeper than mere affection or surface infatuation.

Let the matchless love of God sweep away your doubt and fears. You already have God's attention and you will never lose it.

I will lift up my eyes to the mountains;
From whence shall my help come?
My help comes from the Lord.
Psalm 121:1–2 NASB

STAND BY YOUR GOD
Emilie Barnes

I will call on him as long as I live.
PSALM 116:2 NIV

God greatly desires to spend time alone with you. After all, you are His child (John 1:12; Galatians 3:26). He created you, He loves you, and He gave His only Son for your salvation. Your heavenly Father wants to know you, and He wants you to know Him. The Creator of the universe wants to meet with you alone daily. How can you say no to such an opportunity?

So make it your priority to spend time with God daily. There's not a single right time or one correct place. The only requirement for a right time with God is your willing heart. Your meeting time with God will vary according to the season of your life and the schedules you are juggling. Jesus often slipped away to be alone in prayer (Luke 5:16), but even His prayer times varied. He prayed in the morning and late at night, on a hill and in the upper room (Mark 1:35; Luke 22:45; Matthew 14:23; John 17).

Time with your heavenly Father is never wasted. If you spend time alone with God in the morning, you'll start your day refreshed and ready for whatever comes your way. If you spend time alone with Him in the evening, you'll go to sleep relaxed, resting in His care and ready for a new day to serve Him.

GOD CARES
Hannah Whitall Smith

Who is the best cared for in every household? Is it not the little children? And does not the least of all, the helpless baby, receive the largest share? We all know that the baby toils not, neither does it spin; and yet it is fed, and clothed, and loved, and rejoiced in more tenderly than the hardest worker of them all.

This life of faith, then, consists in just this —being a child in the Father's house. And when this is said, enough is said to transform every weary, burdened life into one of blessedness and rest.

Let the ways of childish confidence and freedom from care, which so please you and win your heart in your own little ones, teach you what should be your ways with God; and, leaving yourself in His hands, learn to be literally "careful for nothing"; and you shall find it to be a fact that the peace of God, which passeth all understanding, shall keep (as with a garrison) your heart and mind through Christ Jesus.

Therefore take no thought, saying, What shall we eat? or, What shall we drink? or, Wherewithal shall we be clothed? . . .for your heavenly Father knoweth that ye have need of all these things.
MATTHEW 6:31–32

Any Woman Can
Marabel Morgan

But godliness with contentment is great gain.
1 Timothy 6:6

Last year, while driving home from vacation in the mountains, we covered four states in one day. That night as we put the weary little travelers to bed, Charlie said, "Michelle, today we had breakfast in North Carolina, lunch in South Carolina, dinner in Georgia, and we're sleeping in Florida tonight. Which state did you like the best?"

Michelle reached up from her bed to hug her daddy. She smiled happily, obviously enjoying the moment, and piped, "Daddy, I like whatever state I'm in right now the best!"

Saint Paul said it this way almost two thousand years earlier, "I have learned in whatsoever state I am, therewith to be content."

And that's the secret of life: living contentedly in the moment—not dwelling on the good ol' days, nor wistfully dreaming about what might be, but living now, today.

Any woman who is filled with joy, His joy, can also tell her Heavenly Father, "I like whatever state I'm in right now the best." And not just tell Him—but shout for joy!

HE ALLOWS ME TO HUNGER

Amy Carmichael

The son found himself in a barren place.

His Father said, "In this place I will give you the peace you are longing for. Here I will give you spiritual food that will nourish you. You are always with Me—no matter what the circumstances—and all that I have is yours."

Then the Father, with great gentleness, drew the son to himself. Quietly, He said, "I am the One who allowed you to come into these humbling circumstances, and allowed you to hunger. I did this so that I might feed you with manna—My bread from heaven! Only in this way could I help you to know that you cannot live by bread alone, but by every word that proceeds from My mouth."

The son said, "Give me this bread always!"

And when he grew thirsty he learned to cry, "The light of Your face is my life!"

Later still, the son wondered why one like himself, who is so richly fed and cared for at times, should at other times feel so poor and needy and thirsty.

His Father replied: "Can someone who has never discovered rivers of these living waters flowing on barren heights—can he ever lead his thirsty friend to those rivers?

"Can someone who has never seen burning sands in the wilderness turn into a refreshing pool—can he speak in praise of My marvels, or My power?"

O God, thou art my God;
early will I seek thee:
...my flesh longeth for thee in a dry and
thirsty land, where no water is.
PSALM 63:1

TRAVELING LIGHT
Ruth Bell Graham

Wherefore seeing we also are compassed about with so great a cloud of witnesses, let us lay aside every weight, and the sin which doth so easily beset us, and let us run with patience the race that is set before us.
HEBREWS 12:1

"I'd like to see you gain a few pounds," I said to our tall, lanky son, Ned.

"No way," he replied. "It would be just that much more to haul up the rock." Rock climbing had become his latest enthusiasm.

I watched him chin himself, using only his fingertips curled over the top of the kitchen door frame. Then he repeated the process using only one arm. Finger grips are important in rock climbing and so is keeping in shape. And I was learning as I listened and watched.

The Christian life is a climb. For Christians, keeping in shape spiritually and traveling light are important. To keep in shape spiritually, we need spiritual nourishment and exercise.

The definition of traveling light may vary from one individual to another. But most of us need to trim off some excess weight. We have too many social involvements, an overabundance of good but unnecessary meetings. We are on more boards than one person can adequately or usefully serve. Remember the caution: "Beware of the barrenness of a busy life."

It is up to us to keep in shape and travel light.

Our "God" Reigns

Jane Hansen

Whatever we set our desire on will rule us. You have only to look around you to see how women, even Christian women, set their desire on men. They have turned to them to gain their approval, to be found acceptable, worthy, admired, and chosen. As a result, they are ruled by them. They take their cues for life from them. Whatever women believe the male race wants, they will try to become.

Women's obsession with thinness, anorexia, bulimia, and the fitness craze all have their roots in this desire. (Men, on the other hand, seem far more interested in impressing other men.)

In spite of living in this "age of enlightenment," with few exceptions, a woman still gets married having unspoken expectations that the man she has chosen will meet all her needs for security, purpose, worth, and identity.

What a colossal disappointment when this self-centered dream is not realized, when the woman's husband is not able to "fill up the grand canyon" inside of her. Ultimately hurt and disillusionment will set in, followed by anger and then bitterness. A great chasm will develop between them. It will take divine surgery to rectify it.

Unto the woman he said, I will greatly multiply thy sorrow and thy conception; in sorrow thou shalt bring forth children; and thy desire shall be to thy husband, and he shall rule over thee.

Genesis 3:16

CHERISH THE GIFTS
Lyn Klug

I will offer to thee the sacrifice of thanksgiving, and will call upon the name of the Lord.
PSALM 116:17

Along with most of my friends, I used to complain about grocery shopping. "Everything is so expensive! Hauling those heavy bags through the snowdrifts is such a hassle. Why does the store have to be jammed just when I go?"

Then we went as missionaries to Madagascar for four years. The shelves in the tiny stores were often empty. The market provided good food but few choices. When we returned to the United States, I pushed my cart down the supermarket aisles with a grateful heart.

Although my perspective was radically altered, I was aware that it wasn't my job to start telling everybody how grateful they should be. But I do know that for me, gratitude has made my life much happier. It has also acted as a magnet for blessings: The more grateful I've become, the more I've had to be grateful for.

An ancient prayer expresses this thanks: "Blessed art Thou, O Lord, who givest us this bread and this wine, the fruit of man's labor." This prayer recognizes that our blessings depend in part on our labor: We shape ourselves, our world, and our history. But all, finally, is a gift of God, and we ourselves are the finest of His gifts. Our gift to God is our gratitude.

A New and Living Way

Sheila Walsh

One of the greatest steps in discovering who we are is discovering who God is. God is a God of justice and righteousness without guilt or sin. He is pure and holy in a way we cannot begin to grasp with our human understanding.

After Moses had been with God, his face glowed. When Isaiah saw the Lord high and lifted up, he was overwhelmed with the reality of his own sinfulness. Mortal man cannot stand before this awesome God. But in the heart of God a way had been prepared from the beginning. Desiring a relationship with His people, God gave a gift. Through Christ's sacrifice on the cross blood has spilled on the doorframe of the hearts of every man and woman who trust in Him.

The New Testament writer of Hebrews reminds us of who we are and where we stand. He exhorts us to draw near to God with a sincere heart in full assurance of faith, because we have been washed clean by the blood of God's perfect Lamb. Who we are in ourselves is not enough, but who we are in Christ is everything.

Therefore, brothers, since we have confidence to enter the Most Holy Place by the blood of Jesus, by a new and living way opened for us through the curtain, that is, his body, and since we have a great priest over the house of God, let us draw near to God with a sincere heart in full assurance of faith, having our hearts sprinkled to cleanse us from a guilty conscience and having our bodies washed with pure water.

HEBREWS 10:19–22 NIV

January 13
CONFLICTS CHANGED TO BLESSINGS
Mrs. Charles E. Cowman

In all these things we are more than conquerors through him who loved us.
ROMANS 8:37 NIV

How can we be "more than conquerors"? We can get out of the conflict a spiritual discipline that will greatly strengthen our faith and establish our spiritual character. Temptation is necessary to settle and confirm us in the spiritual life. It is like the fire which burns in the colors of mineral painting, or like winds that cause the mighty cedars of the mountain to strike more deeply into the soil. Our spiritual conflicts are among our choicest blessings, and our great adversary is used to train us for his ultimate defeat. The ancient Phrygians had a legend that every time they conquered an enemy the victor absorbed the physical strength of his victim and added so much more to his own strength and valor. It is possible thus not only to defeat our enemy, but to capture him and make him fight in our ranks. Just as the wise sailor can use a head wind to carry him forward by tacking and taking advantage of its impelling force, so it is possible for us in our spiritual life through the victorious grace of God to turn to account the things that seem most unfriendly and unfavorable and to be able to say continually, "The things that were against me have happened to the furtherance of the Gospel."

—*Life More Abundantly*

STRETCHING
Jill Briscoe

Reaching leads to stretching. Getting involved expands you as a person. "I could never go to Asia as a missionary," expostulated a single woman. "But couldn't you help us find eating utensils and blankets for a refugee family from Laos that will be coming to Milwaukee tonight?" she was asked. "Sure, I can do that," she responded. Guess what happened. Starting where she was, she reached out and touched a need. And those needy Asian people reached right back and touched her. Two years later she is being stretched beyond her wildest dreams as she proposes to go to Hong Kong with a relief organization! It's a pretty stretching thing to fill needs—real needs. You discover a God-given capacity for caring concern that leads to loving actions you would not have believed you were capable of.

We have to start out by reaching what we can reach and touching what we can touch. Then look out. The choice will come! "Will you be stretched?" God will ask, and we will have to answer that question.

A yes may take us to the uttermost parts of the earth, or it may involve us in the great need on our doorstep—only God knows where it will all end up—but the choice is ours.

Then saith he to the man, Stretch forth thine hand. And he stretched it forth; and it was restored whole, like as the other.
MATTHEW 12:13

JOY, JOY, JOY, FOREVER
Luci Swindoll

Now when a man works, his wages are not credited to him as a gift, but as an obligation. However, to the man who does not work but trusts God who justifies the wicked, his faith is credited as righteousness.
ROMANS 4:4–5 NIV

Here's what I hate: You open up your mailbox, and crammed in with the mail you want to receive is a huge envelope with your name in big letters on the front. Luci Swindoll, You have just won one million dollars. Congratulations! ! ! Inside the envelope is the postscript in little tiny letters: if your number is called. Oh, boy! And your immediate thought is, you can't get something for nothing.

Then, you pick up your New Testament and turn to Ephesians 2:8–9 (NIV), and there in bold print you read these comforting words: "For it is by grace you have been saved, through faith—and this not from yourselves, it is the gift of God—not by works, so that no one can boast."

The wonderful thing about the Christian life is that we all enter freely. No matter who you are, where you're from, what your experience has been, Jesus Christ invites you to freely come. No conditions. No restrictions. No small print. No waiting. About this, you can be certain.

GOD IS INGENIOUS
Ruth Bell Graham

I was chatting with a clerk in a jewelry store.

"Here's one you'll never believe," she said, leaning across the display case. I leaned forward to listen.

A regular customer had not dropped by for some time. When she finally came in, she was on crutches.

"What on earth. . . ?" the clerk wanted to know.

And the friend told her. They were having some landscaping done in the yard with a bulldozer. She had slipped somehow and had broken her leg. While recuperating, she found herself alone in the house one Sunday, propped up in bed. Lonely and bored, she decided to call a friend and found the phone was just out of reach. She made several swipes at it but only succeeded in knocking it off the cradle, onto the floor, out of reach. And from the receiver came "The Hour of Decision."

She wasn't interested in listening to "The Hour of Decision," but she couldn't reach the phone, so she had no choice. She was a captive audience.

"And would you know!" the clerk said to me. "She came in here to tell me she had asked the Lord Jesus into her life and heart and to make her a new person. And I, who've known her a long time, could tell that He had!"

To say that God is ingenious is an understatement!

Now unto him that is able to do exceeding abundantly above all that we ask or think, according to the power that worketh in us.
EPHESIANS 3:20

AMAZING GRACE
Mary W. Tileston

I have blotted out, as a thick cloud, thy transgressions, and, as a cloud, thy sins: return unto me; for I have redeemed thee.
ISAIAH 44:22

He will turn again, he will have compassion upon us; he will subdue our iniquities; and thou wilt cast all their sins into the depths of the sea.
Micah 7:19

If my shut eyes should dare their lids to part, I know how they must quail beneath the blaze Of Thy love's greatness. No; I dare not raise One prayer, to look aloft, lest it should gaze On such forgiveness as would break my heart.
—H. S. Sutton

O Lord God gracious and merciful, give us, I entreat Thee, a humble trust in Thy mercy, and suffer not our heart to fail us. Though our sins be seven, though our sins be seventy times seven, though our sins be more in number than the hairs of our head, yet give us grace in loving penitence to cast ourselves down into the depth of Thy compassion. Let us fall into the hand of the Lord. Amen.
—Christina G. Rossetti

A Calming Faith
Patsy Clairmont

I wonder if David had to be led because he was naturally drawn to the excitement of the rushing waters? It certainly is that way with us. Left to our own agendas, we either run at breakneck speeds right past the pasture, enamored with our frenzied pace, or sit in parched desert. The Shepherd, who understands our naiveté and our humanity (not to mention our sheeplike stupidity), intervenes on our behalf to guide us with a strong hand onto a quiet path and into a calmer faith.

Yep, a calmer faith. That's the quiet place within us where we don't get whiplash every time life tosses us a curve. Where we don't revolt when His plan and ours conflict. Where we relax in the midst of an answerless season. Where we accept (and expect) deserts in our spiritual journey as surely as we do joy. Where we are not intimidated or persuaded by other people's agendas but moved only by Him. Where we weep in repentance, sleep in peace, live in fullness, and sing of victory.

We all know what it feels like to be at rest. And we all long for that more sane lifestyle rather than being overwhelmed. But are we willing to leave the press long enough to lie down in the soothing green pastures and to be led by the still waters of His provision? That, my friend, is not resort living but restored living. And each of us needs it.

He maketh me to lie down in green pastures: he leadeth me beside the still waters.
Psalm 23:2

IF YOU WANT JOY
Hannah Whitall Smith

Thou wilt shew me the path of life: in thy presence is fulness of joy; at thy right hand there are pleasures for evermore.
PSALM 16:11

"In thy presence is fulness of joy," and fullness of joy is nowhere else. Just as the simple presence of the mother makes the child's joy, so does the simple fact of God's presence with us make our joy. The mother may not make a single promise to the child, nor explain any of her plans or purposes, but she is, and that is enough for the child. The child rejoices in the mother; not in her promises, but in herself. And to the child, there is behind all that changes and can change the one unchangeable joy of mother's existence. While the mother lives, the child will be cared for; and the child knows this, instinctively, if not intelligently, and rejoices in knowing it. And to the children of God as well, there is behind all that changes and can change the one unchangeable joy that God is. And while He is, His children will be cared for, and they ought to know it and rejoice in it, as instinctively and far more intelligently than the child of human parents. For what else can God do, being what He is? Neglect, indifference, forgetfulness, ignorance are all impossible to Him. He knows everything, He cares about everything, He can manage everything, and He loves us! Surely this is enough for a "fullness of joy" beyond the power of words to express, no matter what else may be missed besides.

WHEN THE ANSWERS DON'T COME

Stormie Omartian

If your child has made poor choices, don't berate yourself and stop praying. Keep communication lines open with your child, continue interceding for him or her, and declare God's Word. Instead of giving up, resolve to be even more committed to prayer. Pray with other believers. Stand strong and say, "I've only begun to fight," keeping in mind that your part of the fight is to pray. God actually fights the battle. Remember, too, that your fight is not with your child, it's with the Devil. He is your enemy, not your child. Stand strong in prayer until you see a breakthrough in your child's life.

One of the most encouraging Scriptures I have read with regard to such perseverance is when David said, "I have pursued my enemies and overtaken them; neither did I turn back again till they were destroyed. I have wounded them, so that they could not rise; they have fallen under my feet. For You have armed me with strength for the battle." (Psalm 18:37–39 NKJV). He didn't stop until the job was done, and neither should we.

Above all, don't let any disappointment over unanswered prayer cause you to stop praying.

Arise, cry out in the night: in the beginning of the watches pour out thine heart like water before the face of the Lord: lift up thy hands toward him for the life of thy young children, that faint for hunger in the top of every street.

LAMENTATIONS 2:19

THE DESIRES OF MY HEART

Elisabeth Elliot

Wherefore I beseech you that ye would confirm your love toward him. For to this end also did I write, that I might know the proof of you, whether ye be obedient in all things.
2 CORINTHIANS 2:8–9

I had been praying for something I wanted very badly. It seemed a good thing to have, a thing that would make life even more pleasant than it is, and would not in any way hinder my work. God did not give it to me. Why? I do not know all of His reasons, of course. The God who orchestrates the universe has a good many things to consider that have not occurred to me, and it is well that I leave them to Him. But one thing I do understand: He offers me holiness at the price of relinquishing my own will.

"Do you honestly want to know Me?" He asks. I answer yes. "Then do what I say," He replies. "Do it when you understand it; do it when you don't understand it. Take what I give you; be willing not to have what I do not give you. The very relinquishment of this thing that you so urgently desire is a true demonstration of the sincerity of your lifelong prayer: Thy will be done."

So instead of hammering on heaven's door for something which it is now quite clear God does not want me to have, I make my desire an offering. The longed-for thing is material for sacrifice. Here, Lord, it's Yours.

He will, I believe, accept the offering. He will transform it into something redemptive.

INTO THE CLOSET
Linda Dillow

The best time to build your relationship with Christ through prayer and Bible study is during a devotional time. I know how many of us really struggle with this! We manage to carve out the time for maybe a week, and then we give up. I think one reason for our failure is that we set our goals too high: "I'll be up every morning at six!" I've tried this and by the third day I'm so exhausted that I can't even find the Bible, let alone study it!

God wants us to be realistic. Evaluate your life and set a goal that is realistic for you. Don't feel guilty if you read about some dear saint who gets up at five every morning to pray for her nine children! A devotional time is not a law but a relationship. Your relationship with the Savior will be different from everyone else's.

You may have a set time for it, or it may happen several times during the day. You may take five minutes, or five hours, as the Spirit and circumstances lead, but vital personal contact with the Lord is necessary in order that you may have a constant inpouring of the life of Christ and that He may channel it through you to others.

Wherefore the law was our schoolmaster to bring us unto Christ, that we might be justified by faith. But after that faith is come, we are no longer under a schoolmaster. For ye are all the children of God by faith in Christ Jesus.
GALATIANS 3:24–26

WHAT IS BEAUTY?
Ruth Youngdahl Nelson

Your beauty should not come from out-
ward adornment, such as braided hair
and the wearing of gold jewelry and fine
clothes. Instead, it should be that of your
inner self, the unfading beauty of a gentle
and quiet spirit, which is of great worth
in God's sight.
1 PETER 3:3–4 NIV

What qualities make a person beautiful? Are you more concerned about what your body is going to wear than how your soul is clothed? Do you hang the giant share of your salary on your back?

The Lord made his standard of judgment very clear when he said to Samuel, "The Lord does not see as man sees: men judge by appearances but the Lord judges by the heart."

When I was leading Bible studies at the women's reformatory of Washington, D.C., I was startled the first time I heard the women sing this song as they returned to their cells:

> *Let the beauty of Jesus be seen in me,*
> *All His wondrous passion and purity;*
> *O Thou Savior divine, All my nature refine*
> *Till the beauty of Jesus be seen in me.*
> —Albert Osborn

Scripture puts it this way: "The King's daughter is all glorious within!"

You'll Never, Ever, Be Alone Again

Kay Arthur

One of the enemy's tactics is to isolate people, to cut them off from fellowship with one another, to convince them that they are alone and that no one really cares about them. (I believe that's one reason families are under such attack today.)

One of our basic needs is to belong—to be part of something beyond ourselves. Ephesians 2:11–22 tells you that now that you have been saved by grace, you are in Christ Jesus. You belong. You'll never be alone again. If you are a Gentile like most of the citizens of Ephesus were, you have been brought near to God through the blood of Jesus Christ. God is not some distant, supreme sovereign you can never communicate with. Jesus has brought you into peace with the Father, and, now through the gift of the indwelling Holy Spirit, you have access to Him. You are no longer an alien or a stranger; you are part of God's forever family. You've come home. You are in Christ, and He's in you. You're His dwelling place.

You'll never, ever, be alone again. You are bone of His bone—an indispensable member of His body.

Behold, I have graven thee upon the palms of my hands; thy walls are continually before me.
ISAIAH 49:16

OUR THOUGHTS
Hannah Whitall Smith

Whatsoever things are true, whatsoever things are honest, whatsoever things are just, whatsoever things are pure, whatsoever things are lovely, whatsoever things are of good report; if there be any virtue, and if there be any praise, think on these things.
PHILIPPIANS 4:8

The things we think on are the things that feed our souls. If we think on pure and lovely things, we shall grow pure and lovely like them; and the converse is equally true. Very few people at all realize this, and consequently there is a great deal of carelessness, even with careful people, in regard to their thoughts. They guard their words and actions with the utmost care, but their thoughts, which, after all, are the very spring and root of everything in character and life, they neglect entirely. So long as it is not put into spoken words, it seems of no consequence at all what goes on within the mind. No one hears or knows, and therefore they imagine that the vagrant thoughts that come and go as they list do no harm. Such persons are very careless as to the food offered to their thoughts and accept haphazardly, without discrimination, anything that comes.

Every thought we think, in every hour we live, must be, not necessarily about Christ, but it must be the thought Christ would think were He placed in our circumstances and subject to our conditions. This is what it means really to feed on Him and be nourished by the true bread of life that cometh down from heaven.

LIFT UP YOUR HEARTS
Twila Paris with Robert Webber

I not only love to worship, I love to watch people who are worshipping. The psalmist says, "It is fitting for the upright to praise him" (Psalm 33:1 NIV). I read that verse one day, and as I meditated on it, it struck me with its truth. Sometimes when I'm in a group of people who are worshipping, particularly if they are singing with their eyes closed and their hands raised, I'll take a peek at them. And I'm always impressed by how beautiful they look. People seem to glow and radiate when they worship.

I remember my grandmother used to say to me, "Oh, Twila, blue is so becoming on you." She meant that I look good in blue. This idea also pertains to worship. Praise is becoming to the upright. When we worship, praise produces a radiant beauty on our faces because of our contact with God.

More important, in worship we are especially beautiful to God. Worship is a sweet aroma to God. For me, the fact that God loves our worship is a very challenging and motivating truth. In my song, "This Celebration," I have tried to capture how our worship is pleasing to God. The song names who God is and praises God for God's person. Of course, this is what we do when we gather together to worship: We lift up our hearts in response to God.

Sing for joy in the Lord,
O you righteous ones;
praise is becoming to the upright.
PSALM 33:1 NASB

THE OPEN DOOR
Lilian Whiting

Where there is no vision, the people perish: but he that keepeth the law, happy is he.
PROVERBS 29:18

There is something about hesitation and reconsiderations that is curiously fatal to successful achievement. Good fortune is in going on—not in going back. The parable of Lot's wife, who turned into a pillar of salt because she looked back, is by no means inapplicable to the life of today. Let one on whom the vision has shone look backward instead of forward, and he becomes paralyzed and immovable. He has invoked inimical influences. He is impeded by the shallows and the miseries. He has withdrawn himself from all the heavenly forces that lead him on. The fidelity to the vision is the vital motor. It gives that exhilaration of energy which makes possible the impossible.

Each recurring New Year is an open door. However arbitrary are the divisions of time, there is inspiration and exaltation in standing on the threshold of an untried year, with its fresh pages awaiting record. It is, again, the era of possibilities. The imaginative faculty of the soul must, indeed, be "fed with objects immense and eternal." Life stretches before one in its diviner unity—even in the wholeness of the life that is and that which is to come. There is not one set of motives and purposes to be applied to this life, and another set to that which awaits us. This is the spiritual world, here and now. It is well to drop the old that one may seize the new.

GETTING CLEAN

Evelyn Christenson

After we become Christians we commit sins. What do we do with them? Do we live with them? The answer is that we get rid of them. God gives Christians the formula through John, "If we confess our sins, he is faithful and just to forgive us our sins, and to cleanse us from all unrighteousness" (1 John 1:9). This is written to Christians and tells us how we may be cleansed and ready for an effectual intercessory prayer life.

Even little sins can muddy up our communication system. We try to get through to God and there's something in the way. It may be an attitude, a spoken word. God wants these things cleared up. He doesn't want anything between Him and us. If there is, it's our fault, not His, when His ears are closed to our prayers.

This, then, is the first prerequisite—nothing between God and ourselves when we approach intercessory prayer.

If we confess our sins, he is faithful and just to forgive us our sins, and to cleanse us from all unrighteousness.
1 JOHN 1:9

RELEASE OUR BURDENS TO JESUS

Betty Malz

Cast thy burden upon the Lord, and he shall sustain thee: he shall never suffer the righteous to be moved.
PSALM 55:22

We should release our burdens to Jesus along the way.

Jesus said, "Come to Me and I will give you rest for the journey." You will find that the cares don't disappear, but the burden of the cares and work will.

I have found that burdened spirits often lead to physical problems, notably, for some reason, with digestion. I don't think our systems can work properly if we try to carry a load too heavy for them. We need to learn to rest in our Father's ability to take our abilities and bring us security. After His rest, we can perform our responsibilities and continue the journey toward the goal.

Not all burdens have to be big, important ones in order to weigh us down. Small frustrations affect us, too. If you don't think little things mean a lot, try pulling your thumb out of a noose of Scotch tape or tripping on a shoestring while you're jogging! It's not usually the big mountains in our paths that make life hard, it's the small pebbles in our shoes.

It will help us on the journey to remember that even Jesus "for the joy set before Him endured the cross, despising the shame" (Hebrews 12:2 NASB). He remained faithful during His walk through the earth because He knew heaven was waiting for Him at the end of His journey here.

YOU ARE WOMAN. . .GOD'S WOMAN

Mary Hollingsworth

Do you ever get tired of being a woman? Do you sometimes wish you could just be somebody else for a few days?

When you see mountains of laundry, a list of errands as long as your arm, and a stack of paperwork that needed attention yesterday, would you just like to scream and run out the door? "Here, honey, you be the woman this week. Bye!"

And then you would escape to the freedom of no responsibilities—lunch with a friend at the new bistro down the street and a few hours surfing the Net just for fun at www.calm. Peace. Quiet. No phones. No beepers. No problems to solve. No PMS. No stress. Ahhhh. . . Still, think about it. After a few days with no responsibilities, wouldn't you miss the chubby little arms that wrap tightly around your neck? Wouldn't you miss the secret smile that your husband has just for you? Wouldn't you miss your boss's open admiration for the excellent work you do? Wouldn't you miss being "the one in charge" of the community's Fourth of July event? Wouldn't you miss just being you—an amazing, creative, needed, capable, blessed, and loved woman?

Celebrate! You are God's extended feminine presence in this world. Without you, the world would have an incomplete picture of God. You are woman. . .God's woman.

Being enriched in every thing to all bountifulness, which causeth through us thanksgiving to God.
2 CORINTHIANS 9:11

FEAR OF THE LORD
Jo Berry

The fear of the Lord is the beginning of wisdom, and the knowledge of the Holy One is understanding.
PROVERBS 9:10 NASB

Proverbs 9:10 says, "The fear of the Lord is the beginning of wisdom." So, if we want to be wise enough to properly interpret God's practicalities for good living, first we need to fear Him.

What is fear of the Lord? When I was a child, I thought it meant I was to be afraid of Him, which made it very difficult for me to relate to Him, because it is hard to get close to someone who frightens you. "Fear" was an awesome-sounding word that conjured up images of hell fire and brimstone.

Fortunately, that isn't what the word "fear" means. It means to respect, revere, and worship. A wise person holds God in high esteem and worships Him in both attitude and action.

Solomon recorded that, "The fear of the Lord is to hate evil" (Proverbs 8:13 NASB). God is holy, separate, and set apart from all that is sinful and evil. He hates sin. Therefore, if we fear Him, we incorporate His value system into our lives and hate everything that is wicked, immoral, or iniquitous.

FAILURES: ANGELS IN DISGUISE
Ellyn Sanna

Sooner or later, motherhood brings us to this point where we can no longer rely on our own strength and ability. We don't like the dark cloud that surrounds us, for letting go of our self-illusions is painful. Without them, the world is terrifying. We struggle to find some other comfort, some other source of light. When we fail to find anything to restore our sense of security, we sink into depression. But if we wait quietly, "naked," as Catherine of Genoa says, "without any emotional clothing," God finds us even here. Our only hope is to surrender ourselves to His love. When we do, the light that bursts upon us is brighter than any we have yet seen.

The Old Testament tells the story of Jacob wrestling in the night with an angel. The angel first wounds him, then both blesses him and gives him a new identity.

As mothers, perhaps we can look at our failures as God's angels. In the midst of our darkest nights, God radically touches us, wounding our pride and self-confidence. But He does not leave us there. Instead, when we at last abandon our comforting images, when we allow ourselves to drop naked into His hands, He blesses both us and our children. And then He calls us by our new names, the names that will make us whole, and leads us into the light.

And Jacob was left alone; and there wrestled a man with him until the breaking of the day. . . .And he blessed him there.
GENESIS 32:24, 29

SEARCH FOR TREASURES IN THE DARKNESS
Gail MacDonald

Blessed be the God and Father of our Lord Jesus Christ, the Father of mercies and God of all comfort; who comforts us in all our affliction so that we may be able to comfort those who are in any affliction with the comfort with which we ourselves are comforted by God.
2 CORINTHIANS 1:3–4 NASB

One of the greatest get-acquainted exercises we enjoy using when we entertain new friends in our home is to ask a series of questions for each guest to answer in turn. The final question asks, "At what point in your life have you felt closest to God?"

I am impressed that the majority of the answers focus on a moment when life seemed its darkest, when one passed through some sort of anguish or calamity. It was in that terrible time, many say, that God touched their lives with a promise, a personal insight, a sense of supernatural strength or courage. It's not unusual for someone to add that it was an encounter never to be forgotten and for which one will always be deeply thankful. What does that mean?

It probably means that our intimacy with the Lord reaches some of its highest peaks when we are at points of greatest personal need.

That is exactly why we have to train ourselves to a new view of pain if we are to keep climbing. We must discipline our minds to the notion that all pain can be a school in which one can learn.

TENSIONS
Jean Fleming

Living the Christian life means living with tensions. Real Christianity cannot be lived by principles alone; real Christianity is lived in relationship to God. Even if we strive to live under God's direction and to make Him our audience, unplanned situations arise, complicating the neat pattern.

Jesus experienced interruptions, too. A leper approached Jesus, fell at His feet, and begged, "Lord, if you are willing, you can make me clean" (Luke 5:12 NIV).

In this situation Jesus was willing. He touched the man, said, "Be clean," and healed him. Whatever Jesus was doing at the time, He interrupted to redirect His energies.

In my study of the Gospels, I find that Jesus did not respond positively to every interruption or suggested use of His time. How, then, did He determine which requests to fill, which to postpone, which to neglect completely?

Jesus chose often to pull away from the demands of life to pray, to refresh Himself, to get clear direction, and perhaps to avoid further interruptions. That may be the reason that despite frequent interruptions, He moved through life decisively and without irritation.

And it came to pass, when he was in a certain city, behold a man full of leprosy: who seeing Jesus fell on his face, and besought him, saying, Lord, if thou wilt, thou canst make me clean.
LUKE 5:12

AGAINST THE CURRENT
Hannah Whitall Smith

So likewise, whosoever he be of you that forsaketh not all that he hath, he cannot be my disciple.
LUKE 14:33

You must remember that our God has all knowledge and all wisdom, and that therefore it is very possible He may guide you into paths wherein He knows great blessings are awaiting you, but which, to the shortsighted human eyes around you, seem sure to result in confusion and loss. You must recognize the fact that God's thoughts are not as man's thoughts, nor His ways as man's ways; and that He alone, who knows the end of things from the beginning, can judge of what the results of any course of action may be. You must, therefore, realize that His very love for you may perhaps lead you to run counter to the loving wishes of even your dearest friends. You must learn, from Luke 14:26–33 and similar passages, that in order to be a disciple and follower of your Lord, you may perhaps be called upon to forsake inwardly all that you have, even father or mother, or brother or sister, or husband or wife, or it may be your own life also. Unless the possibility of this is clearly recognized, you will be very likely to get into difficulty, because it often happens that the child of God who enters upon this life of obedience is sooner or later led into paths that meet with the disapproval of those he best loves; and unless he is prepared for this and can trust the Lord through it all, he will scarcely know what to do.

SAMPLE DAY OF A PASSIONATE HEART

Gwen Shamblin

The Bible says to "pray without ceasing." Therefore, every hour is spent talking to Him, looking for His opinion, asking Him to rule my day, asking Him to find my keys, thanking Him for something that just happened, coming to Him for comfort from pain in the heart, and looking to Him for His attention or approval and leading any way I can get it. After all, He is the CEO of this world.

He opens my eyes daily to new information from His Word or from life that confirms He is the source of everything. So I love Him as a teacher, a comforter, a constant companion, a trustworthy leader, a husband/defender when I am slandered or falsely accused, an hour-by-hour boss, the source of life, and the love of my life to whom I can confidently give my love and passion.

It means everything to have His love returned to me. I long to see His face. I have no doubt that I will know Him.

When I think about how involved He is in my life, I sometimes want to cry. Obviously, there are hurting and sad times, too; but even in the low points, my heart always runs to the Father and finds peace only in Him.

"Love the Lord your God with all your heart and with all your soul and with all your mind and with all your strength."
MARK 12:30 NIV

THE LIFTING POWER OF PRAISE

Amy Carmichael

*I will bless the Lord at all times;
his praise shall continually
be in my mouth.*
PSALM 34:1

My sight faileth me for waiting so long upon my God."

So long? "Ye have need of patience, that, after ye have done the will of God, ye might receive the promise" (Hebrews 10:36).

"It is written, 'As for me, when I am poor and in heaviness: Thy help, O God, shall lift me up.' I waited to be lifted up."

"But it is also written, 'As for me, I will patiently abide always: and will praise Thee more and more.' Hast thou tried the lifting power of praise?"

"My sight faileth me because of trouble. How can I praise when I cannot see?"

"We can sing when we cannot see; even a little bird will sing in the grey dusk before the dawn breaks."

"My soul melteth away for every heaviness. Who can sing when his soul melteth?"

"Then there is only one way for thee. Thou must look steadfastly through the visible till the invisible opens to thee."

"Live by the grace of thy Lord in the spirit of these words for in them is the quality of eternity. Say of the will of thy God, 'I am content to do it.' Go through that depressing dimness without yielding to depression and without depressing others. All the resources of heaven are at thy command to enable thee to do this."

WORKING WONDERS
Mrs. Charles E. Cowman

God with power and might at His disposal yet works in this wise. His quiet performances are indirect, deep, serene, and seemingly slow and have to be explored to be understood and appreciated. He quietly and confidently moves, working wonders day after day. In every experience, at work, in church, and in society, it sometimes appears as though God were being defeated, and the movements of His grace and providence were failures, and that all His plans were reversed, flowing upstream in the opposite direction from the ocean of blessings. One has but to look up and cast his gaze out from the shore of frustrating encirclements of the present and consider the entire stream of God's purpose among His people in order to see that He is continually winning the battle in quiet, circuitous ways.

God works through individuals, conquering some heart, and through that heart He pours His purpose like a mighty river. The Lord makes His conquests by keeping His saints in utter dependence upon Him, making them live by faith. There is to be none of self in His program, but all of Christ instead.

—M. Taylor

Not by might, nor by power, but by my spirit, saith the Lord.
ZECHARIAH 4:6

VALLEY OF THE SHADOW

Marabel Morgan

Verily, verily, I say unto you, If a man keep my saying, he shall never see death.
JOHN 8:51

My baby was dead. How could this happen to me? Why? Why? Bitterness welled up toward God. I felt as if He had slapped me hard across the face. But immediately I "heard" that familiar quiet voice down in my soul. "Marabel, don't you know that I love you?"

I whispered through my tears, "Jesus, I know You love me. I will trust You." I felt the loss just as keenly as before, and yet now I knew God had control of the situation. Though I continued to cry, I felt peace.

Then an odd thing occurred. I was aware that deep down inside my innermost being, joy was pushing up through me. The only way I know to describe it is a bubble of joy. I was shocked. How could I feel joy when my baby had just died? It was barbaric, and yet the joy kept coming until I thought I would burst out laughing—for joy.

Suddenly I realized. Jesus was showing me once again that He alone is my Source of joy. He can take an awful situation, a hopeless situation such as death, and bring joy in the midst.

God was able to turn sorrow into joy. Heaven became much more real because I had someone there waiting for me. My little girl is there, and we're all anxious to be there with her. The certainty of that family reunion when we step over into eternity takes the sting out of death.

REPENTANCE
Helen Roseveare

The Holy Spirit can make us want to be holy, revealing what things are sin (conviction) and giving us a hatred for these things and a great desire to be rid of them (true repentance). As I grew up, I had only hated the consequence of sin; as I sought to go on with God, however, I had a growing hatred of sin itself.

Then an urge began to grow in me to put right all I could of the wrong that I had inflicted on others—restoring what was stolen, confessing to what was untrue, forgiving where I had borne a grudge, loving where before I had felt hatred. This "putting right" of wrongs committed can never merit or earn forgiveness, any more than we can gain salvation by good works; but it is the outcome of a contrite heart. As the Holy Spirit convinces us of sin and grants to us godly repentance, so also He brings to birth in us this desire to make restitution.

There are times when there is nothing we can do to repair the damage we have caused, yet it is still true that a "broken and contrite heart, O God, you will not despise" (Psalm 51:17 NIV). His forgiveness is dependent only on the finished work at Calvary. Spirit-given repentance only brings about my personal identification with the redeeming grace of God—nothing else.

The sacrifices of God are a broken spirit:
a broken and a contrite heart,
O God, thou wilt not despise.
PSALM 51:17

February 10

LET MY ROOTS SINK DEEP
Anita Corrine Donihue

The Lord is my shepherd;
I shall not want. He maketh
me to lie down in green pastures:
he leadeth me beside the still waters.
PSALM 23:1–2

Lord, I sit alone by a quiet stream. My thoughts turn to Psalm 23. The waters gently ripple by. Trees gracefully bow their branches and teasingly rustle their leaves in the pure, fresh breeze. A bird lilts a beckoning call to its mate. A distant falcon pierces the air with its echoing screech.

Peace. Thank You, Lord. But what about when I must return to the hustle and bustle? How can I be prepared?

I look at the trees; their roots sink deep by the stream. In the same way, let my roots sink deep into You. Let me feed on Your Word. As we commune in prayer, let me drink from the living water of Your spirit. Let me jump in and be bathed by Your cleansing power. I will rely on You rather than things that are shallow and temporary. I can't depend on my own abilities and strength, but I'm confident in Your care and direction.

I will take special notice of the good things when they come. I will fix my mind on what is pure and lovely and upright.

When the heat and winds of life's storms come, I will not fear; I know You are near. I will not worry but keep on producing a life that is a blessing for You and others.

Let me take time often to come drink from Your quiet stream. I thank You for it.

Joy Beads
Barbara Johnson

When I bought some new makeup recently, the salesgirl told me that if I dropped a little BB in the bottle and shook it before each use, the makeup wouldn't get thick and gooey. Not having BBs on hand at home, I told my husband I needed a BB.

A day or so later, Bill came in smiling broadly and looking like he had something wonderful to show me. What he had was a huge plastic carton. Inside were 10,000—that's ten thousand!—BBs.

"BBs only come in tens of thousands," he told me proudly. I smiled appreciatively and took one.

Recently I saw that plastic carton full of 9,999 BBs lying on a shelf in our garage. I got to thinking how much it's like the riches of God in Christ Jesus. We have more than enough. Much, much more than we'll ever be able to use: forgiveness, grace, mercy, love.

We have abundant resources just waiting for us to use! God's riches are beyond anything we could ask or ever dare to imagine! If my life gets gooey and stale, I have no excuse.

God has given us good measure, pressed down, shaken together, and running over. But most of the time, we need only one BB.

Now to him who is able to do immeasurably more than all we ask or imagine, according to his power that is at work within us.
EPHESIANS 3:20 NIV

HOW'S YOUR SOUL-ESTEEM?
Mary Hollingsworth

I can do all things through Christ which strengtheneth me.
PHILIPPIANS 4:13

For several years I've been searching for the right term to replace self-esteem in our vocabulary. I want a word that says, "I can do all things through Christ who gives me the strength." I want a word that says, "God knows that we are made of dust," but "our bodies are the temples of the living God." I want a word that shows that even though we are flawed and weak as human beings, we are strong and capable because the Holy Spirit lives and works through us. I believe that term is soul-esteem.

Our selves may be imperfect, incapable, and weak, but our souls are perfect, capable, and strong through brotherhood with Christ. Our souls are the image of the living God.

When I look in the mirror, I still see self, but I also look beyond self to my soul. I can finally look the real me in the eye and smile. I'm reminded of 1 Corinthians 13:12 (NIV): "Now we see but a poor reflection as in a mirror; then we shall see face to face."

So, the next time you look at yourself in the mirror, look past the poor reflection and into the eyes of your soul. And hear Jesus whisper in your ear, "How's your soul-esteem?"

DEALING WITH BITTERNESS
Martha Peace

Bitterness grows when you "take into account a wrong suffered" (1 Corinthians 13:5 NASB). In other words, as you think about the bad, hurtful things your husband has done, you are feeding bitterness. You may be like so many women who sit and brood over what has happened or lie awake at night replaying it over and over in their minds.

If you dwell on what your husband has done, your emotional pain will greatly intensify, becoming seemingly unbearable at times. You will begin to feel like the prophet Jeremiah.

"And my soul has been rejected from peace; I have forgotten happiness. So I say, 'My strength has perished, And so has my hope from the Lord' " (Lamentations 3:17–18 NASB).

At this point, your husband will be unable to do anything right in your eyes even if he is trying.

Your bitter feelings will improve as you clear your conscience and then begin to make second-mile investments. A second-mile investment is doing something extra special for your husband. The Lord Jesus put it this way, "And whoever shall force you to go one mile, go with him two" (Matthew 5:41 NASB).

And my soul has been rejected from peace; I have forgotten happiness. So I say, "My strength has perished, And so has my hope from the Lord."
LAMENTATIONS 3:17–18 NASB

LOVE IS EXTRAVAGANT

Joni Eareckson Tada

But some were indignantly remarking to one another, "Why has this perfume been wasted?"
MARK 14:4 NASB

I had just finished packing my bags. Ken had packed his things, too, including his rods and reels. We had to be away from one another for several days, I on a speaking engagement and he on a fishing trip. We knew we'd really miss each other.

Wheeling through the living room that afternoon, I was surprised to see a beautiful red rose in a bud vase on the table. That Ken! So thoughtful. Moving into the bedroom to gather my things, I spotted another rose in a bud vase on my dresser. I was shocked. I glanced in the bathroom and to my amazement yet another red rose—a fresh, delicate, little bud—adorned the counter.

By the third rose, I have to admit my excitement turned sour. It wasn't that I didn't appreciate his gifts, it was just that. . .well, both he and I were ready to leave. Nobody but our miniature schnauzer Scruffy would be in the house to enjoy such lovely flowers. Expensive flowers, at that, I pointed out.

Ken gave me a big hug that melted my protests.

As I went off on that speaking trip, I thought of the quality that marks the ministry of love. And that is its sheer extravagance. Love is extravagant in the price it is willing to pay, the time it is willing to give, the hardships it is willing to endure, and the strength it is willing to spend.

And that is what God has given to us.

LEARNING TO SAY NO
Colleen Townsend Evans

If you are caught, as I was, in the barrenness of a too-busy life, look to Jesus. The gospels reveal Him as a man who had learned the importance of saying no. There were times when He said no to the demands and requests made of Him, times when He said no to the crowd and got away to be alone with His disciples, times when He left the disciples to be alone with His Father.

Jesus looked to God for guidance and direction for His days. He listened for that one voice over the roar of all other voices calling for His time and energy and help. And so must we. For Jesus that meant that sometimes He did not get to those close to Him in their time of need. He did not get to his cousin John in prison before Herod took off his head, nor did He heed the call of Mary and Martha to be with Lazarus as he lay ill and dying. (And can't you just see Martha pacing the floor and muttering, "Where's that Jesus when we need Him most?")

And so we, like Jesus, must listen for that one voice above every other, and let God guide us in every aspect of our daily lives. But that will mean learning the important lesson of being willing to say no to people in order to say yes to God.

Martha, Martha, thou art careful and troubled about many things: But one thing is needful; and Mary hath chosen that good part, which shall not be taken away from her.
LUKE 10:41–42

MEEK AND LOWLY
Hannah Whitall Smith

Take my yoke upon you, and learn of me;
for I am meek and lowly in heart:
and ye shall find rest unto your souls.
MATTHEW 11:29

What can be more delicious to a delicate self-love than to hear itself applauded for having none! The truly meek and lowly heart does not want to talk about its me at all, either for good or evil. It wants to forget its very existence. As Fenelon writes, it says to this me, "I do not know you, and am not interested in you. You are a stranger to me, and I do not care what happens to you nor how you are treated." If people slight you or treat you with contempt or neglect, the meek and lowly heart accepts all as its rightful portion. True humility makes us love to be treated, both by God and man, as we feel our imperfections really deserve; and, instead of resenting such treatment, we welcome it and are thankful for it. I remember being greatly struck by a saying of Madame Guyon's that she had learned to give thanks for every mortification that befell her because she had found mortifications so helpful in putting self to death. It is undoubtedly true, as another old saint says, that there is no way of attaining the grace of humility but by the way of humiliations. Humiliations are the medicine that the Great Physician generally administers to cure the spiritual dropsy caused by feeding the soul on continual thoughts of me.

SORROW'S SCARS
Mrs. Charles E. Cowman

Sorrow came to you yesterday and emptied your home. Your first impulse is to give up and sit down in despair amid the wrecks of your hopes. But you dare not do it. You are in the line of battle and the crisis is at hand. . . .

Weeping inconsolably beside a grave can never give back love's banished treasure, nor can any blessing come out of such sadness. Yet there is a humanizing and fertilizing influence in sorrow that has been rightly accepted and cheerfully borne. Indeed, they are poor who have never suffered and have none of sorrow's marks upon them. The joy set before us should shine upon our grief as the sun shines through the clouds, glorifying them. God has so ordered that in pressing on in duty, we shall find the truest, richest comfort for ourselves. Sitting down to brood over our sorrows, the darkness deepens about us and creeps into our heart, and our strength changes to weakness. But, if we turn away from the gloom, and take up the tasks and duties to which God calls us, the light will come again, and we shall grow stronger.

—J. R. Miller

Now after the death of Moses the servant of the Lord it came to pass, that the Lord spake unto Joshua the son of Nun, Moses' minister, saying, Moses my servant is dead; now therefore arise, go over this Jordan, thou, and all this people.
JOSHUA 1:1–2

February 18

BEGINNING TO SINK

Amy Carmichael

But when he saw the wind, he was afraid and, beginning to sink, cried out, "Lord, save me!" Immediately Jesus reached out his hand and caught him.

MATTHEW 14:30–31 NIV

"And immediately Jesus stretched forth his hand, and caught him" (Matthew 14:31). How many seconds lie between a man's beginning to sin and his sinning? A single second or less, I suppose. How swift, then, was the movement of love! And as He was, so He is.

"Must we wait till the evening to be forgiven?" a child once asked.

Do we not all know that feeling? It seems too good to be true that at the very moment of the sorrowful consciousness of sin, or even the shadow of sin, there is pardon, cleansing, the light of His blessed countenance. But nothing can ever be too good to be true with such a Lord as ours.

The use of the word "immediately" has been life and peace to me of late.

They were troubled, those poor men in the boat. "And immediately He talked with them" (verse 27). How needless their trouble seems to us as we read. Does ours seem as needless to the heavenly watchers?

We can find honey in this honeycomb: "Immediately Jesus stretched forth his hand, and caught him."

THE PRINCIPLES OF TRUST

Jo Berry

Wisdom would be unnecessary if life were lived in black and white and consisted of a simple system of dos and don'ts, yeses and nos, with no gray or Technicolor areas. Then we would face only rudimentary choices of right and wrong.

But life isn't like that. Life is complex, and obedience is not as simple as doing one thing or its exact opposite. God's rules and principles may be clear-cut, but acting them out is not. Without His guidance, we would be lost in a maze of indecision and confusion.

Most of us are not aware of how many hundreds, perhaps thousands, of choices we must make every day. Decisions made in a moment can affect a lifetime.

Without God's superintendence, our lives would be so complicated and we would be going in so many different directions that we could not function. He has one perfect thing He wants each of us doing at any given time, and if we are trusting Him, He can reveal His will to us. Placing confidence in the Lord simplifies life and makes it immensely easier. "He who trusts in his own heart is a fool, but he who walks wisely will be delivered" (Proverbs 28:26 NASB) from confusing complexities.

Trust in the Lord with all thine heart;
and lean not unto thine own understanding.
In all thy ways acknowledge him,
and he shall direct thy paths.
PROVERBS 3:5–6

SHINING HIS LIGHT

Karen Mains

God is light, and in him is no darkness at all. If we say that we have fellowship with him, and walk in darkness, we lie, and do not the truth: But if we walk in the light, as he is in the light, we have fellowship one with another, and the blood of Jesus Christ his Son cleanseth us from all sin.
1 JOHN 1:5–7

What unseen incandescence rolls back the gloom when I open this my door and stand silhouetted against the warmth inside! Often I've wondered at the soft glow that fills the rooms only on hospitality nights. Is it the candles? Or is it a presence totally apart from myself, the true Light that enlightens everyone? What shadows are actually dispelled when we share Him with those in bondage, those with broken spirits, those strangers in prisons of their own making?

When I open my door, do I send rays to dispel the night? When I open my eyes and see the suffering, is my soul flooded with an unknown shimmering because I am seeing now with the eyes of Christ? When I open my heart, does it shine somewhere like the flame in a cavern, one living pinprick warding off the monstrous cavity of nothingness? Am I a light in the world and is this house set on a hill for the city to see? I hope so. I fervently hope so.

INFECTIOUS FEAR
Amy Carmichael

Have you ever thought how infectious fear can be? It spreads from one person to another more quickly and certainly than any of the fevers we know so well.

You can refuse the spirit of fear, which never comes to us from God. (And if He does not send it to us, who does?) Instead, open your heart wide to the spirit of "power and love and a calm and well-balanced mind and discipline and self-control" (2 Timothy 1:7 Amplified). Because fear is so infectious, let us, for the sake of others and ourselves, refuse it.

Thank God! Courage is as "infectious" as discouragement. Haven't you often felt the cheer and strength that seem to flow from a person whose mind is fixed and firm on God? I have.

And I have been thinking of another, a greater reason for refusing the spirit of fear.

When we are downhearted or fearful or weak, we are saying to everybody (by the way we look and by our timidity, if not by our words), "After all, the Lord can't be absolutely trusted."

We have a Savior who has never once failed us. He never will fail us. He has loved and led and guarded us all these years.

Look to Him now, and pray from the barren bedrock of your heart, if that is the "ground" you are standing on—"Lord, give me courage!"

If God is for us, who can be against us?
ROMANS 8:31 NIV

WASTELANDS

Elisabeth Elliot

And he said, The Lord is my rock, and my fortress, and my deliverer.
2 SAMUEL 22:2

There are dry, fruitless, lonely places in each of our lives, where we seem to travel alone, sometimes feeling as though we must surely have lost the way. What am I doing here? How did this happen? Lord, get me out of this!

He does not get us out. Not when we ask for it, at any rate, because it was He all along who brought us to this place. He has been here before—it is not wilderness to Him, and He walks with us. There are things to be seen and learned in these apparent wastelands which cannot be seen and learned in the "city"—in places of comfort, convenience, and company.

God does not intend to make it no longer a wasteland. He intends rather to keep us—to hold us with His strength, to sustain us with His sure words—in a place where there is nothing else we can count on.

"God did not guide them by the road towards the Philistines, although that was the shortest. . .God made them go round by way of the wilderness towards the Red Sea" (Exodus 13:17–18 NEB).

Imagine what Israel and all of us who worship Israel's God would have missed if they had gone by the short route—the thrilling story of the deliverance from Egypt's chariots when the sea was rolled back. Let's not ask for shortcuts. Let's keep alert for the wonders our Guide will show us in the wilderness.

A SACRED CHAMBER
Lilian Whiting

Let us make a little chamber.
2 KINGS 4:10

"If I could uncover the hearts of you who are listening to me this morning," said Phillips Brooks in a memorable sermon, "I should find in almost all—perhaps in all—of them a sacred chamber where burns the bright memory of some loftiest moment, some supreme experience, which is your transfiguration time. Once on a certain morning you felt the glory of living, and the misery of life has never since that been able quite to take possession of your soul. Once for a few days you knew the delight of a perfect friendship. Once you saw for an inspirited instant the idea of your profession blaze out of the midst of its dull drudgery. Once, just for a glorious moment, you saw the very truth, and believed it, without the shadow of a cloud. And so the question comes—What do they mean?"

On the personal answer to that question depends all the success or the failure; all the nobleness or the unworthiness of the individual life. No one can estimate too ardently, or too earnestly, the spiritual salvation of keeping faith with the exalted moment—

"Delayed, it may be, for more lives yet,
Through worlds I shall traverse—not a few,
With much to learn and much to forget"—
ere the golden hour of fulfillment shall come;
but faith in the exalted moment is
but another name for faith in God.

WHAT WONDERS!

Eileen Egan and Kathleen Egan, O.S.B

Let this mind be in you, which was also in Christ Jesus: Who, being in the form of God, thought it not robbery to be equal with God: But made himself of no reputation, and took upon him the form of a servant, and was made in the likeness of men.

PHILIPPIANS 2:5–7

To mark the twenty-fifth anniversary of the arrival of the Missionaries of Charity in Venezuela, I wrote to Mother Teresa telling her of my joy at the founding of many houses since that date.

I received a reply from Mother Teresa which put into a few words the very core of her belief and message. Experiencing the utmost in poverty of spirit, she detached herself completely from the achievement. She rejoiced that since Cocorote, the Sisters had opened four hundred houses, one hundred sixty-four in India and two hundred seventy-six houses overseas in ninety-four countries. Then she made a simple, characteristic comment, "What wonders God has done with nothingness."

A stupendous achievement, if viewed in human terms, was seen, with the eye of the spirit, as something else—as the work of a loving Creator. At the same time, Mother Teresa sees herself as the instrument of the Creator, repeating: "I am only a pencil in God's hand. God writes through us, and however imperfect instruments we may be, God writes beautifully."

THE SOURCE OF YOUR VALUES
Linda R. McGinn

Your biblical values can have profound effects on a culture drowning in the sea of situational ethics, neutralism, subjectivism, relativism, and many other "isms." Many of your friends, neighbors, and loved ones have been denied the security of a single standard for determining ethical attitudes and behavior. They carry the crushing burden of creating their own standard for right and wrong, a standard doomed certain to lead them to destruction.

Paul said, "Therefore, I urge you, brothers, in view of God's mercy, to offer your bodies as living sacrifices, holy and pleasing to God—this is your spiritual act of worship. Do not conform any longer to the pattern of this world, but be transformed by the renewing of your mind. Then you will be able to test and approve what God's will is—his good, pleasing and perfect will" (Romans 12:1–2 NIV).

How can you form values that more accurately represent God's character and truth? By spending time reading and discussing His Word with Him. As your thinking changes, your values, attitudes, responses, and actions will follow. Rather than allowing the world's value system to "squeeze you into its own mould" (Romans 12:2), as the Phillips translation describes, God's Word shapes your thoughts and, in turn, your values.

And his disciples remembered that it was written, The zeal of thine house hath eaten me up.
JOHN 2:17

GOD IS THE REWARDER

Evelyn Christenson

But without faith it is impossible to please him: for he that cometh to God must believe that he is, and that he is a rewarder of them that diligently seek him.
HEBREWS 11:6

We are not dropping our prayers into a bottomless barrel. How do we know? One way is by the specific answers to specific requests.

One morning we missed one of our prayer seminars steering committee members. Someone said, "She's taking her mother, who has TB, to the hospital."

Another woman suggested immediately, "Let's stop right now and pray."

To that another steering committee member added, "But that isn't her mother's greatest need. Neither her mother nor her father knows Christ as Savior."

Instead of doing much planning that morning, we spent most of the time praying for the mother and father of our committee member. A couple of weeks after the seminar was over, still another member of the steering committee stopped me on the street and asked, "Ev, did you hear the good news? Do you know that within two weeks after the steering committee prayed, both the mother and father found Christ?" In just two weeks! "The effectual fervent prayer of a righteous man availeth much" (James 5:16).

FOR THY LOVE IS BETTER THAN WINE

Cora Harris MacIlravy

In this place, the word "love" means the continual proofs and tokens of His love, which are said to be better than wine. Wine is a figure of prosperity and of all good and desirable things. The wine from the grape exhilarates and gives strength, but it only strengthens for a time; the love of Christ is better than all earthly good and gives divine strength that abides. It is not only the love that He had to usward when He came and died for us; not only the love that He has for those whom He has redeemed; but that enjoyment of His love, which each of those may have who have felt His kiss of reconciliation.

It is entering into deep communion with Him; it is lying at His feet during those moments that are spent alone with Him; it is the consciousness of being well-pleasing to Him and having His love upon us; it is the holy familiarity with which we pour out our own love at His feet and tell Him all things concerning ourselves. It is at such times that our enraptured souls cry: "Thy love is better than wine!"

No earthly good can allure the one who has pressed close to the side of her Beloved and has tasted and found that the Lord is good. All the joy and delight, all the pleasures a thousand worlds could offer, are as dust in the balance when weighed against one hour of this mutual exchange of love and communion with the Lord.

For thy love is better than wine.
SONG OF SOLOMON 1:2

A Longing to Be Accepted

Mary Graham

Wherefore receive ye one another, as Christ also received us to the glory of God.
Romans 15:7

I wanted to understand God's grace. I wanted to experience His unconditional love for me. I wanted to believe His promise in John 15:9 (NASB): "Just as the Father has loved Me, I have also loved you." And in Romans 15:7: "I have accepted you." And in Matthew 6: "I will care for you."

In my mind, I grasped the truth of these promises and clung as tightly as possible to their reliability. But somehow I could not always make them work in my life. They needed to go deeper into the foundation of my soul, to find solid ground.

"Unmerited favor," a definition of God's grace, was simply not in my vocabulary. Total acceptance and unconditional love were only terminology to me. I struggled to apply those terms personally.

The apostle Paul made it clear in Ephesians 2:8 that it is "by grace" that we have been saved. He spent most of his time in the book of Galatians explaining that just as we are saved by God's grace, we are also perfected (brought to maturity) by His grace.

As I focused my mind on this, I began to comprehend that grace means God accepts me just as I am. He does not require or insist that I measure up to someone else's standard of performance. He loves me completely, thoroughly, and perfectly. There's nothing I can do to add to or detract from that love.

SHAKE US TO WAKE US
Lisa Bevere

When God shakes us to wake us, we often find ourselves surrounded by the unfamiliar and unfriendly. God wakes us up from the secure by pushing us out of our comfort zone. By comfort zone I am referring to all that is familiar, expected, constant, and under our own control.

We are comfortable when what we expect happens. We enjoy being understood and supported by those around us. We prefer to have a constant source of financial provision. But when we get all this comfort and support, we are easily lulled into a false sense of security.

God is more concerned with our condition than our comfort. At times He stirs our nests to make our comforting things uncomfortable.

This is how young eagles get their flight training. The mother eagle grabs the nest with her talons and flaps her wings up and down, blowing all the nice, comfortable padding out of the nest. She tears up what she had so carefully provided. Then she takes each baby eagle and carries it outside of the nest into the wind. This is where young eagles learn to fly. You can't try your wings if you're sitting in the nest.

As an eagle stirreth up her nest, fluttereth over her young, spreadeth abroad her wings, taketh them, beareth them on her wings.
DEUTERONOMY 32:11

AN INFLEXIBLE WILL
Elizabeth Prentiss

For it is God who works in you to will and to act according to his good purpose.
PHILIPPIANS 2:13 NIV

It has been said "that a fixed, inflexible will is a great assistance in a holy life."

You can will to use every means of grace appointed by God.

You can will to spend much time in prayer without regard to your frame at the moment.

You can will to prefer a religion of principle to one of mere feeling; in other words, to obey the will of God when no comfortable glow of emotion accompanies your obedience.

You cannot will to possess the spirit of Christ; that must come as His gift; but you can choose to study His life and imitate it. This will infallibly lead to such self-denying work as visiting the poor, nursing the sick, giving of your time and money to the needy, and the like.

If the thought of such self-denial is repugnant to you, remember that it is enough for the disciple to be as his Lord. And let me assure you that as you penetrate the labyrinth of life in pursuit of Christian duty, you will often be surprised and charmed by meeting your Master Himself amid its windings and turnings and receive His soul-inspiring smile. Or, I should rather say, you will always meet Him, wherever you go.

SETTING TIME ASIDE DAILY
Cheryl Biehl

I am not suggesting that you rush to God each morning to have Him put a check mark by your name for some righteous ritual you've completed. I am suggesting, however, that you come to Him in prayer each morning to draw close to Him. . .to focus on Him. . .to receive your focus for the day.

I prefer coming before God each morning so that I can reflect on my time with God throughout the day. Perhaps you're a "night person." You may prefer evening time with God so you can "sleep on it" and think about it the next day as well. Choose the time of least distractions for you.

Spending time with God does take time. It is a commitment. Let me emphasize again, however, that the spiritual exercises described are not "shoulds" intended to inflict guilt if you are not able or don't care to execute them. They are simply options from which you may choose those which suit your personality and particular needs at this time in your life.

It still isn't easy. My bed still entreats me to linger there each morning, but years of experience convince me each morning that I want to get up more than I want to sleep. For me, nothing can exceed the joy of spending time at the feet of our Lord.

Delight thyself also in the Lord; and he shall give thee the desires of thine heart.
PSALM 37:4

THE GIFT OF LIFE
Hannah Whitall Smith

Every good gift and every perfect gift is from above, and cometh down from the Father of lights.
JAMES 1:17

I would say, first of all, that this blessed life must not be looked upon in any sense as an attainment, but as an obtainment. We cannot earn it, we cannot climb up to it, we cannot win it; we can do nothing but ask for it and receive it. It is the gift of God in Christ Jesus. And where a thing is a gift, the only course left for the receiver is to take it and thank the giver. We never say of a gift, "See to what I have attained," and boast of our skill and wisdom in having attained it; but we say, "See what has been given me," and boast of the love and wealth and generosity of the giver. And everything in our salvation is a gift. From beginning to end, God is the giver and we are the receivers; and it is not to those who do great things, but to those who "receive abundance of grace and of the gift of righteousness," that the richest promises are made.

THE WIFE'S CHOICE
Martha Peace

Since most wives are "in love" with their husbands when they marry, what happens to that love? If you analyze each individual situation biblically, many would fall into one of three categories of sin that will destroy love: selfishness (1 Corinthians 13:5), bitterness (1 Corinthians 13:5), or fear (1 John 4:18). Often, it is a combination. However, no matter what has happened and what she is feeling, God can work in her life and her husband's life, and He can give them a love for each other that they never dreamed possible. God's love is righteous and unselfish. When godly love is expressed between husband and wife, they will often experience tender feelings and a "sweetness" between the two of them. Their biblical love can draw them together in a more lasting intimate bond than all of the intensity of their early days of infatuation put together. The bond of love between a husband and wife is special because of the "one flesh" intimacy that God has given them (Genesis 2:24). And even if her husband does not respond in love, it is a choice the wife must make because of Christ's command.

A new commandment I give unto you, That ye love one another; as I have loved you, that ye also love one another.
JOHN 13:34

FULLNESS OF JOY
Marabel Morgan

These things have I spoken unto you, that my joy might remain in you, and that your joy might be full.
JOHN 15:11

Joy. That's where Jesus comes in. My joy depends solely upon Him who said, "These things have I spoken unto you, that my joy might remain in you, and that your joy might be full." The joy of God Almighty, constant and reliable and all encompassing, becomes my own joy. Not bits and pieces—but full. Complete. Total.

He promises to supply all my needs. When I go to Him admitting my lack, He fills me up. He alone restores my soul. Secure in His love, I know who I really am, a child of the King. At last, free. Truly liberated. As Jesus said, "If the Son therefore shall make you free, ye shall be free indeed."

When I invited Jesus of Nazareth into my life, I became a child in His Forever Family, forgiven and assured of life eternal. And that wasn't all. God also had a plan for my life and what a plan! I started down the road on a great adventure, which He calls "the abundant life." Jesus Himself said, "If you abide in me and my words abide in you, you shall ask what you will, and it shall be done unto you. . . . Ask and you shall receive that your joy may be full."

I have learned the condition to having constant joy. The condition is allowing Jesus to sit at the control center of my life. To relinquish those controls, I say, "Jesus, my Lord, please guide me in Your perfect plan today."

HIS APPOINTMENT
Mary W. Tileston

I love to think that God appoints
My portion day by day;
Events of life are in His hand,
And I would only say,
Appoint them in Thine own good time,
And in Thine own best way.
—A. L. Waring

Thy servants are ready to do whatsoever
my lord the king shall appoint.
2 SAMUEL 15:15

If we are really, and always, and equally ready to do whatsoever the King appoints, all the trials and vexations arising from any change in His appointments, great or small, simply do not exist. If He appoints me to work there, shall I lament that I am not to work here? If He appoints me to wait indoors today, am I to be annoyed because I am not to work out-of-doors? If I meant to write His messages this morning, shall I grumble because He sends interrupting visitors, rich or poor, to whom I am to speak, or "show kindness" for His sake, or at least obey His command, "Be courteous"? If all my members are really at His disposal, why should I be put out if today's appointment is some simple work for my hands or errands for my feet, instead of some seemingly more important doing of head or tongue?
—Frances Ridley Havergal

IN THE FAMILY

Joni Eareckson Tada

"I no longer call you servants. . . . Instead, I have called you friends."
JOHN 15:15 NIV

Let me tell you about my sisters.

You've heard the phrase, "Blood is thicker than water." When I was a girl an expression like that would have sounded gross. But I instinctively understood its meaning. For even though I loved my friends, there was nobody who could match the importance of my three older sisters.

Throughout the course of His life on earth, the Lord Jesus had special names for those who followed Him. He called them His servants, His sheep, or His beloved. At the last supper, He must have encouraged His men mightily when He named them "friends."

It wasn't until after His resurrection, however, that Christ referred to His disciples as His brothers.

Even though He was as close as a good friend could be to the men and women who followed Him through His earthly ministry, He couldn't call them blood relatives until after He paid the penalty for sin and welcomed them into the family. Christ's death and resurrection opened the door for men and women to share the same genes, so to speak, with the Son of God. To share the same Father and family.

Blood is thicker than water. And if you have found salvation through Jesus Christ, you can never be an only child. You're in the family of Jesus.

Let me tell you about my big Brother.

No Fear
Hannah Whitall Smith

A friend of mine told me that her childhood was passed in a perfect terror of God. Her idea of Him was that He was a cruel giant with an awful "Eye" that could see everything, no matter how it might be hidden, and that He was always spying upon her and watching for chances to punish her and to snatch away all her joys.

With a child's strange reticence, she never told anyone of her terror; but one night Mother, coming into the room unexpectedly, heard the poor little despairing cry, and, with a sudden comprehension of what it meant, sat down beside the bed, and, taking the cold little hand in hers, told her God was not a dreadful tyrant to be afraid of, but was just like Jesus; and that she knew how good and kind Jesus was, and how He loved little children, and took them in His arms and blessed them. My friend said she had always loved the stories about Jesus, and when she heard that God was like Him, it was a perfect revelation to her and took away her fear of God forever. She went about all that day saying to herself over and over, "Oh, I am so glad I have found out that God is like Jesus, for Jesus is so nice. Now I need never be afraid of God anymore."

The little child had got a sight of God "in the face of Jesus Christ," and it brought rest to her soul.

If ye had known me, ye should have known my Father also: and from henceforth ye know him, and have seen him.
JOHN 14:7

THE LORD'S DIEHARDS

Amy Carmichael

Why boastest thou thyself in mischief,
O mighty man? the goodness of God
endureth continually.
PSALM 52:1

"Die hard, my men, die hard!" shouted Colonel Inglis of the 57th to his men on the heights behind the river Albuhera. The regiment was nicknamed the Diehards after that. The tale may have been forgotten but the name lives on, and in spite of foolish uses, it is a great name. It challenges us.

We are called to be the Lord's diehards to whom can be committed any kind of trial of endurance and who can be counted upon to stand firm whatever happens. It is written of Cromwell: "He strove to give his command so strict a unity that in no crisis should it crack." With this aim in view he made his Ironsides. The result of that discipline was seen not only in victory but in defeat; for his troops, "though they were beaten and routed, presently rallied again and stood in good order till they received new orders" (*Oliver Cromwell* by John Buchan).

This is the spirit that animates all valiant life: to be strong in will—to strive, to seek, to find, and not to yield—is all that ever matters. Failure or success, as the world understands these words, is of no eternal account. To be able to stand steady in defeat is in itself a victory. There is no tinsel about that kind of triumph.

There is a curious comfort in remembering that the Father depends upon His child to not give way. It is inspiring to be trusted with a hard thing.

THE NEED FOR INTIMACY

Jane Hansen

Right things from the wrong source constitute lusts.

The desire of the woman springs from this root; it is a form of lust. It is a way of objectifying the man in her own way, wanting him for herself, to find her life in him. It is looking to him for what only God can supply. As long as her desire is set upon him, the needs she so desperately longs for cannot be met. Even if it were possible for the woman to grasp onto the man and somehow mold him into the image she wants him to be, it would not be enough because lust is never satisfied.

When a woman's heart is turned, when she sets her desire back on God, a new freedom will come. The grasping will be gone from her voice and her attitude. She will be able to move into relationship with her husband based on wholeness rather than inappropriate neediness, hurt, and woundedness. She will be able to speak into her husband's life with more effectiveness because her worth and identity no longer depend on his response. Free now, she is able to be the help to him God designed her to be.

When the woman stops looking to her husband for the needs he cannot meet, she frees him to meet the ones he can: the need for intimacy and the shared responsibility for the marriage and family.

She took of the fruit thereof, and did eat, and gave also unto her husband with her; and he did eat.
GENESIS 3:6

STONE SOUL SEARCH
Corrie ten Boom

For the sake of Christ, then, I am content with weaknesses, insults, hardships, persecutions, and calamities; for when I am weak, then I am strong.
2 CORINTHIANS 12:10 RSV

It has been said that the removal of small stones which frequently encumber the fields does not always increase the crop. In many soils they are an advantage, attracting the moisture and radiating the heat. In one experiment, the results of removing the stones were so unfavorable to the crop that they were brought back again. We often cry to God, as Paul did, for the removal of some thorn in the flesh. Later experience teaches us that it was better for it to remain.

Your strength, my weakness—
here they always meet,
When I lay down my burden at Your feet:
The things that seem to crush will in the end
Be seen as rungs on which I did ascend!
Thank You, Lord.

FEELING LOVED AND ACCEPTED
Stormie Omartian

Even though it is God's love that is ultimately most important in anyone's life, a parent's love (or lack thereof) is perceived and felt first. Parental love is the first love a child experiences and the first love he (she) understands. In fact, parental love is often the means by which children actually open themselves to God's love and come to understand it early in life.

Ask God to show you what you can do to communicate love to your child—and don't listen to the Devil weighing you down with guilt about past failure. You know his tactics:

"If you weren't so dysfunctional, you'd be able to communicate love to your child."

"No one ever loved you, so how can you love anyone else?"

These lies are from the pit of hell and part of Satan's plan for your child's life.

If you are being tormented by guilt or feelings of failure in this area, confess your thoughts to God, pray about it, put it in God's hands, and then stand up and proclaim the truth. Say, "God loves my child. I love my child. Other people love my child. If my child doesn't feel loved, it's because he (she) has believed the lies of the enemy. We refuse to live according to Satan's lies."

And hope maketh not ashamed; because the love of God is shed abroad in our hearts by the Holy Ghost which is given unto us.
ROMANS 5:5

GOD-MADE TREES
Millie Stamm

And he shall be like a tree planted by the rivers of water, that bringeth forth his fruit in his season; his leaf also shall not wither; and whatsoever he doeth shall prosper.

PSALM 1:3

We are familiar with the poem that ends with the line, "But only God can make a tree." The psalmist compares the Christian to a tree, a God-made tree.

We are planted trees—"he shall be like a tree planted." When we plant a tree, we select the spot where we want it and the type of tree best suited for that location and for the purpose we had in mind. God knows where He wants to plant us, and He has a purpose in planting us there.

God provides for His trees—He plants them "by the rivers of water."

We are to be productive trees—"that bringeth forth his fruit in his season." We must be productive in due season, bringing forth God's fruit in God's season. When our lives take deep rootage in Christ, we will bring forth rich fruitage for Him.

God's trees will be perpetually alive—"his leaf also shall not wither." We will be ever-living trees of unfading beauty radiating the loveliness of our lovely Lord.

We are prosperous trees—"whatsoever he doeth shall prosper." Rooted in Christ, nourished by the Word, and refreshed by the Spirit, our lives become blessings to others.

A BOUNTIFUL BLENDING
Mrs. Charles E. Cowman

How wide is this assertion of the Apostle Paul! He does not say, "We know that some things" or "most things," but "all things." From the minutest to the most momentous; from the humblest event in daily providence to the great crisis-hours in grace.

And all things "work"—they are working; not all things have worked, or shall work; but it is a present operation.

At this very moment, when some voice may be saying, "Thy judgments are a great deep," the angels above, who are watching the development of the great plan, are with folded wings exclaiming, "The Lord is righteous in all his ways, and holy in all his works" (Psalm 145:17).

And then all things "work together." It is a beautiful blending. Many different colors, in themselves raw and unsightly, are required in order to weave the harmonious pattern.

Many separate wheels and joints are required to make the piece of machinery. Take a thread separately, or a note separately, or a wheel or a tooth of a wheel separately, and there may be neither use nor beauty discernible.

But complete the web, combine the notes, put together the separate parts of steel and iron, and you see how perfect and symmetrical is the result. Here is the lesson for faith: "What I do thou knowest not now, but thou shalt know hereafter" (Macduff).

And we know that all things work together for good to them that love God.
ROMANS 8:28

WHAT THINK YE OF CHRIST?
Hannah Whitall Smith

What think ye of Christ?
MATTHEW 22:42

The crucial question for each one of us in our everyday life is just this, "What think ye of Christ?" To some, the question may seem to require a doctrinal answer, and I do not at all say that there is no idea of doctrine involved in it. But to my mind, the doctrinal answer, valuable as it may be, is not the one of most importance for every day. The vital answer is the one that would contain our own personal knowledge of the character of Christ; not what He is doctrinally, but what He is intrinsically, in Himself. For, after all, our salvation does not depend upon the doctrines concerning Christ, but upon the person of Christ Himself, what He is and upon what He does.

"For the which cause I also suffer these things: nevertheless I am not ashamed: for I know whom I have believed, and am persuaded that he is able to keep that which I have committed unto him against that day" (2 Timothy 1:12).

Paul knew Christ; therefore, Paul could trust Him; and if we would trust Him as Paul did, we must know Him as intimately. I am afraid a great many people are so taken up with Christian doctrines and dogmas and are so convinced that their salvation is secured because their "views" are sound and orthodox, that they have never yet come to a personal acquaintance with Christ Himself.

AUTHORITY IS ACCOUNTABLE

Jill Briscoe

One of the most helpful thoughts, as I consider servant leadership, has been the realization that however many people I have under me, I, myself, am under authority and am accountable. Even if I end up to be queen of England (unlikely)—I will be accountable to Parliament! If I am to be a woman that fears the Lord, I well know I must give an account to Him of how I have exercised that leadership role.

Ephesians 6:7 (NKJV) tells me that "with goodwill doing service, as to the Lord, and not to men." This helps me to keep a servant spirit in mind as I lead.

If I am in authority, I also need to know this does not mean I am better than my servants. It is the position that is different, not the people in the positions. A true spirit of meekness tells me I am to esteem others better than myself and not to think highly of myself. We are simply called to different functions in society and in the church, and I need to acknowledge the equality of my peers, yield to the authority of my superiors, and thoughtfully care for those for whom I am responsible—all in a spirit of meekness.

So then every one of us shall give account of himself to God.
ROMANS 14:12

With Eyes Shut Tight
Doris Coffin Aldrich

The eyes of your understanding being enlightened; that ye may know what is the hope of his calling, and what the riches of the glory of his inheritance in the saints.
Ephesians 1:18

The click of the latch, a gust of cold air, a resounding slam! . . .and Joe was home to lunch.

"Mommie!" shouted Joe, bursting into the kitchen, "Mommie, I. . ."

"Where's Jon and Jane?" she interrupted.

"They're coming. And Mommie, all the way home I shut my eyes and asked the Lord to lead me. I really did."

"Well, what was the sense of that? The Lord gave you eyes to see with and He expects you to use them, not to do foolish stunts." And Mommie carried the tray of soup to the table.

"Sometimes I only shut one eye," countered Joe, somewhat subdued.

"But why shut any eyes. . . ? Then if you'd stumbled you would have blamed the Lord and it would not have been His fault. Now better get your hands washed."

"But, Mommie, I wanted to pray!" Joe shouted while walking to the washbowl.

"My! How many times I've done just that," she thought. "Shut my eyes and asked the Lord to lead me when I should have left them open and walked along with Him on the path made plain before my feet."

ANGELS
Anita Corrine Donihue

Angels are all around us in the form of gold pins on shoulders, other kinds of jewelry and pictures, and in stores, books, poetry, and even movies.

The Bible tells us real angels are here with us. Some of us have even experienced angels working personally in our lives. The Bible also teaches we are a little lower than the angels, but God has appointed both angels and us to be servants for Him.

We must be careful that our praise does not go to the angels, but only to God who made them. Remember, the Scriptures tell us we are to put nothing or no one before God. This includes angels.

God is the Master of all. Him only are we to worship and serve.

Let's be thankful for angels, but be thankful to God, who made them.

Take heed that ye despise not one of these little ones; for I say unto you, That in heaven their angels do always behold the face of my Father which is in heaven.
MATTHEW 18:10

EVEN THIS. . .

Amy Carmichael

"Who is this? He commands even the winds and the water, and they obey him."
LUKE 8:25 NIV

Is there something you are facing—whether in your outer circumstances or in your inner character—that seems impossible to command? Something that has baffled you and outwitted you a thousand times and appears that it will win over you in the end?

Don't despair. Don't shrug and give up.

Our Lord—your Lord and mine—can command even the most difficult, unruly thing that seems as if it will never be commanded.

Let His word "even" be a comfort to you. He who commands even the winds and water (and they must obey Him)—He can say to that "even" of yours, "Peace, be still."

And there will come for you "a great calm" (Mark 4:39).

Remember that there is nothing you are asked to do in your own strength. Not the least thing, nor the greatest.

Isn't that amazing?

How utterly foolish it is to plead weakness when we—even you and I—may move into the stream of that power. If only we will.

HELP. . .NOW!

Patsy Clairmont

Life has a way of mounting up until we are slumping down. Soon our joyful noises turn into grumpy groans.

I watch young moms board airplanes toting babies and all the endless, yet necessary, paraphernalia, and I wonder how they do it. I do catch glimpses of their frayed nerves and exhaustion, and I sometimes see in their eyes neon signs that flash, "Gimme a break. . . please!"

I'm not sure David said "please," but I do hear him plead frequently in the Psalms for a reprieve from his enemies. Check out Psalm 70:1, 5 (NIV): "Hasten, O God, to save me; O Lord, come quickly to help me. . . . You are my help and my deliverer; O Lord, do not delay."

David needed a break now. He was pleading with the Lord of the universe to drop everything else He was doing and rescue him. Now is usually when I need my help as well. That's because I tend to let things—activities, demands, mail, dishes, bills, laundry, telephone messages, people's expectations—pile up until I'm howling for help and blubbering the blues.

It's obvious that, as long as we can find a reflection in the mirror, we will long for a break. And that's not wrong. But when we reach the end of our strength, wisdom, and personal resources, we enter into the beginning of His glorious provisions. And that's a wonderful place to be.

Make haste, O God, to deliver me.
PSALM 70:1

INTERCESSION FOR OTHERS
Quin Sherrer and Ruthanne Garlock

I exhort, therefore, that, first of all, supplications, prayers, intercessions, and giving of thanks, be made for all men.
1 TIMOTHY 2:1

"Without God, we cannot. Without us, God will not." St. Augustine's succinct statement sums up the twofold nature of intercession. God empowers us by the Holy Spirit to intercede for others' needs; without that empowerment, our prayers would be empty words.

God also invests us with Christ's authority to restrain satanic forces that are blinding and hindering the person for whom we're praying. God could restrain those forces without us if He chose to. But He has equipped us and commissioned us to intercede by pushing back the enemy, thus allowing the Holy Spirit to bring conviction that leads to repentance.

Two Old Testament verses depict the need for an intercessor to do battle for sinful man: "[God] was appalled that there was no one to intervene" (Isaiah 59:16 NIV); "I looked for a man among them who would build up the wall and stand before me in the gap on behalf of the land so I would not have to destroy it, but I found none" (Ezekiel 22:30 NIV).

Of course, Jesus ultimately filled that gap. He became the mediator between God and man by giving Himself as a sacrifice for sin. But believers should also see themselves as intercessors: standing between God and the person(s) for whom we are praying, pleading for God to intervene.

BOREDOM OR ABUNDANT LIVING
Ruth Youngdahl Nelson

Housewives bored with life are top drug users, concludes a study.

It is sad when people find life boring and take to artificial means to either stimulate or dull their God-given senses. It is particularly sad because the One who brings fulfillment and excitement and joy stands at each heart's door knocking. But the thief is also there, the thief who comes to steal and kill and destroy. Who is this thief?

As simplistic as it sounds, it is nevertheless eternally true, that thief is embodied in the one letter "I." "Navel gazing" is no newfangled occupation. Since the beginning of time it has been man's chief foe. The "poor me" attitude, the stench of self-pity, repels other people and shuts out God.

That big "I" is the only vowel and the middle letter in the word "sin." How well I remember my confirmation pastor writing those three letters on the chalkboard. Then he told us this same "I" is the blockade between us and heaven. If we permit the Holy Spirit to take hold of the "I" and bend it around until each end meets, it becomes "0"—zero, nothing. Then the transformation happens, and "sin becomes son," God's Son. As He takes over our lives, heaven enters our hearts here and now. He is also the means for the gate to be wide open to the hereafter.

The thief cometh not, but for to steal, and to kill, and to destroy: I am come that they might have life, and that they might have it more abundantly.
JOHN 10:10

CONTENTMENT
Jean Fleming

I can do all things through Christ who strengthens me.
PHILIPPIANS 4:13 NKJV

We face an unknown future. We do not know what the days ordained for us contain, but we can prepare for whatever lies ahead.

View life as a learning opportunity. Ask God what He wants you to learn from the situations you face. Daily Bible reading and prayer prepare us to receive instruction and direction from God. When we set aside specific time to listen, He often encourages us with His presence and promises and interprets to some degree the circumstances of life. Take advantage of the natural lull after hard times when you're pulling together the pieces to sort through the events and ferret out the lessons.

The situations we face today can build a greater God confidence in our life and give us assurance that in Christ we can tackle what lies ahead. Incident after incident, lesson after lesson, year after year, as we experience God's great faithfulness, grace, and power, we will gain the confidence to say, "I can do all things through Christ who gives me strength."

In tough times, Paul was stretched beyond his human capacity, yet he experienced deliverance. From the abyss Paul asked not, "Why me, Lord?" but "What do you want me to understand from this situation?" Paul concluded that everything happened "that we might not rely on ourselves but on God."

WHEN YOUR GUILT'S GONE, YOU HAVE PEACE

Kay Arthur

Jesus doesn't turn the clock back on your life when you're saved by grace through faith. He doesn't change what you've done. But He does take away the guilt! When your guilt's gone, you have peace.

If peace eludes you, one or both of two things may be hampering you—unbelief (which is sin) or the devil.

If it's unbelief, you'll remain miserable and probably ineffective until you determine to believe God's Word. What more can God say, what more can He do than what He's done to blot out your sins and convince you of His forgiveness? Until you decide in faith to believe God, you're in sin, "for whatsoever is not of faith is sin" (Romans 14:23).

That's a strong statement, isn't it? Let me show you why I said it. Look up Hebrews 3:18–19, and note what is synonymous with unbelief.

The other possibility for why you feel guilty is the enemy. If he can heap guilt on you, he'll flatten you with it. Remember, Satan means adversary—he'll get you any way he can.

However, don't make him your focus. Don't live in fear of his attacks. Simply be aware of his devices—and remember one of those schemes is unremitting guilt.

And their sins and iniquities will I remember no more.
HEBREWS 10:17

I Am Unable to Save Myself

Twila Paris with Robert Webber

In my distress I called upon the Lord, and cried unto my God: he heard my voice out of his temple, and my cry came before him, even into his ears.
PSALM 18:6

No matter how many songs I write, no matter how successful my career is, I can't save myself. I need the Cross and Resurrection; I need Christ to save me. When God comes to save us, we are relocated in God and now able to respond in worship. This is what "Running to the Rescue" is about.

"Running to the Rescue" expresses the message of so many of the Psalms. For example, in Psalm 40 the psalmist is in a deep depression. Then God comes to rescue him, and the psalmist bursts forth with praise. "He lifted me out of the slimy pit, out of the mud and mire; he set my feet on a rock and gave me a firm place to stand. He put a new song in my mouth, a hymn of praise to our God" (Psalm 40:2–3 NIV). I think the movement of this psalm is so significant. Notice that first he was in despair (dislocated), then God brought him out of the mud and mire (relocated), and finally there was a new song in his mouth (worship).

This movement happens over and over again in life. It doesn't mean that a person gets saved again and again, but that the pattern of being in distress, being brought out, and praising God is not only the pattern of salvation, it is the pattern of the Christian life.

The Romance of the Religious Life

Hannah Whitall Smith

My soul had started on its voyage of discovery, and to become acquainted with God was its unalterable and unceasing aim. I was as yet only at the beginning, but what a magnificent beginning it was. God was a reality, and He was my God. He had created me, and He loved me, and all was right between us. All care about my own future destiny had been removed from my shoulders. I could say with Paul, "I know whom I have believed, and am persuaded that he is able to keep that which I have committed unto him against that day." I needed no longer to work for my soul's salvation, but only to work out the salvation that had been bestowed upon me. All the years of my self-introversion and self-examination were ended. Instead of my old fruitless searchings into my feelings and emotions for some tangible evidence of God's favor, the glorious news, declared in the Bible, that He so loved the world as to have sent His only begotten Son to save the world, absorbed every faculty.

It was no longer "How do I feel?" but always "What does God say?" And He said such delightful things, that to find them out became my supreme delight.

For the which cause I also suffer these things: nevertheless I am not ashamed: for I know whom I have believed, and am persuaded that he is able to keep that which I have committed unto him against that day.
2 Timothy 1:12

HOW LONG, O LORD?
Lyn Klug

Let him bury his face in the dust—
there may yet be hope.
LAMENTATIONS 3:29 NIV

A teenager rebels and wastes his life on alcohol and drugs. A marriage goes through years of painful struggle. An aging parent suffers disability and pain. Some problems go on for so long and seem so hopeless that we can hardly bear to ask God for help anymore.

We may never be able to answer that question: Why does God allow such bad things to happen to us? But we begin to realize that we can learn and grow through them. A seed sprouts always in the darkness of the earth, and much spiritual growth begins in the darkness of pain, loss, sickness, and disappointment. In this life, suffering will never be eliminated, but we believe that God can work in all things for our good (Romans 8:28).

"Faith sometimes falters, because He does not reward us immediately," wrote St. Augustine. "But hold out, be steadfast, bear the delay, and you have carried the cross." God is never a God of hopelessness. Even if God does not change the situation, He can change us. This is most certainly true.

MY FOUNDATION AND MY BUILDING

Anna J. Lindgren

Now if any man build upon this foundation gold, silver, precious stones, wood, hay, stubble; Every man's work shall be made manifest: for the day shall declare it, because it shall be revealed by fire; and the fire shall try every man's work of what sort it is.
1 CORINTHIANS 3:12–13

I think I have feared a wrong foundation as much as I have feared anything in life. It was primarily this fear that led me to question and doubt everything. For already as a child I had witnessed old people die who did not want to die, who feared death with a terrible fear. And the reason, I found, was that they had made a failure of life—and knew it. I did not want a repetition of that. I did not want to stand on the brink of eternity and see my whole house crumble to dust because its foundation was "sinking sand." Long did I search and far did I wander before I found that "Other foundation can no man lay than that is laid, which is Jesus Christ," and so I found Thee again, Master of mine. And the strongest thing in my soul is the consciousness that I am on the foundation that neither the wild roaring sea nor the floods of hell can engulf or shake.

So I ask Thee, dear Master, let the searchlight from Thy face fall on my building today; lay bare its every weakness, reveal its every fault. Touch it with a live coal from off Thy altar, that it may stand secure and unhurt, honoring Thee, in the day that will show forth gain or irreparable loss.

"Do You Know of Any Pill to Cure Loneliness?"

Betty Malz

Our soul waiteth for the Lord: he is our help and our shield.
Psalm 33:20

Carolyn has a wonderful perspective on helping others.

Early one morning I decided to walk my three miles before it got too hot. There was Carolyn down on the beach picking up cans and trash. I asked her if she was the beach angel.

"No," she said, "I'm the original bag lady. I come every morning and evening and tidy up the beach. While I'm here I get to enjoy the sunrise and sunset. I don't guess I've missed a single one in twenty-six years."

This woman lives alone but isn't lonely. She has a merry heart and in giving of herself receives enjoyment from the beauty of the world around her.

Little things can mean a lot when we invest in others. Last February I sent a valentine to the most despised, hateful, selfish woman in the state of Illinois.

It broke her heart. The neighbors tell me she has made a drastic change since then.

Our perspectives on heaven and the people we help find it are important to the way we live our lives now. We can keep that perspective aligned by praising Jesus for the joy of eternity with Him and by sharing that good news with others.

Few things can be more exciting!

MRS. SIT TIGHT

Jean Lush with Pam Vredevelt

Jean, I am disgusted with the way you are raising the children. Robin talks all the time. . . . And. . .you mark my word, Jean. David will end up delinquent. . . . And another thing. Your children never have nice clothes. . . ."

All right, Mother, you need not ever see them again, I thought. *No matter what I do, I'll never please you.*

The rest of the day was a blur, but. . .after the children were in bed, I turned to Psalm 37 for comfort. As in times past, God told me to wait, sit still, and not take action.

Three weeks later another letter arrived. It was from my sister. "Jean, Mother is very depressed over hurting you and fears you will never forgive her."

Shortly after receiving my sister's letter, I invited Mother to our home for lunch.

Over lunch Mother said, "Jean, please forgive me for all the nasty things I said. I need you."

Often we are caught off guard when someone hurts us, and our immediate angry impulses are deadly vicious. These are times when we must pull back the reins on those wild urges and look to God for strength to sit tight until He shows us what to do next.

But that on the good ground are they, which in an honest and good heart, having heard the word, keep it, and bring forth fruit with patience.
LUKE 8:15

MADE AND REPAIRED BY THE MASTER

Corrie ten Boom

All things were made by him;
and without him was not any thing
made that was made.
JOHN 1:3

There is only One who can cleanse us from our sins—He who made us.

In Russia, many people lived in a certain apartment house. The basement of the house was filled with the junk of all the families. Amongst the junk was a beautiful harp, which nobody had been able to fix.

One snowy night, a tramp asked if he could sleep in the building. The people cleared a space for him in the corner of the basement, and he was happy to stay there.

In a little while, the people heard beautiful music coming from the basement. The owner of the harp rushed downstairs and found the tramp playing it.

"But how could you repair it? We couldn't," he said.

The tramp smiled and replied, "I made this harp years ago, and when you make something, you can also repair it."

Lord, You made me.
What a joy that You are willing
and able to repair me.

DEALING WITH ANNOYING PEOPLE
Elizabeth Prentiss

You forget perhaps the indirect good one may gain by living with uncongenial, tempting persons. . .such people do good by the very self-denial and self-control their mere presence demands.

"But suppose one cannot exercise self-control and is always flying out and flaring up?"

"I should say that a Christian who was always doing that. . .was in pressing need of just the trial God sent."

"It is very mortifying and painful to find how weak one is."

"That is true. But our mortifications are some of God's best physicians and do much toward healing our pride and self-conceit."

"We look at our fellow men too much from the standpoint of our own prejudices. They may be wrong, they may have their faults and foibles, they may call out all the meanest and most hateful in us. But when they excite our bad passions by their own, they may be as ashamed and sorry as we are irritated. And I think some of the best, most contrite, most useful of men and women, whose prayers prevail with God and bring down blessings into the homes in which they dwell, often possess unlovely traits that furnish them with their best discipline. The very fact that they are ashamed of themselves drives them to God; they feel safe in His presence."

Judge not according to the appearance, but judge righteous judgment.
JOHN 7:24

CHRIST'S INEFFABLE LOVE
Cora Harris MacIlravy

Let him kiss me with the kisses of his mouth.
SONG OF SOLOMON 1:2

This is the heart-cry of the soul who would receive the kiss of reconciliation, which only the Son can give. The meaning, however, which finds a deep response in the hearts of those who have already met the Prince of Peace and who have accepted Him as their Savior, is the expression of that deep longing for a closer touch with the Lord.

How our hearts have cried to the Lord that we might approach Him and enter into such fellowship, such humility, as would constrain us to abide continually at His feet!

The "kisses of the mouth" is the symbol of the close relation that is between a bride and a bridegroom. There may be kisses upon the hand, signifying respect and friendship; but the mouth is kept by the bride for the bridegroom, and the bridegroom keeps these kisses for his bride. Here it is a token of the highest, closest communion and relation that one can have with the Lord. She is longing for the kiss of betrothal, which will be an earnest from Him that she is to be His bride. Who can tell the joy of those who approach close enough to receive this kiss, which is the seal of the closer relation with the Lord!

Thou Hast Enlarged Me
Amy Carmichael

"Thou hast enlarged me when I was in distress" (Psalm 4:1).

The more one thinks of these words, the more they reveal their wonderful meaning. Darby renders it, "In pressure, Thou hast enlarged me," and Kay, "In straits Thou madest wide room for me." Whatever the pressure be, in that pressure—think of it—enlargement; the very opposite of what the word "pressure" suggests. And room, plenty of room, in a strait place.

We may sometimes feel distressed. Here, then, is a word of pure hope and strong consolation. No distress need cramp us, crowd us into ourselves, or make us smaller and poorer in anything that matters. Largeness, like the largeness of the sea, is His gift to us. We shall not be flattened in spirit by pressure, but enlarged. In the narrow ways of pain or of temptation He will make wide room for us.

Hear me when I call, O God of my righteousness: thou hast enlarged me when I was in distress; have mercy upon me, and hear my prayer.
PSALM 4:1

SOMETHING IS MISSING

Marabel Morgan

And the peace of God, which passeth all understanding, shall keep your hearts and minds through Christ Jesus.
PHILIPPIANS 4:7

Several weeks ago, a confused military wife wrote telling of her inner turmoil. "I'm all mixed up inside," she said. "I want to know the joy and peace you speak of. I want to give my love freely to my husband and children. I'm desperate. I feel as if something is missing no matter what I do."

The ache of that woman's heart is universal. The ache comes from being on the outside looking in—like a child looking in the candy-store window. Something is missing, but what?

Getting married or raising children doesn't completely fulfill a woman. Having a career does not produce peace. Neither prestige nor power brings purpose. Money can't make a happy atmosphere at the breakfast table.

What is the purpose of it all? I believe a woman is just spinning her wheels until she is fulfilled by the Ultimate, God Himself. He is the only One who can get it all together. He is the only One who can keep it there. He is the only One who can make you complete—total. He is the only One who can give you a good attitude all the time. And best of all, He offers to you the possibility of a life of no regrets.

His name: Jesus of Nazareth, the God-Man.

JESUS IN GETHSEMANE (HOW TO ENTER IN)
Hannah Whitall Smith

And he went a little farther, and fell on his face, and prayed, saying, O my Father, if it be possible, let this cup pass from me: nevertheless not as I will, but as thou wilt.
MATTHEW 26:39

I was once trying to explain to a physician who had charge of a large hospital the necessity and meaning of consecration, but he seemed unable to understand. At last I said to him, "Suppose, in going your rounds among your patients, you should meet with one man who entreated you earnestly to take his case under your especial care in order to cure him, but who should at the same time refuse to tell you all his symptoms or to take all your prescribed remedies, and should say to you, 'I am quite willing to follow your directions as to certain things because they commend themselves to my mind as good, but in other matters I prefer judging for myself and following my own directions.' What would you do in such a case?" I asked.

"Do!" he replied with indignation. "I could do nothing for him unless he would put his whole case into my hands without any reserves and would obey my directions implicitly."

"It is necessary, then," I said, "for doctors to be obeyed if they are to have any chance to cure their patient?"

"Implicitly obeyed!" was his emphatic reply.

"And that is consecration," I continued. "God must have the whole case put into His hands without any reserves."

April 6

EASTER WEEK
Mrs. Charles E. Cowman

Jesus therefore, knowing all things that should come upon him, went forth, and said unto them, Whom seek ye?
JOHN 18:4

The days before Easter teach us that applause must be accepted humbly, that it can swiftly fade into the twilight of forgetfulness. They teach us that we should be meek in our moments of triumph and that we should rely not upon the fanfare of the crowd, but upon the unspoken praise of the Greatest Judge. They teach us tolerance—never the tolerance of a Pilate who washed his hands and let it go at that, but the sort of Christian tolerance that offers sympathy and help and refuses to take part in any wrongdoing. They teach us that God's will is not always our will, but that we must accept it. They teach us that life and love can survive even scorn and crucifixion.

"Sometimes we know that there are barriers ahead and that pain will be a part of the future. Christ knew, all too well, that torture was His heritage—that, during Holy Week, He was rapidly approaching a moment of extreme grief. And yet the knowledge did not make Him a specter at the feast. He kept His appetite and His philosophy and His good cheer, and His trust in the Father. He was able, by so doing, to join in the festivity that filled the city!"

—Margaret Sangster, *Christian Herald*

COMING BEFORE THE HOLY GOD OF HEAVEN

Cheryl Biehl

He chose you to be His child for all eternity. He made this possible through His Son, Jesus Christ. Not only has He forgiven your sin, but He has transferred Jesus' righteousness to you.

You are His child. He cares about you even more than we as human mothers know how to care for and love our own children. He cares about your problems, your hurts, your victories, and your defeats. He invites you to spend time in His presence because He loves you.

My response to this is, "Why me, Lord? Why did You choose me to be Your child?" I am eternally grateful. Love overwhelms my heart as I fall to my knees before Him. I am ready to worship Him. I am ready to listen to Him. I am ready to give Him complete control of my life.

All that I am—my assets. . .my strengths. . . my liabilities. . .my fears. . .anxieties. . .hurts. . . past sins. . . reputation—all of these I leave with Him.

All that I have, everything we have comes from God. He can take it away at any moment. Today, how does He want to use what He has given me for His glory?

All that I hope to be—my dreams. . .fantasies. . .goals . . .He is free to eliminate or change any of them. Or He may choose to expand them to greater heights than I have ever dreamed.

When I kept silent about my sin,
my body wasted away.
PSALM 32:3 NASB

EVEN THE DEATH OF THE CROSS

Amy Carmichael

In the day when I cried thou answeredst me, and strengthenedst me with strength in my soul.
PSALM 138:3

I find much comfort in Psalm 138:3: "In the day when I cried thou answeredst me, and strengthenedst me with strength in my soul."

"In the day that I cried." That does not mean the day after, but that very day, that very hour, that very minute. God hears us the moment we cry and strengthens us with the only kind of strength that is of any use at all.

To each of us there is something that seems simply impossible to get on top of. I know my special foe and all this week I have had to live looking off to Jesus, the author and (thank God) the finisher of our faith. (I have just now turned to Hebrews 12:2 to make sure that word is really there.) Psalm 138:8 is another standby. Oh! blessed be the eternal Word of God. Feelings may change (they do), we may change and fall (we do), but His Word stands steadfast. It cannot fail.

Don't you think that some of us must know the trials of misty weather if we are to be enabled to understand when others are in the mist?

My word yesterday was "Even the death of the cross" (Philippians 2:8). There is an "even" in most lives. God help us not to shrink back from that "even."

WHEN YOU'VE LOST YOUR THIRST
Sheila Walsh

I see my soul as being like my car. As a vehicle needs clean oil, I need intimate contact with God. Our souls were made for this. When we deprive our souls of that very life force, we can survive—but that is all we are doing. We were not created to merely survive but to thrive in God.

Sometimes we know we need refreshment but are too lazy in the routine of life—or too preoccupied with what we think is "important"—to stop for spiritual replenishment. Sometimes life may crowd in on us enough that we simply are not aware of our need. Think of the need for intimacy with God in terms of physical thirst. In the routine demands and distractions of the day we can forget this most basic of all needs. I notice that on a hot day my dog, Bundle, is always returning to his water bowl for a drink. Sometimes it's only in watching him that I realize how thirsty I am. I have the beginnings of a headache caused by dehydration. It's not wise to wait to drink a glass of water until after the headache is so bad you have to go and lie down in a dark room.

It's the same in our relationship with God. Start with an honest confession to God that you have been distracted or negligent. Thank Him for reminding you of your need—your thirst. We have forgotten how well we were meant to run.

"I will pour water on him who is thirsty."
ISAIAH 44:3 NKJV

HE LIVES!

Mrs. Charles E. Cowman

I am he that liveth, and was dead; and, behold, I am alive for evermore.
REVELATION 1:18

Flowers! Easter lilies speak to me this morning the same dear old lesson of immortality that you have been speaking to so many sorrowing souls.

Tree and blossom and bird and sea and sky and wind whisper it, sound it afresh, warble it, echo it, let it throb and pulsate through every atom and particle.

Let it be told and retold and still retold until hope rises to conviction, and conviction to certitude of knowledge; until we, like Paul, even though going to our death, go with triumphant mien, with assured faith, and with serene and shining face.

A well-known minister was in his study writing an Easter sermon when the thought gripped him that his Lord was living. He jumped up excitedly and paced the floor repeating to himself, "Why Christ is alive, His ashes are warm, He is not the great 'I was,' He is the great 'I am.'" He is not only a fact, but a living fact. Glorious truth of Easter Day!

We believe that out of every grave there blooms an Easter lily, and in every tomb there sits an angel. We believe in a risen Lord. Turn not your faces to the past that we may worship only at His grave, but above and within that we may worship the Christ that lives. And because He lives, we shall live also.

—Abbott

RESURRECTION SUNDAY

Mrs. Charles E. Cowman

There is an Easter Sunrise Service every year at the famed Hollywood Bowl in Southern California. To this particular service there arrived a dear sister who was sorely bereaved.

"I was among the first to arrive," she related. "I meditated on the story of the first Easter, when they came and found the empty tomb, and I wondered how the women felt when they found the stone rolled away. That morning I had an awakening in my soul before the buglers on the hillside announced the arrival of the dawn! The sun did not shine, but the assurance of the resurrection of Jesus impressed me as never before! Suddenly the darkness within the shell on the stage turned to a white cross, and the children began to sing, 'Christ is Risen!' Then something within me burst forth in praise, and for the first time of my entire lifetime I experienced the full significance of that revelation that came to the women on their first visit to the tomb! Then thousands of voices took up the song, 'All Hail the Power of Jesus' Name!'—and I could understand why the women were perplexed on that first Easter morn—so overwhelming had been to them the demonstration of His power over death. I now know the power of the Risen Lord! He lives! And they live whom I hold most dear! The dawn of Easter broke in my own soul! My night was gone!"

He is not here: for he is risen, as he said.
MATTHEW 28:6

I Am Human, Too!
Ruthe White

I am forgotten as a dead man out of mind:
I am like a broken vessel.
PSALM 31:12

I'm tired of being strong! Weary of being a leaning post. If people really knew how weak I was, they would never look to me for support.

But I am afraid to tell them!

Afraid to let them know I hurt, too. I don't want anyone to know I struggle with some of the same problems everyone else does. It makes me look so good, so spiritual, to pretend.

Have I made myself appear to others as a great pillar of strength, a spiritual authority standing with outstretched arms, inviting people to look up to me?

I dare not tell them what I really am!

Perhaps, I should hide the fact behind a gilded layer of superficial piety.

If they only knew how fragile I was, how easily broken, they would never believe in me again.

Perhaps, perhaps not!

Maybe confession is what is needed. To allow myself to be exposed. Broken! Then there would be no reason for others to come to me or hold me in esteem.

Yes, that is it. Brokenness is what is needed—to lose the pieces of my own identity! Let self be lost so a new person can emerge.

One that is honest, glued together with love, unafraid to be exposed and obviously human.

A Vexation Arises
Mary W. Tileston

My mind was ruffled with small cares
today,
And I said pettish words, and did not keep
Long-suffering patience well, and now
how deep
My trouble for this sin! In vain I weep
For foolish words I never can unsay.
> —H. S. Sutton

A vexation arises, and our expressions of impatience hinder others from taking it patiently. Disappointment, ailment, or even weather depresses us; and our look or tone of depression hinders others from maintaining a cheerful and thankful spirit. We say an unkind thing, and another is hindered in learning the holy lessons of charity that thinks no evil. We say a provoking thing, and our sister or brother is hindered in that day's effort to be meek. How sadly, too, we may hinder without word or act! For wrong feeling is more infectious than wrong doing; especially the various phases of ill temper—gloominess, touchiness, discontent, irritability—do we not know how catching these are?
> —Frances Ridley Havergal

Let us not therefore judge one another any more: but judge this rather, that no man put a stumbling-block or an occasion to fall in his brother's way.
> ROMANS 14:13

FAITH IS HOLDING OUT YOUR HAND
Elisabeth Elliot

Every good gift and every perfect gift is from above, and cometh down from the Father of lights, with whom is no variableness, neither shadow of turning.
JAMES 1:17

Sometimes when I was a child my mother or father would say, "Shut your eyes and hold out your hand." That was the promise of some lovely surprise. I trusted them, so I shut my eyes instantly and held out my hand. Whatever they were going to give me I was ready to take. So it should be in our trust of our heavenly Father. Faith is the willingness to receive whatever He wants to give or the willingness not to have what He does not want to give.

From the greatest of all gifts, salvation in Christ, to the material blessings of any ordinary day (hot water, a pair of legs that work, a cup of coffee, a job to do and strength to do it), every good gift comes down from the Father of Lights. Every one of them is to be received gladly and, like gifts people give us, with thanks.

Sometimes we want things we were not meant to have. Because He loves us, the Father says no. Faith trusts that no. Faith is willing not to have what God is not willing to give. Furthermore, faith does not insist upon an explanation. It is enough to know His promises to give what is good—He knows so much more about us than we do.

PRESSURES
Ruth Bell Graham

There are pressures and pressures. This is about necessary, even creative pressure; not pressure that destroys and debilitates. Capstones, not compactors.

Have you ever studied an old stone arch? The capstone supports the weight of the whole: it bears the pressure.

We appreciate the value of pressure when we see a tourniquet stopping the flow of blood and thus saving a life.

J. Hudson Taylor, that great pioneer missionary to China, used to say we should not mind how great the pressure is—only where the pressure lies. If we make sure it never comes between us and our Lord, then the greater the pressure, the more it presses us to Him.

It may be one more request than we think we can fulfill, one more responsibility than we think we can manage, one more phone call, one more pile of dishes to wash, one more bed to make, one more room to clean, one more complaint to listen to, or one more interruption.

Interruptions never distracted Jesus. He accepted them as opportunities of a richer service.

Brethren, I count not myself to have apprehended: but this one thing I do, forgetting those things which are behind, and reaching forth unto those things which are before, I press toward the mark for the prize of the high calling of God in Christ Jesus.
PHILIPPIANS 3:13–14

April 16

YOUR TRUST IN HIM

Hannah Whitall Smith

I am crucified with Christ: nevertheless
I live; yet not I, but Christ liveth in me:
and the life which I now live in the flesh
I live by the faith of the Son of God,
who loved me, and gave himself for me.
GALATIANS 2:20

Do you, then, now at this moment, surrender yourself wholly to Him? You answer, "Yes." Then, my dear friend, begin at once to reckon that you are His, that He has taken you, and that He is working in you to will and to do of His good pleasure. And keep on reckoning this. You will find it a great help to put your reckoning into words and say over and over to yourself and to your God, "Lord, I am Thine; I do yield myself up entirely to Thee, and I believe that Thou dost take me. I leave myself with Thee. Work in me all the good pleasure of Thy will, and I will only lie still in Thy hands and trust Thee."

Make this a daily, definite act of your will, and many times a day recur to it, as being your continual attitude before the Lord. Confess it to yourself. Confess it to your God. Confess it to your friends. Avouch the Lord to be your God, continually and unwaveringly, and declare your purpose of walking in His ways and keeping His statutes; and sooner or later, you will find in practical experience that He has avouched you to be one of His peculiar people, and will enable you to keep all of His commandments, and that you are being made into "an holy people unto the Lord, as he hath spoken."

DIVINE CONNECTION
Lynne Ricart

While driving my five-speed sports car down the road, I was experiencing great difficulty shifting gears. I stopped at a red light and couldn't get into first gear again. After a few beeps from the cars behind me, I finally succeeded in getting my car into gear and proceeded down the highway.

At the next intersection, every woman's greatest fear became my life! Not only would my car not go into gear, but the engine died right in the middle of a major intersection. I turned on my flashers and headed for the convenience store to use their phone. The man behind the counter, seeing my plight, offered to push my car into the store's parking lot. Not only could this guy operate a cash register, but he turned out to be a proficient auto mechanic. Thank you, Lord! He quickly assessed my problem as a loose battery connector and had my car running within minutes.

How often do we as Christians concern ourselves with what gear or direction we are in when what God really wants is for us to be connected to Him? Just as my car malfunctioned when its battery connector was loose, we cannot function well as Christian women without being connected to our heavenly Father. Seeking His presence daily in prayer, study, fellowship with other Christians, and outreach, we must plug into His power so He can lead us down the road of life and use our journey for His honor and glory!

But the one who joins himself to the Lord is one spirit with Him.
1 CORINTHIANS 6:17 NASB

COME FORTH AS GOLD

Amy Carmichael

Everyone who has this hope in him purifies himself, just as he is pure.
1 JOHN 3:3 NIV

"My grace is sufficient for you, for my power is made perfect in weakness" (2 Corinthians 12:9 NIV). Such words lead straight to a land where there is gold, and the gold of that land is good.

Gold—the word recalls Job's affirmation: "But he knows the way that I take; when he has tested me, I will come forth as gold" (Job 23:10 NIV). And it recalls the ringing words of the apostle Peter: "[All kinds of trials come] so that your faith—of greater worth than gold, which perishes even though refined by fire—may be proved genuine" (1 Peter 1:7 NIV). And it brings the quiet words in Malachi: "He will sit as a refiner and purifier of silver" (Malachi 3:3 NIV).

The Eastern goldsmith sits on the floor by his crucible. For me, at least, it is not hard to know why the heavenly Refiner has to sit so long. The heart knows its own dross.

"How do you know how long to sit and wait? How do you know when it is purified?" we asked our village goldsmith.

"When I can see my face in it," he replied.

Blessed be the love that never wearies, never gives up hope that, even in such poor metal, our Father may at last see the reflection of His face.

WHO IS THE HELPER?
Catherine Marshall

Most of us begin by thinking of the Holy Spirit as an influence, something ghostly, floating, ethereal that produces a warm and loving feeling in us. We betray this misconception by using the impersonal pronoun "it" when speaking of the Spirit.

But the Helper is no influence; He is rather a Person—one of the three Persons of the Godhead. As such, He possesses all the attributes of personality. He has a mind; He has knowledge; He has a will.

In addition, the Spirit acts and forms relationships only possible with a person. Check for yourself these texts:

He speaks (Acts 1:16). He prays (Romans 8:26–27). He teaches (John 14:26). He works miracles (Acts 2:4; 8:39). He can be resisted (Acts 7:51). He commands (Acts 8:29; 11:12; 13:2). He forbids (Acts 16:6–7).

The Helper's work on earth today is also to administrate the Church, Christ's body on earth. For instance, He sets ministers over churches. He distributes varying gifts and ministries to individual members of the Church, and so on.

To crown all this, the Spirit, being a Person, is a Friend whom we can come to know and to love. One of His most lovable characteristics is that He deliberately submerges Himself in Jesus; He works at being inconspicuous.

And I will pray the Father, and he shall give you another Comforter.
JOHN 14:16

SENSITIVITY SIGNALS
Gail MacDonald

And do not grieve the Holy Spirit of God, by whom you were sealed for the day of redemption.
EPHESIANS 4:30 NASB

Sensitivity. . .is the development of an ability to look beneath the surface of events and people and ask the questions: What do these things mean? What is needed? And what can I contribute?

When there is a lack of sensitivity, people can be deeply hurt. We see that sad fact all the time.

I have borrowed a term from Esther Howard, who, years ago, wrote in *Faith at Work* magazine about what she called IALAC. I-A-L-A-C, meaning, I am lovable and capable, is that sense of self-assurance necessary to the inner health of every one of us. When we know God personally, we draw this sense of belonging and competence most powerfully from Him. In the more immediate sense, however, most of us receive it through other people, just as Benjamin West received a portion of it from his mother when she looked over his shoulder. But we only receive it when people are sensitive.

It is possible to build this IALAC into one another, and, sadly enough, it is possible for us to take it away from each other in our insensitive moments. In other words, this IALAC is generally increased or diminished according to the sensitivity of those about us, who, reading our signals, contribute to our sense of value and usefulness, just as we hope we will to them.

Our Life Is Hid With Christ in God

Lilian Whiting

In the most literal sense we live and move and have our being in the realm of spiritual forces. Our "life is hid with Christ in God" (Colossians 3:3). That assertion is no more a mystic phrase, but a plain and direct assertion of an absolute spiritual truth. Our real life, all our significant action, is in the invisible realm, and the manifestation in the physical sphere is simply the results and effects of which the processes and causes are all in the ethereal world. Prayer, in all its many and varied phases, is simply activity on the spiritual side, and because of this, it is the motor life. It is the key to that intense form of energy that is the divine life, and its highest development is reached when the soul asks only for one thing—the one that includes all others—that of union with God.

"Anxiety and misgiving," wrote Fenelon, "proceed solely from love of self. The love of God accomplishes all things quietly and completely; it is not anxious or uncertain. The Spirit of God rests continually in quietness. Perfect love casteth out fear. It is in forgetfulness of self that we find peace. Happy is he who yields himself completely, unconsciously, and finally to God. Listen to the inward whisper of His Spirit and follow it—that is enough; but to listen one must be silent, and to follow one must yield."

Your life is hid with Christ in God.
COLOSSIANS 3:3

I Want to Leave My Mark for You
Anita Corrine Donihue

I press on toward the goal to win the prize for which God has called me heavenward in Christ Jesus.
PHILIPPIANS 3:14 NIV

I know not what each day holds or what time I have left to serve. This I do know, dear Lord, I want to leave my mark for You.

Help me make every day count. Remind me to lay aside my own wants, to be willingly inconvenienced and used for You. Let me not put anything before You, no matter how good it seems. Help me shed bad habits that slow me down from doing Your will.

I can only leave my mark for You by replacing idle time with purposeful movement. When I rest, I open my heart that You may fill me with Your strength and spirit.

Teach me to let go of yesterday, live fully today, and look with excitement toward tomorrow. I am awed as I daily come to know You more. I feel You shower love upon me like a refreshing summer rain.

Even though I am unworthy, I long to reach the end of life's journey and see You face-to-face. In the meantime, Lord, may I use each day, each hour, each moment to leave my mark for You. Amen.

MAKING HIM MORE ROMANTIC

Jean Lush with Pam Vredevelt

When women ask me "How can I change my husband? How can I get him to meet my needs?" I have to say, "It's not easy, but he was very well-conditioned before he ever met you. More romance from him may well depend on your choice to accept and treasure him as he is. If he doesn't sense acceptance and feels you are pushing him to change, he may simply become more resistant. He needs to feel loved as he is. When this is firmly established, then changes may come slowly."

I also believe that too much discussion about unmet needs in a marriage can rob romance of its mystique. Treat romance as you would a delicate and beautiful flower that can be scorched by the hot sun (quarreling and harsh words) or withered by frost (coldness and indifference). Like a beautiful flower, romance must be nurtured, fertilized, and watered on a regular basis. Then the blooming will come naturally.

The grass withereth, the flower fadeth: but the word of our God shall stand for ever.
ISAIAH 40:8

WINGS OF GROWTH
Mrs. Charles E. Cowman

They shall mount up with wings as eagles.
ISAIAH 40:31

There is a fable about the way the birds got their wings at the beginning. They were first made without wings. Then God made the wings and put them down before the wingless birds and said to them, "Come, take up these burdens and bear them."

The birds had lovely plumage and sweet voices; they could sing, and their feathers gleamed in the sunshine, but they could not soar in the air. They hesitated at first when bidden to take up the burdens that lay at their feet, but soon they obeyed, and taking up the wings in their beaks, laid them on their shoulders to carry them.

For a little while the load seemed heavy and hard to bear, but presently, as they went on carrying the burdens; folding them over their hearts, the wings grew fast to their little bodies, and soon they discovered how to use them and were lifted by them up into the air—the weights became wings.

The fable is a parable. We are the wingless birds, and our duties and tasks are the pinions God has made to lift us up and carry us heavenward. We look at our burdens and heavy loads and shrink from them; but as we lift them and bind them about our hearts, they become wings; and on them we rise and soar toward God.

WISING UP
Jo Berry

A large portion of the first ten chapters of Proverbs is devoted to sexual attitudes. The book is laced with warnings about sexual excess. We are admonished to stay away from any adulterous person who has forsaken his or her marriage vows; to avoid "the strange woman, . . .the adulteress who flatters with her words; that leaves the companion of her youth, and forgets the covenant of her God" (Proverbs 2:16–17 NASB).

The first fourteen verses of chapter 5 caution us to steer clear of improper sexual behavior.

Conversely, Solomon extols sex within the marriage relationship. He sets forth, through the power of the Holy Spirit, a beautiful case for monogamy and marital sex, emphasizing that fidelity makes for a joyful, exhilarating relationship.

It is clear that sex within the proper context is not dirty. God invented it. "Male and female He created them. . . . And God saw all that He had made, and behold, it was very good" (Genesis 1:27, 31 NASB). The Lord instituted the one-flesh relationship. He meant for sex within marriage to be a pleasurable, fulfilling experience; a God-given gift to enhance the love relationship between man and wife.

Sex is not dirty, but misuse of it tarnishes and defiles it.

And they were both naked, the man and his wife, and were not ashamed.
GENESIS 2:25

JOCHEBED
Gien Karssen

And Jesus answering saith unto them, Have faith in God.
MARK 11:22

Jochebed had received the meaning of her name, "Jehovah is her glory." Had that name been given to her by believing parents in the hope that she would work for God's glory in her life? Did she choose it herself as a public witness of her deepest thoughts, or was it a name of honor granted to her by God?

The Bible mentions her name only twice, but it is forever engraved in history as the name of one of the most important mothers who ever lived. Probably never in history have three children of one mother, Jochebed, ever had such an influence at the same time.

Her children demonstrated to the world the place that God had in their mother's heart. His honor had been her highest purpose. They also illustrated that principle with their own lives. When Moses was the leader of the Israelite nation, Aaron was its high priest who symbolized God's holiness and grace toward His people. As the high priest, he also represented God to the people and the people to God. As the intercessor for his people, he also foreshadowed Christ.

Miriam also played a part in the leadership of God's people, which, for a woman, was a rare exception in Israel's history. She was the nation's first prophetess and used her gifts in music and song to allow the Hebrew women to bring honor to God.

THE WEAVER'S WORK
Corrie ten Boom

"Does God always give us what we ask in prayer?"

Sometimes His answer is no. He knows what we do not know. He knows everything and His negative answer is part of His plan for our lives.

> My life is but a weaving, between my
>   God and me.
> I do not choose the colors.
>   He worketh steadily.
> Ofttimes He weaveth sorrow, and I,
>   in foolish pride,
> Forget He sees the upper, and I,
>   the underside.
> Not till the loom is silent and
>   the shuttles cease to fly,
> Will God unroll the canvas and
>   explain the reason why,
> The dark threads are as needful in
>   the skillful Weaver's hand.
> As the threads of gold and silver in the
>   pattern He has planned.

Lord, it is hard to accept a negative answer, but keep us humble enough, patient enough, and faithful enough to trust. Thank You that You always answer our prayers in Your way with a yes or a no. How good it is to know that You never make a mistake.

I know, O Lord, that thy judgments are right, and that in faithfulness thou hast afflicted me.
PSALM 119:75 RSV

April 28

CONCERNING CONSECRATION
Hannah Whitall Smith

Thou hast avouched the Lord this day to be thy God, and to walk in his ways, and to keep his statutes, and his commandments, and his judgments, and to hearken unto his voice.
DEUTERONOMY 26:17

"Every devoted thing is most holy unto the Lord" (Leviticus 27:28). This is so plain as not to admit of a question.

But if the soul still feels in doubt or difficulty, let me refer you to a New Testament declaration that approaches the subject from a different side, but which settles it, I think, quite as definitely. It is in 1 John 5:14–15, and reads, "And this is the confidence that we have in him, that, if we ask any thing according to his will, he hear-eth us; And if we know that he hear us, whatsoever we ask, we know that we have the petitions that we desired of him." Is it according to His will that you would be entirely surrendered to Him? There can be, of course, but one answer to this, for He has commanded it. Is it not also according to His will that He should work in you to will and to do of His good pleasure? This question also can have but one answer, for He has declared it to be His purpose. You know, then, that these things are according to His will; therefore, on God's own word, you are obliged to know that He hears you. And knowing this much, you are compelled to go farther and know that you have the petitions that you have desired of Him.

I Don't Like My Job
Anita Corrine Donihue

Dear Father, I pray You will help me with my job. Things aren't going right. I dread going to work, and I need Your direction. On days I feel I'm doing more than my share, may my attitudes be right. Give me wisdom, I pray. When I do menial tasks, help me remember when Your Son, though King of kings, came down from heaven and often acted as a servant. Let me not be too proud to serve.

Help me to be honest in estimating my own abilities, to not put myself down or become a braggart. Teach me to appreciate a job well done, to feel an inner sense of accomplishment. I lean on You, not only on my skills. I know I can earn my pay and make a living; or I can give of myself and make a life.

Go before me when there is friction and backbiting. Let my motives be pure and uplifting, depending on Your help, so Your light can shine through.

Whatever you do, work at it with all your heart, as working for the Lord, not for men, since you know that you will receive an inheritance from the Lord as a reward. It is the Lord Christ you are serving.
COLOSSIANS 3:23–24 NIV

FATIGUE
Mary W. Tileston

For which cause we faint not;
but though our outward man perish,
yet the inward man is renewed day by day.
2 CORINTHIANS 4:16

Let my soul beneath her load
Faint not through the o'erwearied flesh;
Let me hourly drink afresh
Love and peace from Thee, my God!
—Richter

In my attempts to promote the comfort of my family, the quiet of my spirit has been disturbed. Some of this is doubtless owing to physical weakness; but, with every temptation, there is a way of escape; there is never any need to sin. Another thing I have suffered loss from—entering into the business of the day without seeking to have my spirit quieted and directed. So many things press upon me, this is sometimes neglected; shame to me that it should be so.

This is of great importance, to watch carefully—now I am so weak—not to overfatigue myself, because then I cannot contribute to the pleasure of others; and a placid face and a gentle tone will make my family more happy than anything else I can do for them. Our own will gets sadly into the performance of our duties sometimes.

—Elizabeth T. King

CHRISTIAN SERVICE
Ellyn Sanna

Our families are small communities, and within them we experience a "magnitude" of opportunities for service. We are accustomed to thinking of Christian service in terms that are nobler, more dramatic, more like Mother Teresa in the slums of Calcutta or Florence Nightingale on the battlefields of the Crimea. But even for women like Mother Teresa and Florence Nightingale, service boils down to simple assistance in "trifling, external things." For us as mothers, this means things as trivial as matching socks, packing lunches, or wiping kitchen tables. "Be faithful in little things," Mother Teresa advises, "for in them our strength lies."

Self-righteous, self-centered service demands visible, external rewards, but the sort of service that Jesus modeled does not concern itself with results. Instead, it is contented even with obscurity.

Jeremy Taylor's *Rule and Exercises of Holy Living,* written in the seventeenth century, says that we should "love to be concealed, and little esteemed; be content to lack praise, never be troubled when thou art slighted or undervalued."

We need to remind ourselves that our value springs from God's love. We find our truest identities in the midst of his unmerited grace.

With good will doing service, as to the Lord, and not to men.
EPHESIANS 6:7

RUTH
Gien Karssen

"Your God shall be my God, your people shall be my people," Ruth had declared to Naomi on the road to Bethlehem. She decided to do what Naomi had proposed.

She lay down at Boaz's feet, a woman who once again had adorned herself as a bride for a man. She waited expectantly, wondering how Boaz would react.

He was willing to marry her. There was a problem, however, for another man was more closely related to Ruth than he was. If that man waived his rights by not redeeming her, then the way was free for him. Through this test, God would clearly show which of the two men He intended to be Ruth's husband.

Early in the morning while it was still dark, Ruth left Boaz and went out into the empty streets. Boaz had not touched her. His deep love and respect for her had been expressed through his control over his desires.

He had also protected her good name. No one would need to know that she had been on the threshing floor.

Boaz not only guarded himself against evil, he was also conscious of the ideas other people might have. His conversation and attitude proved that God was foremost in his thoughts.

AUTHORITY
Jill Briscoe

Our loving Lord told us that happiness was to be found in following His example and serving others. So many people in this day and age consider this to be a ludicrous concept. The very idea of serving others flies in the face of the constant encouragement we receive from our world to serve ourselves! Self-serving is the name of the game today. In fact, the abundance of leisure time afforded this affluent society has produced a torrent of suggestions from the media as to what to do with all those spare moments. . . .

Jesus, however, took a towel, knelt down, and washed His disciples' feet. Remember, this was His leisure time. Here He was at the end of a busy day, relaxing with His friends, and the first thing He did was to take the form of a slave and busy Himself with a menial task. What's more, He told us if we looked for and engaged in such acts of service, we would be happy indeed.

What does it take to make you happy? A bigger boat in which to cruise the oceans of the world? A longer pleasure trip to faraway places? More weekend outings to the ballpark? Light beer—a few drugs—expensive clothes and jewelry? A better camper or membership in the country club? Try finding some dirty, smelly, sticky, needy feet; and kneeling in the dust of other people's distress, attend to them—then, surprise, surprise—happy you will be! Yes, Jesus left us an example.

Ye call me Master and Lord:
and ye say well; for so I am.
JOHN 13:13

KNOWING GOD
Hannah Whitall Smith

In the beginning was the Word, and the Word was with God, and the Word was God.
JOHN 1:1

To know God, therefore, as He really is, we must go to His incarnation in the Lord Jesus Christ. The Bible tells us that no man has seen God at any time, but that the only begotten Son of the Father, He has revealed Him. When one of the disciples said to Christ, "Shew us the Father, and it sufficeth us," Christ answered, "Have I been so long time with you, and yet hast thou not known me, Philip? he that hath seen me hath seen the Father; and how sayest thou then, Shew us the Father? Believest thou not that I am in the Father, and the Father in me? the words that I speak unto you I speak not of myself: but the Father that dwelleth in me, he doeth the works" (John 14:9–10).

Here then is our opportunity. We cannot see God, but we can see Christ. Christ was not only the Son of God, but He was the Father. Whatever Christ was, that God is. All the unselfishness, all the tenderness, all the kindness, all the justice, and all the goodness that we see in Christ is simply a revelation of the unselfishness, the tenderness, the kindness, the justice, and the goodness of God.

Someone has said lately, in words that seem to me inspired, "Christ is the human form of God." And this is the explanation of the Incarnation.

AND AT BEDTIME
Marabel Morgan

Just before putting our children to bed, we set aside time for spiritual nourishment. Charlie and I believe a spiritual foundation will give our girls the confidence that nothing else on earth can give. Knowing that God loves them and has a wonderful plan for them gives them stability in the face of temptation.

Michelle's first answered prayer was a thrill to us all. When she was very little, she and I spent one afternoon lying in our hammock watching fluffy clouds glide by. She said, "I wish the sky would turn pink."

I said, "Maybe the Lord would paint a pink sunset for you tonight. Do you want to ask Him?"

She prayed fervently, "Dear Jesus, will You make a pink sunset for me tonight?"

I prayed silently and earnestly, too. "Lord, she's only a little child, and this will make such an impression if You do this. Please do it."

We had nearly finished dinner when Laura glanced out the window and said, "Wow! Look at the sunset!" We all looked up at the rosiest, glowingest sunset I had ever seen—many shades of pink vibrantly colored the sky.

Michelle was absolutely awestruck. Excitedly, she told of her prayer that afternoon, and we all reveled in God's answer to a little girl. I knew Michelle would never forget that sunset—her first answered prayer—and the fact that she knew her God cared personally about her.

And all things, whatsoever ye shall ask in prayer, believing, ye shall receive.
MATTHEW 21:22

IS ANYBODY HOME?

Doris Coffin Aldrich

Behold, I stand at the door, and knock.
REVELATION 3:20

It was time for evening devotions. Mommie suggested a song in order to quiet them a bit. (When they get a silly streak, it is easier to keep eight bobbing corks submerged than to get them all quiet at once.) They joined heartily in singing, "Behold, behold, I stand at the door and knock, knock, knock!" This was sung with appropriate motions and great vim.

At the third singing, Jon added a line just after the "knock, knock, knock." While the children were knocking earnestly on the palms of their hands, he asked quizzically, "Is anybody home?"

We laughed until we fairly wept, and then we began to think that his remark wasn't so unreasonable after all.

The Lord does stand and knock at our heart's door—not once or twice, but many times, and the door remains closed, closed to the One who stands without, waiting to bring forgiveness, cleansing, and love to a needy, needy heart.

He will not force His way in—He knocks, and asks entrance. Are you "at home" to His love? Or is He to be left outside? Can you afford to deny Him entrance?

He said, "Behold, I stand at the door, and knock: if any man hear my voice, and open the door, I will come in to him, and will sup with him, and he with me" (Revelation 3:20). He's knocking. Is anybody home in your heart? Home. . .to Him?

GOD'S HEART
Jane Hansen

Restoration is the reason Jesus came to earth. He came not only to redeem us from the fall—to buy us back from death and hell—as essential and wonderful as that was. In great reverence, I say that redemption was just the first step in God's ultimate plan for us. It was, as DeVern Fromke says in *The Ultimate Intention*, "parentheses incorporated into the main theme. Redemption was not the end but only a recovery program," incorporated to return us to God's larger purposes, which He planned from the beginning. Luke's gospel opens by telling us, "[He] has raised up a horn of salvation for us" (Luke 1:69 NKJV). "Salvation" is an all-inclusive term. It means "to deliver, protect, heal, preserve, make whole." In other words, "restore."

God wants to make us whole; that's why Jesus suffered and died! Jesus, the Creator of the universe, died to restore that which He created; and He bore more than just our sins. He suffered death that we might experience peace, healing, and a sense of purpose or destiny, all of which are necessary for wholeness. Restoration is at the heart of the gospel because it expresses the very heart of the Father.

Hear the word of the Lord, O ye nations, and declare it in the isles afar off, and say, He that scattered Israel will gather him, and keep him, as a shepherd doth his flock.
JEREMIAH 31:10

CONTENTMENT
Mrs. Charles E. Cowman

I have learned, in whatsoever state I am, therewith to be content.
PHILIPPIANS 4:11

Paul, denied of every comfort, wrote the above words in his dungeon. A story is told of a king who went into his garden one morning and found everything withered and dying. He asked the oak that stood near the gate what the trouble was. He found it was sick of life and determined to die because it was not tall and beautiful like the pine. The pine was all out of heart because it could not bear grapes like the vine. The vine was going to throw its life away because it could not stand erect and have as fine fruit as the peach tree; and so on all through the garden. Coming to a heart's-ease, he found its bright face lifted, as cheery as ever. "Well, heart's-ease, I'm glad, amidst all this discouragement, to find one brave little flower. You do not seem to be the least disheartened."

"No, I am not of much account, but I thought that if you wanted an oak, or a pine, or a peach tree, or a lilac, you would have planted one; but as I knew you wanted a heart's-ease, I am determined to be the best little heart's-ease that I can."

They who are God's without reserve are in every state content; for they will only what He wills and desire to do for Him whatever He desires them to do; they strip themselves of everything and in this nakedness find all things restored an hundredfold.

I Won't Worry for the Future

Anita Corrine Donihue

Sometimes I feel overwhelmed, wondering what the future holds. Then I remember that worry and fear are not from You. I praise You, Lord, for having control of my future.

Why should I be anxious over what tomorrow or the next day brings when I'm Your child and You have my needs and best interests at heart? Thank You for caring for me, not only now but always. Thank You for caring for those I love. I trust You that now—and even someday when I leave this perishable body and join you in heaven—You will be answering my prayers for my loved ones down through generations.

I read of how, although Abraham's faith was strong, sometimes he doubted Your promises for his future. Sometimes he created disasters by taking things into his own hands. In spite of all that, You still blessed him and Sarah in their later years with a wonderful son.

You have authority over all, so I will not worry for the future. I will trust in You with all my heart and I won't depend on my own understanding. Instead, in all my ways I'll be in tune with You and Your will to guide and direct my paths.

Thank You for the future, Lord. I praise You for going before me and making a way.

"Who of you by worrying can add a single hour to his life? Since you cannot do this very little thing, why do you worry about the rest?"
Luke 12:25–26 NIV

WHEN GOD MADE MOTHERS
Ruthe White

A woman that feareth the Lord, she shall be praised. Give her of the fruit of her hands; and let her own works praise her in the gates.
PROVERBS 31:30–31

He made them as something special!

Their hands are delicately formed; they can create an exquisite piece of art while binding the imaginary wound of a child's broken heart. A mother's soothing touch to a feverish brow is like a "magic cure" to the inner soul.

Kings have been transfused by the plasma of her dreams. Nations are still being conquered through the inspiration of her ideals. Weak leaders are often supported by her feminine mystique. Her offspring have walked on the moon, tilled the soil, explored planets, and plumbed the ocean depths.

She is a paradox! Unpredictable. Not easily understood by the male species. They have studied her, used her body, written pages of scientific data about her. Yet, no one has discovered the mystery of the woman herself.

Nor will they ever!

God and God alone is able to contemplate her worth. For it was she He chose to bear His Son, tutor Him in childhood, and to minister to Him at the cross.

She was the very last of all God's creative acts. When He had finished with His original "Masterpiece" called woman, it was as if God said: "Now that I have made mothers, I can rest."

MOTHER
Doris Coffin Aldrich

Perhaps there will be some willing angel who could take this message up to you, Mother, or maybe they will tell you of it up there where all the glory is.

It makes my heart fill with thankfulness to remember what you did for me, what you were to me, and what you gave me of yourself. From you I learned the beauty of soft yellow and brown, the loveliness of the lines of tree trunks, the way white puffy clouds go scudding across a blue sky.

That night you left us, Mother, Daddy knelt by your bed just after you had gone and wept, "Oh Mother, you've had such a hard life, I had so little to give you." I stood and looked at you both with a great swelling lump in my throat. But now I doubt that it was true. You lived a full life, Mother, and you had so much to give. You enjoyed such dear companionship, and you had your children. And so have I.

There is One who gave and who gives more than any mother. And how mothers need that which He has to give—for those times of weariness there is the gentleness of the Lord and the knowledge of His loving-kindness. For the sense of inadequacy there is His sufficiency, and for the joy of being a mother there is the delight of sharing it all with Him.

As one whom his mother comforteth, so will I comfort you; and ye shall be comforted in Jerusalem.
ISAIAH 66:13

THE HEART OF THE HOME
Mary Hollingsworth

For we are his workmanship,
created in Christ Jesus unto good works,
which God hath before ordained
that we should walk in them.
EPHESIANS 2:10

A woman is not just a person; she's a miracle! Like a cosmic shape-shifter of *Star Trek,* she can transform into anything she needs to be in an instant.

She turns into a nurse at the sight of a scrape or a scratch; in larger emergencies, she's instantly a paramedic.

When trouble comes or the enemy attacks, she becomes the fortress behind which the whole family—even Dad—huddles for protection.

Or she snaps her fingers and changes into a Little League coach, a Girl Scout leader, a homeroom mother, a corporate executive, a financier, a Sunday School teacher, a playmate, a seamstress, a play director, or a volunteer for the March of Dimes. She is, all in the same day, a cook, a taxi driver, a boardroom presenter, a maid, a politician, and a referee.

In addition, she is often the spiritual heart of the home—guiding, encouraging, leading, teaching, and praying. She is God's hands and feet, His laughter and joy, His tears and sorrow. She is the heart of God personified.

There's no doubt about it—a woman is not just a person; she's a miracle!

THE CLOSURE OF FORGET-ME-NOTS
Mrs. Charles E. Cowman

Follow the way of love.
1 CORINTHIANS 14:1 NIV

Love covereth....
PROVERBS 10:12

Rehearse your troubles to God only. Not long ago I read in a paper a bit of personal experience from a precious child of God, and it made such an impression upon me that I record it here. She wrote: "I found myself one midnight wholly sleepless as the surges of a cruel injustice swept over me, and the heart. Then I cried to God in an agony for the power to obey His injunction, 'Love covereth.'

"Immediately the Spirit began to work in me the power that brought about the forgetfulness.

"Mentally I dug a grave. Deliberately I threw up the earth until the excavation was deep.

"Sorrowfully I lowered into it the thing which wounded me. Quickly I shoveled in the clods.

"Over the mound I carefully laid the green sods. Then I covered it with the white roses and forget-me-nots, and quickly walked away.

"Sweet sleep came. The wound which had been so nearly deadly was healed without a scar, and I know not today what caused my grief."

RAINBOW GARDENING

Barbara Johnson

An anxious heart weighs a man down,
but a kind word cheers him up.
PROVERBS 12:25 NIV

When I opened my mail last week, I pulled out a letter with a tiny surprise tucked inside. In a miniature plastic bag was a teaspoon full of colored sprinkles with a label that said: Rainbow seeds. Planting instructions on back. Delighted I quickly turned over the packet and read:

When to Plant: Any season, but rainbows grow best just after a storm.

Where to Plant: In the light of the Son, preferably near a pot of gold.

How to Plant: Assume a kneeling position close to the earth. Dig a hole deep enough to hold the cause of your dark clouds. Place the cause and the seeds in the soil, cover with earth, then rise and stomp down with both feet. Walk away in faith.

Harvest: When needed most.

I got to thinking about how a rainbow is a perfect picture of God's grace. It's a kind of refuge for our mind when storms threaten to rip us apart and flood our dwelling. In the rainbow we see God's promise that He will never again devastate life on earth.

You can be a rainbow gardener by opening your heart even if you're in pain yourself. Let someone know that although you don't have it all together, you find comfort and hope in the Lord.

SAY "YES" TO GOD
Anita Corrine Donihue

Have you come to a fork in your road of life? Do you feel God's call to serve? Do you recognize His voice and know it is Him? Simply wait on Him and say, "Yes."

Don't ponder over the what-ifs or whys, neither question your abilities. Don't worry about timing or the future. Test the calling to be sure it is of God. When you know it is Him, simply tell Him, "Yes."

When the mighty winds blow, He will miraculously place them at your back. When the floods begin to rage, He may tell you to keep paddling in faith, believing, while He calms the seas.

God's calling is sure. We don't have to worry about making a way. If it is His will, He works all things out in His own perfect way and timing.

He calls us through, around, over, and under to serve. No foe can stop us, no poverty can starve us, no evil can diminish His call. For He has a glorious plan!

So, just say, "Yes."

Teach me to do thy will; for thou art my God: thy spirit is good; lead me into the land of uprightness.
PSALM 143:10

THE GREAT SCANDAL
Hannah Whitall Smith

What shall we say then? Shall we continue in sin, that grace may abound?
ROMANS 6:1

Can we, for a moment, suppose that the holy God, who hates sin in the sinner, is willing to tolerate it in the Christian, and that He has even arranged the plan of salvation in such a way as to make it impossible for those who are saved from the guilt of sin to find deliverance from its power?

As Dr. Chalmers well says, "Sin is that scandal which must be rooted out from the great spiritual household over which the Divinity rejoices. Strange administration, indeed, for sin to be so hateful to God as to lay all who had incurred it under death, and yet, when readmitted into life, that sin should be permitted; and that what was before the object of destroying vengeance should now become the object of an upheld and protected toleration. Now that the penalty is taken off, think you it is possible that the unchangeable God has so given up His antipathy to sin as that man, ruined and redeemed man, may now perseveringly indulge, under the new arrangement, in that which under the old destroyed him? Does not the God who loved righteousness and hated iniquity six thousand years ago bear the same love to righteousness and hatred to iniquity still?"

GIVE TIME TO QUIETNESS

Amy Carmichael

The fight to which we have been called is not an easy fight. We are touching the very center of the Devil's power and kingdom, and he hates us intensely and fights hard against us. We have no chance at all of winning in this fight unless we are disciplined soldiers, utterly out-and-out and uncompromising, and men and women of prayer.

So first, give much time to quietness. For the most part we have to get our help directly from our God. We are here to help, not to be helped, and we must each learn to walk with God alone and feed on His Word so as to be nourished. Don't only read and pray; listen. And don't evade the slightest whisper of guidance that comes. May God make you very sensitive and very obedient.

Fill up the crevices of time with the things that matter most. This will cost something, but it is worth it. "Seek ye my face; my heart said unto thee, Thy face, Lord, will I seek" (Psalm 27:8).

All this will be, if you walk with Him as with a visible Companion, from dawn through all the hours till you go to sleep at night. And your nights will be holy, too, for He is watching over your sleep as your mother watched over it when you were a tiny child.

The Lord is my light and my salvation; whom shall I fear? the Lord is the strength of my life; of whom shall I be afraid?
PSALM 27:1

THOUGHTS BY THE SPRING

Joni Eareckson Tada

Do not get drunk on wine,
which leads to debauchery.
Instead, be filled with the Spirit.
EPHESIANS 5:18 NIV

When I was a child on our family's farm, one of my favorite places was the pond down in the pasture by the barn.

As a child, I always wondered where the water in the pond came from. I'd walk all the way around its edge but could never see any stream splashing into it.

My dad patiently tried to explain that the pond was fed by a spring, a source of water from deep down in the earth. That spring, he told me, bubbled up from within and filled the little pond area.

How many of us picture the Spirit being poured into our lives from the outside as if we were hollow mannequins? Just unscrew the cap on top of our heads, Lord, and fill us from the toes on up!

Do we get the idea that God's Spirit is being carried around in a massive pitcher, ready to be ladled out to us for the asking?

That thought reminds me of my old confusion about the farm pond. I kept looking for some stream pouring in. An outside source. Yet, when the Bible talks about us being filled with the Spirit, it's more accurate to picture a spring. When we obey God and yield our lives to Him, emptying ourselves of selfish desires, the Spirit of God is just like a spring bubbling up within us from down deep in our souls. The Spirit source fills us, and we are satisfied.

TRUE HUMILITY
Lyn Klug

Psychologists tell us how important it is that we achieve a high measure of self-esteem. The Christian faith traditionally has emphasized humility. Is there a conflict between these two? Paul tells us not to think more highly of ourselves than we ought, but this implies that we should not think more lowly of ourselves either.

A false humility can be an easy way out. If I put myself down, I need not risk failure or put forth any effort. I can play it safe: "Oh, I'm not good at that; someone else will do it better."

True humility means taking an honest look not only at my limitations and weaknesses, but also at the strengths God has given me.

I'm helped to do this by being part of Christ's body, where there are many members, each with his or her own function. Knowing this, I don't have to exaggerate my strengths or claim gifts that I don't have. I can count on others who have the gifts I don't. But I should not undervalue myself, because my true self-esteem comes from knowing that my unique gifts are as necessary to the body of Christ as anyone else's.

Do not think of yourself more highly than you ought, but rather think of yourself with sober judgment, in accordance with the measure of faith God has given you.
ROMANS 12:3 NIV

EASY LISTENING

Karen Mains

If any man have ears to hear, let him hear.
MARK 4:23

Good conversation is a matter of listening. When Christians filled with the Holy Spirit listen, they listen on three levels. They listen to what words are being said. They listen to what a person really means by those words. And they listen to the voice of the Spirit within, who is giving illumination to their hearing.

Often while sitting in conversations, certain phrases I've heard take on sudden significance. What the speaker meant by a casual expression was deeper than he or she intended to convey. The Spirit has given me knowledge totally apart from the words that were just expressed. Unexpectedly I have come to know some information about this personality; perhaps it is a fear or a problem or the source of the problem. The next step is to ask for spiritual wisdom about what must be done with this information. Am I to confront? Am I to keep quiet and only pray? Am I to wait for more data in order to form a fuller understanding? Am I to reach out in compassionate love?

This complicated capacity for listening deeply cannot be developed apart from learning to listen to the Lord in structured, uninterrupted moments. In order to hear His voice, we must remove ourselves regularly from the busy, overly active, exciting, and troublesome outside world. Contemplation, the fastening of one's mind on one's Creator, is the only method by which we can properly develop this interior silence and openness to the Spirit.

The Measure of the Family

Arvella Schuller

When someone rises to a high position in world leadership and influence, the first information the world wants to know is, "What is the family history?"

Upon reading only a few of the volumes of biographies of well-known people, one will quickly sense that indeed the family—the home and the individuals in it—or the lack of family—greatly influences the actions and life-changing decisions of adults and young persons. It makes them who they are, and, in turn, the family molds and shapes future generations.

Name the person or persons who have shaped our world in art or music, politics or science. Look beyond those persons to the families and homes that molded them. We cannot fully measure the effect of the family, any family. Like the wake of a ship that leaves an unending ripple in an enormous sea, a family's influence can extend far beyond our sight or knowledge.

How can you and I measure the influence upon us of the families that lived before our time? Our ancestors? Or even those who are not in our direct line, but whose lives affected those who were?

And they came with haste, and found Mary, and Joseph, and the babe lying in a manger.
LUKE 2:16

THE MIRACLE-WORKER

Catherine Marshall

But ye shall receive power, after that the Holy Ghost is come upon you: and ye shall be witnesses unto me both in Jerusalem, and in all Judea, and in Samaria, and unto the uttermost part of the earth.

ACTS 1:8

In the early summer of 1944 I found myself curious about what seemed a strange subject indeed—the Holy Ghost. It was not that I had heard any sermon on this topic, or read a book, or been a part of some lively discussion group. Indeed, nothing overt had happened to spark this curiosity.

I decided to go to the one place I could count on for final authoritative truth—the Bible. Scripture had never yet deceived me or led me astray. From long experience I knew that the well-worn words from an old church ordinance had it exactly right—the Bible still is "the only infallible rule of faith and practice."

I discovered that the fullness of the Holy Spirit is not something that happens automatically at conversion. His coming to us and living within us is a gift, the best gift the Father can give us. But the Father always waits on our volition. Jesus told us that we have to desire this gift, ask for it—ask for Him.

Something else shimmered through, too. It's the Spirit who is the Miracle-Worker. When our churches ignore Him, no wonder they are so devoid of answered prayer.

GOING ON A GOD HUNT

Gail MacDonald, Karen Mains, Kathy Peel

Christianity becomes a positive experience when we recognize God at work in our lives. We'd challenge our children to look for God in their everyday lives, using four categories we devised. The first is answered prayer.

The second category is unexpected evidence of His care. For example, Jeremy took the car one day and the motor died. He couldn't get it started. We live by a major highway, right next to a dangerous curve. If the motor had died there, he could have been in a serious accident.

The third "God Hunt" category is unusual linkage and timing. Jeremy demonstrated this when it was time to go away for college. He felt that God was going to do something in the lives of the young people in the Bible study and that he shouldn't leave. So he enrolled at a local junior college instead.

God verified that choice because we saw some of the kids in the Bible study become Christians, as well as some of their friends and parents.

God's help to do His work in the world is the fourth category where we recognize His presence among us. We see this all the time with our work in the radio broadcast *Chapel of the Air*. The children have observed it as well. We have to come up with a new idea for every broadcast—six times a week! And there's always provision.

To every thing there is a season, and a time to every purpose under the heaven.
ECCLESIASTES 3:1

DINAH

Gien Karrsen

Now therefore, if ye will obey my voice indeed, and keep my covenant, then ye shall be a peculiar treasure unto me above all people: for all the earth is mine.
EXODUS 19:5

Dinah, the daughter of Jacob, felt bored, and she had good reason to be. Life in a goatskin tent did not offer much attraction for a girl in her teens, especially since her parents were aged and she had only brothers with whom to talk.

Then they arrived in Canaan. Her father pitched their tents near Shalem, which belong to the city of Shechem, and bought a piece of land. Apparently he wanted to settle in the land God had promised to his forefathers Abraham and Isaac, for through the promise, the land was also his.

Dinah longed for something happier, brighter than the tents of her father. She left the parental tent and began walking toward Shechem.

So she arrived at Shechem. How many, if any, of the local beauties she saw is unknown. But she did end up in the bedroom of the prince of the land. Prince Shechem, the son of Hamor, saw her, took her, and raped her.

Whether Dinah consented to enter the palace or whether she did everything within her power to prevent it remains a secret. Yet within those walls she lost her purity, her virginity. Like every other girl who has shared that experience, she lost something very precious, something that could never be returned.

No Fishing Allowed
Corrie ten Boom

Guilt is a useful experience because it shows where things are wrong. It is dangerous when it is not there at all, just as the absence of pain when someone is ill can be dangerous.

When we belong to Jesus we are not called to carry our guilt ourselves. God has laid on Jesus the sins of the whole world. What you have to do is to tell Him everything, confess your guilt and sin and repent, and then He will cleanse you and throw all your sins into the depths of the sea. Don't forget there is a sign that reads "No fishing allowed." If somebody has suffered through your guilt, then make restitution in the power and wisdom of the Lord.

Lord, thank You that where You have carried our guilt we have not to carry it ourselves. Help us not to listen to the accuser of the brethren, the Devil, anymore, but to Your Holy Spirit, who always points to the finished work on the cross.

As far as the east is from the west, so far does he remove our transgressions from us.
PSALM 103:12 RSV

HIS JOY REFRESHES

Susan Alexander Yates

Neither be ye sorry;
for the joy of the Lord is your strength.
NEHEMIAH 8:10

Happiness is usually caused by circumstances. When things are going great, we feel happy; when life is unpleasant, we are depressed. Supernatural joy, however, enables us to experience a deeper joy that is not so dependent on our circumstances. As we live by correct priorities, cultivating our relationship with Christ on a daily basis, we will begin to experience a quiet joy resulting from a sense of security that we belong to God, and He is indeed in control of our lives. When we focus on this security, we will be free to relax and trust Him in whatever situation we find ourselves. We will not always feel happy, but we will have a deeper sense of joy that we belong to Christ and that His plans for us are good. God's joy is supernatural. His joy is also refreshing.

HE IS ALTOGETHER LOVELY

Cora Harris MacIlravy

It is not when we are following afar off that we find Jesus Christ "altogether lovely"; it is not when we are flirting with the world, nor when we are compromising the Truth of the gospel, that we experience the sweetness of His mouth. It is when we draw close to Him and follow hard after Him; when we constrain Him to come in and sup with us, and we with Him, that we exclaim: "His aspect is like Lebanon, excellent as the cedars. His mouth is most sweet." It is when all else has faded away into insignificance, and He alone fills our vision, that we apprehend the sweetness of His love, which can only be revealed to us as we enter into this place of separation.

It is as we set our faces to know Him; it is as we go through the keenest suffering and persecution for His dear sake, in order to receive all He has for us, that He is altogether lovely. Only as we are without the gate can our eyes be anointed with heavenly eyesalve; only as our eyes are anointed by the Holy Spirit can we see Him clearly. Then do we realize that there is none else who is lovely; and to us, none other is desirable and delightful.

His mouth is most sweet: yea, he is altogether lovely. This is my beloved, and this is my friend, O daughters of Jerusalem.
SONG OF SOLOMON 5:16

NOW
Susan L. Lenzkes

How I wish I could be with you now.
GALATIANS 4:20 NIV

One of my mother's delightful ideas is to write birthday letters to all six of her grown children. These messages warmly and lovingly assure us that we have, indeed, turned out all right.

Musing on my childhood, she recalled that there was never really any friction between us except in my tendency to be in a "dream world." She claimed I still have some of that in my makeup, but she now realizes this is the "creative part" of me.

Imagine that! Just because I occasionally don't hear my kids talking to me when they're two urgent inches in front of my face, she says I'm in a dream world! She wrote:

"I'm sure that you continue to find this creates problems and conflicts as you try to balance the practical everyday world with the ideas and dreams in your head and heart.

"It's a big job, isn't it? Putting practical on one side of the scale and just the right amount of creativity on the other to make a good balance.

"Our time doesn't always have to be divided equally, but our attention needs to be concentrated wholly on one or the other during each encounter!"

Amen to that bit of insight. All we have is now. And the now-moments with our children are as brief as a baby's first smile, as irretrievable as a missed hug.

BELIEVE YOUR FATHER
Hannah Whitall Smith

You are no more under a necessity to be doubtful as to your relationships to your heavenly Father than you are to be doubtful as to your relationships to your earthly father. In both cases the thing you must depend on is their word, not your feelings; and no earthly father has ever declared or manifested his fatherhood one thousandth part as unmistakably or as lovingly as your heavenly Father has declared and manifested His. If you would not "make God a liar," therefore, you must make your believing as inevitable and necessary a thing as your obedience. You would obey God, I believe, even though you should die in the act. Believe Him, also, even though the effort to believe should cost you your life. The conflict may be very severe; it may seem at times unendurable. But let your unchanging declaration be from henceforth, "Though he slay me, yet will I trust in him." When doubts come, meet them, not with arguments, but with assertions of faith. All doubts are an attack of the enemy; the Holy Spirit never suggests them, never. He is the Comforter, not the Accuser; and He never shows us our need without at the same time revealing the Divine supply.

Jesus answered and said unto them, Verily I say unto you, If ye have faith, and doubt not, ye shall not only do this which is done to the fig tree, but also if ye shall say unto this mountain, Be thou removed, and be thou cast into the sea; it shall be done.
MATTHEW 21:21

CALLING ALL TROOPS
Judy Reamer with Donna Arthur

Where no counsel is, the people fall: but in the multitude of counsellors there is safety.
PROVERBS 11:14

When you have made a decision to allow God to work in your heart and in your situation, help is on the way. But let me warn you, you may be in for one of the fiercest spiritual battles you have ever fought. Satan knows your lack of moral strength from the past. He will do everything in his power to keep you in darkness. Remember that "God is faithful; he will not let you be tempted beyond what you can bear. But when you are tempted, he will also provide a way out so that you can stand up under it" (1 Corinthians 10:13 NIV).

Wars are not fought by single soldiers. Armies are sent to win the victory. So you, too, must call on your army of helpers, both heavenly and earthly, to come to your aid.

When your battle becomes fierce, keep the cross (what Jesus Christ accomplished for us at Calvary—freedom from the power of sin, in this case) before you.

If you become weary and drop your guard or see your enemy advancing, open up to one or two spiritual helpers who will support you. Let them know you are not doubleminded and that you desire to be completely healed. You must have help in the beginning. "Confess your faults one to another, and pray one for another, that ye may be healed" (James 5:16).

THE DIFFERENCE CHRIST MAKES IN YOUR DISPOSITION
Eugenia Price

Men and women both excuse their dispositions on the grounds of circumstances. But I believe in all fairness that women have another excuse which is rather exclusively theirs. We don't put it into words. We don't admit it publicly. Usually we aren't even aware of it ourselves. But deep within our feminine personalities is the conviction that we are permitted some temperament simply because we are women!

A woman's disposition is merely an outward sign of what she really is within. An outward sign of what is predominant within her inner self.

If she is predominant there, her disposition shows it.

If Christ is predominant there, her disposition shows that, too.

Then what are we to do? If we know Christ lives within us, and we are still displaying ourselves via our dispositions, what are we to do? First, we are to remember that He works with our minds according to the way He created them. And He created them able to form habits. If we remember this, we will realize that we must form the habit of choosing to let Christ act through us.

But one thing is needful; and Mary hath chosen that good part, which shall not be taken away from her.
LUKE 10:42

HOUSEWORK AND GOD

Ellyn Sanna

Lord, thou hast been our dwelling place in all generations.
PSALM 90:1

Christians today tend to disparage physical appearances. We feel guilty for wanting our private homes to be beautiful, for surely this beauty, benefitting no one but ourselves, would be worldly or selfish. True, our society is obsessed with appearances, and we do not want to make possessions too important or forget those who have so much less. But in the process we have sometimes thrown out the baby with the bath water. We have divorced God from our homes.

God reveals himself intimately in our families. Consequently, our homes are sacred places. They should speak to us of God just as clearly as our churches do. Judaism was more apt to remember the home's holiness, but too often Christians have forgotten. We relegate God to our churches, forgetting that most of Christ's ministry, including the Last Supper, took place in private homes.

Just as in those days, our homes are meant to be welcoming places, places of security and grace that reflect God's nature. "Lord, you have been our dwelling place," says Psalm 90:1. If we remember that our houses are metaphors for God himself, then housework takes on a whole new significance.

HURRY UP, MOM!
Ruth Bell Graham

Ned was not quite tall enough to see over the dashboard of the car I was driving.

"Hurry up, Mom," he urged.

But he was too young to read the road signs that said 45 miles per hour. As I began to apply the brakes, he demanded, "Why are you stopping?"

"There is a school bus that has just stopped," I explained.

As soon as we started again, he urged, "Pass him, Mom." He was too small to see the double yellow line.

I thought to myself, How like me when I pray! Spiritually I am too young to read the road signs, too small to see what lies ahead. Yet how often I am guilty of telling God how to run things.

We may make requests, but never insist on having our own way lest we become one of those of whom it was said, "He gave them their request; but sent leanness into their soul" (Psalm 106:15).

We may pray in simple, childlike faith; urgently, persistently. But we must always pray, "Thy will be done."

Because the foolishness of God is wiser than men; and the weakness of God is stronger than men.
1 CORINTHIANS 1:25

PURPOSE AND PRIORITIES
Gail MacDonald

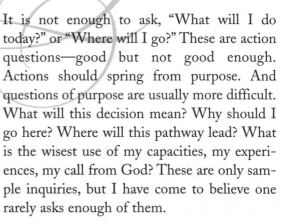

And whatever you do in word or deed,
do all in the name of the Lord Jesus,
giving thanks through Him
to God the Father.
COLOSSIANS 3:17 NASB

It is not enough to ask, "What will I do today?" or "Where will I go?" These are action questions—good but not good enough. Actions should spring from purpose. And questions of purpose are usually more difficult. What will this decision mean? Why should I go here? Where will this pathway lead? What is the wisest use of my capacities, my experiences, my call from God? These are only sample inquiries, but I have come to believe one rarely asks enough of them.

Questions of purpose increase in importance not only with age or struggle but also with the number of things we have to do, the decisions we have to make, the people who make demands on us, the circle of our relationships, and our skills, spiritual gifts, and natural abilities. Purpose questions provide the foundation for the selections we make when it comes to determining when we will say yes and when we will say no.

Harness life with such questions as: What are the truly important things God wants me to do with my years? Where will I seek to make my maximum contributions?

SLOW TO ANGER
Martha Peace

How many times have you burned with anger when you did not have your way? Probably so many times that only God could really keep count. James warned us. First listen. Cultivate the art of listening. Be slow to speak. Think about what you are going to say. Choose words that are edifying instead of angry.

For example, your husband promises to wash the outside windows Saturday. You have a commitment and will be gone all day. It makes you happy just thinking about the windows being sparkling clean! When you arrive home, it is obvious that he did not wash any windows. Immediately, you begin to feel frustrated. By the time you find him, you are boiling on the inside. If you are wise, you remind yourself that you need to listen to his side of the story ("quick to hear"). He will most likely have a reasonable explanation. If not, say, "I need to think about what to say and I'll be back ("slow to speak"). Next, pray and think about what you want to say and how you want to say it. Finally, go back to your husband and talk with him, speaking in a gentle tone of voice. If you have done all of the above, you will be very "slow to anger."

This you know, my beloved brethren. But let everyone be quick to hear, slow to speak and slow to anger.
JAMES 1:19 NASB

LETTING GO
Sheila Walsh

Do not be anxious about anything,
but in every-thing, by prayer and
petition, with thanksgiving,
present your requests to God.
And the peace of God, which transcends
all understanding, will guard your
hearts and your minds in Christ Jesus.
PHILIPPIANS 4:6–7 NIV

What a promise! This is an all-inclusive verse. Do not worry about anything. Don't worry about the children or your car payment or your job or your health. Whatever is on your heart and mind, bring it to the Lord in prayer and in petition and do it with thanksgiving. Thanksgiving is such an important part of the process because it speaks to trust and confidence.

When we take our prayer requests to God and then continue to worry, it is as if we are saying, "Thanks so much for stopping to listen to me, but I'm not sure you can help." In our souls we sense the dissonance in that line of thinking. We believe that God is able to do what He says He will do; why then is it so difficult to rest in this promise that Paul brings before the church in Philippi? Don't be anxious about anything.

What a gift! The Word of God could not be clearer here. If we will relinquish control of our lives and place our trust in God with absolute confidence, then the peace of God, which is beyond human understanding, will cover us, protecting our hearts and minds. This is true joy. Joy that G. K. Chesterton called "the giant secret of the Christian."

No Insignificant People

Amy Carmichael

To some of us, there often comes such a sense of the vastness of things and of our own insignificance it can be a shaking thing. It can even shake our faith in the truth that our Father regards with compassion even the fall of a single sparrow (Matthew 10:29).

To me, one of the proofs that God's hand is behind and all throughout this marvelous book we know as the Bible is the way it continually touches upon this very fear in us—the fear that we are so insignificant as to be forgotten. That we are nothing. Unconsciously, His Word meets this fear and answers it—not always by a direct statement, but often by giving a simple, loving little story.

John, looking through the thin veil of time into eternity, saw his Lord—the Lord he had seen pierced—now holding in His hand seven stars. John declares: "I fell at His feet as though dead." Immediately—just as though this fallen one mattered more than the seven stars, as though there were no stars—"He placed His right hand upon me" (Revelation 1:16–17).

Isn't it beautiful that there was no rebuke at all for their human weakness? And there never is a rebuke for our weaknesses either. "The soul of the wounded calls for help, and God does not regard it as foolish" (Job 24:12 Rotherham).

My God, with his loving kindness,
will meet me.
PSALM 59:10
(Revised Version of 1901)

OFFER HOSPITALITY
Emilie Barnes

*Offer hospitality to one another
without grumbling.*
1 PETER 4:9 NIV

My mother, at seventy-seven, lived in a one-room efficiency apartment on the fifteenth floor of a senior citizen building. She continually shared hospitality with a cup of tea, a cookie, a piece of carrot cake, or some banana bread. Her guests always felt special sipping tea in a real china teacup, eating cookies placed on a pretty plate with a paper doily, and enjoying a few flowers on the table with a lit candle.

Do you grumble at the thought of inviting guests into your home? Many of today's women seem to avoid hospitality due to the pressure of their busy lives.

So many times we feel things have to be perfect—the right time, a clean house, the right food. Yet today's Scripture tells us to cheerfully share our homes. When was the last time you had guests over?

First Peter 4:11 says that if anyone serves, he should do it with the strength God provides. God will provide the strength as we provide the desire. Jesus often fed people before He preached. Having friends in our home gives us the opportunity to let them see Jesus in us, to feel our spirits, to be touched by our love and caring. Many doors have been opened in the hearts of our friends when we've shared a meal together.

ACQUAINTANCE WITH GOD
Hannah Whitall Smith

Who could have anything but peace in coming to know that the God who has created us and to whom we belong forever is a God of love? And what else is there that can bring an unwavering peace?

Acquaintance with doctrines or dogmas may give peace for a time, or blissful experience may, or success in service; but the peace from these can never be trusted to abide. Doctrines may become obscure, experiences may be dulled or may change, we may be cut off by providential circumstances from our work, all things and all people may seem to fail us. The only place therefore of permanent and abiding peace is to be found in an acquaintance with the goodness and the unselfishness of God.

In human relations we may know a great deal about a person without at all necessarily coming into any actual acquaintance with that person; and it is the same in our relations with God. We may blunder on for years thinking we know a great deal about Him, but never quite sure of what sort of Being He actually is, and consequently never finding any permanent rest or satisfaction. And then, perhaps suddenly, we catch a sight of Him as He is revealed in the face of Jesus Christ, and we discover the real God. We no longer need His promises; we have found Himself, and He is enough for every need.

But we have this treasure in earthen vessels, that the excellency of the power may be of God, and not of us.
2 CORINTHIANS 4:7

ROOTED IN LOVE
Gwen Shamblin

I pray that you, being rooted and established in love, may have power, together with all the saints, to grasp how wide and long and high and deep is the love of Christ, and to know this love that surpasses knowledge— that you may be filled to the measure of all the fullness of God.
EPHESIANS 3:17–19 NIV

There is nothing more fun in life than looking for the attention and personal love of the Father. He is waiting to "show off" His love and character to us in totally fresh and unique ways. He is such a genius! It would bore Him to be anything but incredible and mysterious in all of His ways.

I am absolutely delighting in exploring the boundaries of His love. I have not reached the edge of the width or the length, nor have I experienced the height or depth. Have faith and start looking for this love. If you have already found it, then there are still more surprises ahead for you. Just as love between a man and woman will result in the conception and birth of a life, this love of God to you will spring forth life in you.

DIAMONDS IN THE ROUGH
Mrs. Charles E. Cowman

The secret of the Lord is with them that fear him.
PSALM 25:14

There are secrets of Providence which God's dear children may learn. His dealings with them often seem, to the outward eye, dark and terrible. Faith looks deeper and says, "This is God's secret. You look only on the outside; I can look deeper and see the hidden meaning."

Sometimes diamonds are done up in rough packages, so that their value cannot be seen.

God may send you, dear friends, some costly packages. Do not worry if they are done up in rough wrappings. You may be sure there are treasures of love, and kindness, and wisdom hidden within. If we take what He sends, and trust Him for the goodness in it, even in the dark, we shall learn the meaning of the secrets of Providence.

—A. B. Simpson

He that is mastered by Christ is the master of every circumstance. Does the circumstance press hard against you? Do not push it away. It is the Potter's hand. Your mastery will come, not by arresting its progress, but by enduring its discipline, for it is not only shaping you into a vessel of beauty and honor, but it is making your resources available.

TRADITIONS

Quin Sherrer and Laura Watson

A merry heart doeth good like a medicine.
PROVERBS 17:22

Laura is in a regular Thursday-at-three tea-sippers group. They first got together when one of them (Linda) invited a couple of her friends to share her afternoon tea break. Linda had accompanied her husband on a business trip to England where this custom caught her imagination. The news spread, and the three or four of them became nine or ten.

How in the world could they justify taking two hours out of the heart of the week just to drink tea, swap magazines and catalogs, and talk about recipes and roses and "tea bags that are good to lay on puffy eyes"?

Well, aside from "a merry heart doeth good like a medicine" (Proverbs 17:22), "the joy of the Lord is your strength" (Nehemiah 8:10). We do usually take ourselves too seriously. But not this bunch! They have joy!

Their blessing often includes thanking God for the fun they have defusing tension and stress. However, not only do they laugh together—when one of them is hurting, they pray together, too. They have discovered that is what real fellowship is all about. As God draws them closer together, He draws them closer to Himself as well. They truly are strengthened by joy in Him.

Do you need a "family" to share your heart with? Invite someone to tea.

DIFFICULTIES CONCERNING FAITH
Hannah Whitall Smith

I wish you would try to imagine yourself acting in your human relations as you do in your spiritual relations. Suppose you should begin tomorrow with the notion in your head that you could not trust anybody because you had no faith. When you sat down to breakfast you would say, "I cannot eat anything on this table, for I have no faith, and I cannot believe the cook has not put poison in the coffee, or that the butcher has not sent home diseased or unhealthy meat"; so you would go away starving. When you went out to your daily avocations, you would say, "I cannot ride in the railway train, for I have no faith, and therefore I cannot trust the engineer, nor the conductor, nor the builders of the carriages, nor the managers of the road."

Just picture such a day as this, and see how disastrous it would be to yourself, and what utter folly it would appear to anyone who should watch you through the whole of it. Realize how your friends would feel insulted, and how your servants would refuse to serve you another day. And then ask yourself the question, "If this want of faith in your fellowmen would be so dreadful, and such utter folly, what must it be when you tell God that you have no power to trust Him, nor to believe His word; that it is a great trial, but you cannot help it, 'for you have no faith'?"

Jesus said unto him, If thou canst believe, all things are possible to him that believeth.
MARK 9:23

A SERVANT SPIRIT

Jill Briscoe

She riseth also while it is yet night, and giveth meat to her household, and a portion to her maidens.
PROVERBS 31:15

Usually the Servant serves the Master, but the Queen of Hearts "riseth also while it is yet night, and giveth meat to her household, and a portion to her maidens." Now that's because she has a servant spirit. For her, service is a joyful way of life, for there is no question about it, she has made a commitment to be a servant of the Lord. I remember the shock it was to my system to learn that once I had become a Christian I had become a servant! After spending eighteen years of my life serving myself, I learned that there were other people in my world. What was more—they were just as important as I was and did not need to listen to me as I went around speaking with great authority from the depths of my considerable ignorance! I needed to listen to them, and listening, find a way to serve them.

Following on the heels of that surprising discovery came the confirmation of Scripture. As I avidly read my Bible, I found such verses as 2 Corinthians 5:15: "He died for all, that they which live should not henceforth live unto themselves, but unto him which died for them, and rose again"; and Galatians 5:13, "by love serve one another." David and other writers of such psalms as Psalm 116 and 119 sang about being servants, too, and Paul talked constantly about being a "bond slave of Jesus Christ." Yes, I learned being a disciple definitely meant service!

Morning on the Mount

Mrs. Charles E. Cowman

The morning is the time fixed for my meeting with the Lord. The very word "morning" is as a cluster of rich grapes. Let us crush them and drink the sacred wine. In the morning! Then God means me to be at my best in strength and hope. I have not to climb in my weakness. In the night I have buried yesterday's fatigue, and in the morning I take a new lease of energy.

My mother's habit was every day, immediately after breakfast, to withdraw for an hour to her own room and to spend that hour in reading the Bible, in meditation and prayer. From that hour, as from a pure fountain, she drew the strength and sweetness which enabled her to fulfill all her duties and to remain unruffled by the worries and pettinesses which are so often the trial of narrow neighborhoods. As I think of her life and all it had to bear, I see the absolute triumph of Christian grace in the lovely ideal of a Christian lady. I never saw her temper disturbed; I never heard her speak one word of anger, of calumny, or of idle gossip; I never observed in her any sign of a single sentiment unbecoming to a soul which had drunk of the river of the water of life and which had fed upon manna in the barren wilderness.

Give God the blossom of the day. Do not put Him off with faded leaves.

Come up in the morning. . . and present thyself there to me in the top of the mount.
EXODUS 34:2

ROLL, BABY, ROLL
Marabel Morgan

These things have I spoken unto you, that my joy might remain in you, and that your joy might be full.
JOHN 15:11

I hardly ever experience a Plan A day anymore. Life and its upsets seem to gain momentum as I grow older. But I am much more able to cope when I have a workable plan. When the bottom drops out and everything is in chaos, I have two choices: Go bananas or be flexible enough to adjust to Plan B or Plan C or T.

One day, some years ago, I determined to have a "merry heart" even if it killed me. Of course, by starting out with an attitude like that, it almost did. I was already behind the eight ball by breakfast when the baby knocked a pie off the table. Then the cleaners lost Charlie's best shirt. At noon, disgusted, discouraged, and hungry, I headed for the school. While returning home with a carload of little preschoolers plus my baby, the car stopped dead in 89-degree heat in the middle of five lanes of traffic.

I wanted to cry. Then I remembered that I was setting the atmosphere for everyone in the car, so instead I laughed—rather hysterically. The little ankle-biters looked at me surprised, but then they too started to laugh. As we all held hands and raced across the traffic, we laughed. As we trudged for help, we laughed. I told my little charges brightly, "We're having an adventure!"

Remember, when things go wrong, only your plan has failed; you haven't.

ONE REASON FOR DARKNESS
Elisabeth Elliot

Many great saints have experienced what they could only describe as the absence of God, when their souls have entered into a dark night. Abraham was overcome by a horror of great darkness. No doubt this is one of the necessary lessons for some who share most deeply in the sufferings of Christ. He, too, felt that His Father had forsaken Him.

But for the rest of us who are a long way from that most intimate fellowship, there is another, much more common reason for darkness. We find it in the Psalms (107:10–11 NEB): "Some sat in darkness, dark as death, prisoners bound fast in iron, because they had rebelled against God's commands and flouted the purpose of the Most High."

Before we dignify our own experience of darkness by identifying it with the classic mystic experience, it might be well to see if we have not disobeyed the Lord in some way or have been angry at Him because His purpose has been at odds with our cherished plans.

Thank You, Lord, for Your promise: "I am the light of the world. No follower of mine shall wander in the dark; he shall have the light of life" (John 8:12 NEB).

"I am the light of the world. Whoever follows me will never walk in darkness, but will have the light of life."
JOHN 8:12 NIV

PROMISES
Sheila Walsh

God is faithful, through whom you were called into fellowship with His Son, Jesus Christ our Lord.
1 CORINTHIANS 1:9 NASB

I used to have an answer for most problems in life. I had a lot to say on almost any subject. I now have fewer answers, and they might be reduced to the simple phrase, God is faithful. I don't say that lightly or without thought; I say it because I know it is true, and I have discovered that it is true no matter what is happening in my life. With confidence, I add these words to the end of the worst statements in the world: My child is sick and I don't know what to do. . .but God is faithful; I lost my job and I don't know how I will pay my bills. . .but God is faithful; my husband has left me and my heart is torn in two. . .but God is faithful.

Sometimes God does not seem to be faithful because He doesn't answer our prayers as we expected Him to. I have changed my expectations. If the whole purpose of my life is to learn to love God and to show His compassion to the world, then what He is doing in me is more important than what He is doing for me. I have discovered through many tears that if I will bring every jagged edge of my life to Him, He will continue to mold me to become the woman I am called to be.

Whatever is happening with you right now, as your sister in Christ, I urge you to meditate on these words of life: God is Faithful.

Fancy Footwork
Patsy Clairmont

"In the name of Jesus Christ of Nazareth, walk."
Acts 3:6 NIV

Life is full of stuck possibilities. In fact, when you think about it, we are kind of stuck here on planet Earth until further notice. If, as my hymnal puts it, "Till the Roll Is Called Up Yonder," it makes me think we better make the best out of stuck lest life turn into one big rut.

I hate ruts. Ruts are common, unimaginative, and oh, so boring. I know because I've spent time in them. Actually, I even took up emotional residence in a couple. To make them comfortable, I even decorated them. I adorned the walls with excuses: "I can't," "I tried," and "I don't wanna." Those are just a few of the plagues, I mean plaques, I hung in my ruts.

Have you ever observed excavators? First thing they do is send out surveyors to assess. This is where the Holy Spirit and several of your wise friends can assist. The Holy Spirit can reveal to you why you are stuck, and He can empower you to change. Your friends can help strengthen your resolve and pray for you in the process.

Now just imagine what might happen if we were to step out of our old routine and deliberately walk in His ways. Why we might even do a little break dancing on our way up and out of that hard place.

C'mon, sister rut-dwellers, boogie out of there. Risk life!

Jesus, You lead; I want to follow. Amen.

How to Enter In

Hannah Whitall Smith

But thou, when thou prayest, enter into thy closet, and when thou hast shut thy door, pray to thy Father which is in secret; and thy Father which seeth in secret shall reward thee openly.

MATTHEW 6:6

A Christian lady who had this feeling was once expressing to a friend how impossible she found it to say, "Thy will be done," and how afraid she should be to do it. She was the mother of an only little boy who was the heir to a great fortune and the idol of her heart. After she had stated her difficulties fully, her friend said, "Suppose your little Charley should come running to you tomorrow and say, 'Mother, I have made up my mind to let you have your own way with me from this time forward. I am always going to obey you, and I want you to do just whatever you think best with me. I will trust your love.' How would you feel towards him? Would you say to yourself, 'Ah, now I shall have a chance to make Charley miserable. I will take away all his pleasures and fill his life with every hard and disagreeable thing that I can find. I will compel him to do just the things that are the most difficult for him to do and will give him all sorts of impossible commands.' "

"Oh, no, no, no!" exclaimed the indignant mother. "You know I would not. You know I would hug him to my heart and cover him with kisses and would hasten to fill his life with all that was sweetest and best."

"And are you more tender and more loving than God?"

LET JESUS BE LORD
Alma Kern

Some homes have the reminder "Christ is a guest at every meal, the unseen listener to every conversation." Jesus also sees the television programs we watch and the books and magazines we read. He observes the way we use our time, the things we do and say and think. He knows what our income is and how we spend our money.

Sometimes we treat the Lord as an unwelcome guest. We feel uncomfortable knowing He's always around observing everything. At times we ignore Him and wish He'd do the same to us. When a problem arises, we like Him close by. Otherwise, we'd like to confine Him to certain areas of our life and fit Him into our time schedule.

We would be insulted if a guest were to tell us to change our lifestyle, budget and timetable. That's what Jesus does. He's not satisfied to be merely an unseen guest. He wants to be manager. He wants to be in control. That means drastic adjustments on our part. It's not easy to say, "Jesus, I trust You as Savior. I trust You also as Lord of my life. Rule over me."

Only if we really mean that will we become all we can be.

Behold, I stand at the door, and knock: if any man hear my voice, and open the door, I will come in to him, and will sup with him, and he with me.
REVELATION 3:20

WHAT REALLY MATTERS?

Linda R. McGinn

Pray without ceasing.
1 THESSALONIANS 5:17

Have you ever been placed in a situation where you were asked to do something you knew was wrong, and the consequences of refusing were monumental? What did you think? Maybe it won't really matter if I do this once. Only one time, never again. The Lord will understand.

Or did you come to God and pray? Did you say, Lord, what's Your mind about this matter? What instructions do You want to give me through Your guidebook for life, the Bible? Then did you turn to your Bible for answers?

I don't know about you, but sometimes when a crisis arises, I find myself asking others to pray before I've talked to God about the situation myself. I've come to realize that God wants me to read His Word and talk to Him first.

We constantly carry on a personal conversation with ourselves. We evaluate every situation. We review conversations we've had with others over and over in our minds. We carry on an internal discussion about life and our evaluation of it.

I believe God wants us to invite Him into that conversation. That's what I believe Paul means when he tells the Thessalonians to "pray without ceasing" (1 Thessalonians 5:17). God never gives us a command that we can't fulfill. So instead of talking to yourself, why not start talking with God?

THE IMPORTANCE OF DISCIPLINE

Susan Alexander Yates

Through Biblical examples and direct teaching, we see the crucial role of discipline in character development. From Scripture we glimpse the goals of discipline, and we are reminded that the motivation for discipline is love. Practically, what do these principles really mean? How should they actually affect the way we train our children? First, just as God's discipline springs from love, so, too, must ours.

Second, in His relationship with His children, God always took much time to explain and to prepare His children to walk in His ways. Much of what godly discipline involves is training and teaching. Adequate explanation and anticipation of situations can serve to prevent future situations in which punishment is necessary. It is helpful to see discipline as both training and punishment.

Third, our goal in discipline should be twofold: to train in self-discipline and to teach obedience. When our children learn self-discipline at an early age, they will be more likely to withstand the temptations of sin as they grow up. They will also have the personal discipline to be productive adults. Obedience to God is first learned when a child is taught obedience to his parents.

No discipline seems pleasant at the time, but painful. Later on, however, it produces a harvest of righteousness and peace for those who have been trained by it.

HEBREWS 12:11 NIV

"Father," a Relational Term

Jane Hansen

And Jesus increased in wisdom and stature, and in favour with God and man.
LUKE 2:52

God not only wanted to reproduce Himself and fill the earth with His likeness, He also longed for a family. "Father" is a relational term. God wanted children with whom He could share His life. He wanted a people who would love and respond to Him, a people who would have the capacity to know Him and have intimate fellowship with Him.

God began His family with one man, Adam, created in His own image, but soon declared that Adam's solitary condition was "not good." In response to this problem, the woman was brought forth out of the man and at this point, God blessed them, and God said to them, "Be fruitful, and multiply" (Genesis 1:28). In other words, they were to become a family.

The kingdom of God—the nature and character of God, as well as the outworking of God's plan on earth—was to be played out in and through man and woman and the concept of family. There God pronounces His blessing.

Clearly, then, we see that the family is God's design. It was His choice and plan. He gave it His highest endorsement when He placed His own Son within its protective, nurturing walls. Within this framework, His plan for humanity and for Himself will best come to fulfillment. In the context of family, we experience the sense of belonging for which our hearts long. Here we receive love and nurturing.

THE TRANFORMING FRIENDSHIP
Lyn Klug

Two friends asked me to sing in a trio with them. I was glad I'd be singing more, but even happier that I'd be spending time with these two people. The people we choose to spend time with help determine the kind of person we are becoming. They love us, confront us, and help us to do things we never thought we could.

While He was on earth, Jesus changed people's lives by being their friend. A shady tax collector became Saint Matthew, and a quick-tempered fisherman became Saint Peter. They were still themselves, but they were capable of saying and doing things that were quite beyond them until they became His friends.

The heart of the Christian faith is that we, too, can know Jesus, and our friendship with Him can change our lives. Leslie Weatherhead wrote: "Unless the church in all its branches is sadly mistaken, unless the saints were deluded, unless the lives of the world's purest and best are based on illusion, that friendship is still available. . .a friendship capable of making us what we most want to be."

Therefore, if anyone is in Christ, he is a new creation; the old has gone, the new has come!
2 CORINTHIANS 5:17 NIV

SOLITUDE
Jean Fleming

But we all, with open face beholding
as in a glass the glory of the Lord,
are changed into the same image from
glory to glory, even as
by the Spirit of the Lord.
2 CORINTHIANS 3:18

Why solitude? Christians are born complete in Christ, but not mature. We have in Him all we need for life and godliness. But the Christ-life is developed through a process of nourishment and exercise. Our faith must be fed and our obedience given opportunity to express itself. Time alone with God reveals who God is and what He wants done.

Solitude isn't a new idea. The first human couple walked and talked with their Creator in the Garden of Eden. At the heart of life, in all its intended fullness and perfection, man must commune with God. A growing communion with the Lord is the goal of solitude.

Like non-Christians, Christians must exercise, eat a balanced diet, and get fresh air and proper rest if they are to contribute to their good health. In addition, Christians have a secret inner life that must be cared for. Christianity is not an ascetic religion that strips the material world of value, but God does say that what a man is inside is more important than his outward appearance, economic status, or position in society. God looks at the heart (see 1 Samuel 16:7). Christ directed His most stinging rebukes to the Pharisees who neglected their inner life but diligently exercised outward forms to give a spiritual impression.

LITTLE THINGS MEAN A LOT
Linda Dillow

When was the last time you sent a note to your husband at his job, thanking him for taking you out to dinner? Or put a note in his briefcase or lunch box telling him you love him? It only costs a few cents to send a letter, and it only takes a few minutes to write one. We write thank-you notes to everybody, the neighbors who invited us over for hot dogs, to Aunt Grace, who sent the lovely ceramic poodle candy dish, and to Mrs. Duzitall, who so generously gave of her time to address your ladies' club. But what about the fellow who takes you out to dinner when he'd rather collapse on the sofa, who sends you roses even though they make his nose itch, and who spends Saturday afternoons watching your offspring play soccer when the football game on television beckons him?

We somehow feel our husbands just know we appreciate them. Try letting him know by writing or say it explicitly. He may not show any emotion or may even act embarrassed, but inside he'll be thinking you're a pretty smart woman to have figured out what a terrific guy he is! There are hundreds of little things you can say and do to let him know you love him. Use your imagination!

Beloved, let us love one another: for love is of God; and every one that loveth is born of God, and knoweth God.
1 JOHN 4:7

GOD IS REAL

Hannah Whitall Smith

Now faith is the substance of things hoped for, the evidence of things not seen.
HEBREWS 11:1

Because God is not visibly present to the eye, it is difficult to feel that a transaction with Him is real. I suppose that if, when we made our acts of consecration, we could actually see Him present with us, we should feel it to be a very real thing and would realize that we had given our word to Him and could not dare to take it back, no matter how much we might wish to do so. Such a transaction would have to us the binding power that a spoken promise to an earthly friend always has to a man of honor. What we need, therefore, is to see that God's presence is a certain fact always, that every act of our soul is done before Him, and that a word spoken in prayer is as really spoken to Him as if our eyes could see Him and our hands could touch Him. Then we shall cease to have such vague conceptions of our relations with Him and shall feel the binding force of every word we say in His presence.

THE SIMPLE TRUTH
Kathy Kearney

During my first months as a new Christian, I didn't know any other believers.

Then a classmate in my English class invited me to an Intervarsity Christian Fellowship Bible study. One evening John, an acquaintance from high school, came to visit. He invited me to dinner the next weekend at his aunt and uncle's.

His aunt and uncle asked me about my new beliefs. "I accepted Christ about three months ago. I can't describe the joy I have in my heart knowing that every one of my sins is forgiven."

They looked at each other. "Your sins are not forgiven. Christ died only for the sins of Adam. You now have the privilege of earning your salvation by living a good life to gain heaven."

My heart spiraled downward.

Monday one of our Intervarsity counselors came by. I found myself pouring out the events of Saturday evening. She turned to Ephesians 2:8, pointing out that we are saved by grace through faith and not by works.

"Well, then, whom do you believe, Kathy? A nice, friendly couple who look and sound good or God's Word?"

It was a simple true answer. And it was enough.

For God so loved the world, that he gave his only begotten Son, that whosoever believeth in him should not perish, but have everlasting life.
JOHN 3:16

GOD'S KINGDOM IS HERE
Hannah Hurnard

Be ye transformed by the renewing of your mind.
ROMANS 12:2

I was growing very dissatisfied with myself and my life. I meant so well and longed to be of use, but somehow I seemed to be so dreadfully powerless, so unable to help people in their sorrows, sufferings, and sicknesses as I longed to do, and as I believe we are all meant to be able to do.

I talked about this lack of power to the Lord.

"My child, what is your motive? To help or hurt? Instead of blaming people, bless them, speak well of them. Concentrate on discovering the good things in people and on encouraging them to enjoy doing good and lovely things. You can't force people to stop doing bad things, but you can make doing good so attractive that they don't want to waste a minute of time on the wrong and harmful things. Quietly adapt yourself to living happily with the people who aggravate you, rather than trying to force them to change their habits so as to suit you."

Whenever you react with praise and thanksgiving for an opportunity to grow more like Jesus in your way of reacting to things, instead of grumbling or feeling self-pity, you will find that the whole situation will be changed into a great big blessing.

How to Pray in God's Will

Evelyn Christenson

Have you come to the place where you can pray, "Only God's will"? Do you know that you are in absolute oneness with the will of God? Have you come to that place?

What do we mean when we use the expression "praying in God's will"? Is it simply tacking on the end of a prayer the phrase we use perhaps more frequently than any other? You know how it goes. We ask God for a whole string of things, then we piously add, "if it be Thy will, Lord. Amen." Or it may be that we ask God for something we know is not good for us. Let's say, for example, that we ask for a bushel of Hershey bars! God knows very well (and so do we) that if we ate a bushel of Hershey bars we'd die of indigestion, but many times we ask Him for something just as ridiculous and tack on "if it be Thy will," just to get ourselves off the hook. This is not what it means to pray in God's will. Praying in God's will is not easy, yet it's very simple. It involves a commitment of every single thing that comes into our lives to God and His perfect will. And it's exciting to live in complete oneness with the will of God. It is never dull or static because it is not a one-time, once-for-all commitment. It is something we have to work at constantly, moment by moment.

And this is the confidence that we have in him, that, if we ask any thing according to his will, he heareth us: And if we know that he hear us, whatsoever we ask, we know that we have the petitions that we desired of him.
1 John 5:14–15

TO LEARN CHRIST
Elizabeth Prentiss

Looking unto Jesus the author and finisher of our faith.
HEBREWS 12:2

I have just been to see Mrs. Campbell. In answer to my routine lamentations, she took up a book and read me. . . "Wish always, and pray, that the will of God may be wholly fulfilled in you."

I said despondently, "If peace can only be found at the end of such hard roads, I am sure I shall always be miserable."

"Are you miserable now?" she asked.

"Yes, just now I am. I mean that I am in a disheartened mood, weary of going round and round in circles, committing the same sins, uttering the same confessions, and making no advance."

"My dear," she said after a time, "have you a perfectly distinct, settled view of what Christ is to the human soul?"

"I do not know. I understand, of course, more or less perfectly that my salvation depends on Him alone; it is His gift."

"But do you see with equal clearness that your sanctification must be as fully His gift as your salvation is?"

"No," I said after a little thought. "I have had a feeling that He has done His part and now I must do mine."

"My dear," she said with much tenderness and feeling, "then the first thing you have to do is to learn Christ."

"But how?"

"On your knees, my child, on your knees."

FAMILY, WHAT'S THAT?

Arvella Schuller

The very existence and presence of my children make home a pleasure for me. When I've come home tired, only to open the door and hear their feet running toward me and feel their warm arms encircle my legs, I've thanked God for their life. They loved me without noticing when my dress was not the latest fashion, my hair needed attention, or I had a run in my stocking. They never noticed when my face was badly in need of some fresh make-up; they just loved me the way I was.

The pleasure of belonging to a family is a treasure indeed. Each person needs a place where he or she belongs. That is a natural need for every human being. You and I gravitate to a place that we can call our own, a place where we can hang our hat, where we can live in privacy. Where I can be me! We naturally are pulled toward a person or group of persons whom we can trust and where we are accepted as we really are. This, then, is the joy of belonging to a family: We can relax in a private place, whether it is a tent or a tower, a condominium, a cottage, or a castle, with people who love us as we are.

And thy seed shall be as the dust of the earth, and thou shalt spread abroad to the west, and to the east, and to the north, and to the south: and in thee and in thy seed shall all the families of the earth be blessed.
GENESIS 28:14

CLAY AND WAX

Joni Eareckson Tada

Beloved, think it not strange concerning the fiery trial which is to try you, as though some strange thing happened unto you: But rejoice, inasmuch as ye are partakers of Christ's sufferings; that, when his glory shall be revealed, ye may be glad also with exceeding joy.
1 PETER 4:12–13

Hardened clay is brittle, easily damaged. If dropped, it can fracture into a thousand pieces. Dropped wax, however, only bends from the pressure of the fall. Impressionable and pliable, it can be quickly remolded.

People are like that. People who are hardened in their resolve against God are brittle; their emotions are easily damaged. But those who bend to the will of God find perfect expression in however God molds them.

"The same sun that hardens clay, melts wax." That's true. There is no change or variation in the sun itself. It's just the way the clay or wax responds. Trials and suffering will harden some just like breakable clay, baking in bitterness and resentment. The same circumstances can melt others, teaching them patience and endurance. The trials have no value or intrinsic meaning in themselves. It's the way we respond to those trials that makes all the difference.

SAILING BY FAITH

Mrs. Charles E. Cowman

*He went out,
not knowing whither he went.*
HEBREWS 11:8

When we can see, it is not faith, but reasoning. In crossing the Atlantic we observed this very principle of faith. We saw no path upon the sea nor sign of the shore. And yet day by day we were marking our path upon the chart as exactly as if there had followed us a great chalk line upon the sea. And when we came within twenty miles of land, we knew where we were as exactly as if we had seen it all three thousand miles ahead.

How had we measured and marked our course? Day by day our captain had taken his instruments and, looking up to the sky, had fixed his course by the sun. He was sailing by the heavenly, not the earthly, lights.

So faith looks up and sails on, by God's great Sun, not seeing one shoreline or earthly lighthouse or path upon the way. Often its steps seem to lead into utter uncertainty, and even darkness and disaster; but He opens the way and often makes such midnight hours the very gates of day. Let us go forth this day, not knowing, but trusting.

Waiting on God brings us to our journey's end quicker than our feet.

FAMILY—AN OUTFLOW OF THE FATHER'S HEART

Jane Hansen

And God said, Let us make man in our image, after our likeness.
GENESIS 1:26

From the beginning, family was the centerpiece of God's creation. When God created the heavens and the earth, He didn't just reach "out there somewhere" to arbitrarily devise a plan for this new creation. Because He is omnipotent (all-powerful) and omniscient (all-knowing), He could have designed the earth and its inhabitants to function any way He chose.

He wanted to reproduce Himself and fill the earth with His own image—all that He is. All of His characteristics—His love, His gentleness, His mercy, His grace—were attributes of a Father for His children, attributes that He intended to reproduce in them.

This gives greater meaning to the words we read in Genesis 1:26 when God said, "Let us make man in our image, according to our likeness" (that they might bear the stamp of our likeness). Humanity was meant to bear more than a rational or moral likeness to God. He intended that His own Spirit be placed within us. A. W. Tozer agrees:

> *Deep inside every human being there is a private sanctum, a sacred place where only God can dwell. And that which makes him a human being is not his body but his spirit, the place in which the image of God was made to rest.*

PAUSE (SELAH)

Amy Carmichael

We have all been subjected to the wearying voices which flood the very atmosphere around us, complaining, "There is no help."

Pause.

"But You, O Lord, are my helper!"

This is true, not only with the difficult outward circumstances of our lives, but with inward temptations, too. We are tempted. And at once we recall past failures in this same area. This causes us to feel weak and start to fall. The voices within are saying, "There is no help."

Even these inner struggles may be turned to peace. How? Instead of trying to answer the many voices of the enemy or arguing with them (we can never win this type of argument), we must do something else.

We pause. We look away from self, away from the enemy. We look up!

Some believe that selah signifies also a sudden pealing forth of musical instruments. The pause, then, was for praise.

Then let us fill all of our pauses with praise! Let us give all that lies within us, not to the voices of the enemy, but to pure praise, to pure loving adoration, and to worship from a grateful heart—a heart that is trained to look up.

Many there be which say of my soul,
There is no help for him in God. Selah.
PSALM 3:2

HAVE YOU CHECKED YOUR WARDROBE LATELY?

Barbara Johnson

Put on therefore, as the elect of God, holy and beloved, bowels of mercies, kindness, humbleness of mind, meekness, longsuffering.
COLOSSIANS 3:12

Have you checked your spiritual wardrobe lately? The apostle Paul listed the garments of the Holy Spirit in his letter to Colossian believers. First on his list is tender mercies—acts of empathy for weak or hurting people. I call tender mercies the underwear of God's wardrobe—personal and next-to-the-skin. They are the foundation for everything that goes on the outside.

Next on Paul's list is kindness, treating others with honor and significance.

Humility is next. No matter how much we win or lose in life, God wraps us in a beautiful cloak of grace.

Meekness is one of my favorite things to wear. Meekness makes it possible to endure difficult circumstances and poor treatment at the hands of others.

How about longsuffering? Sometimes I wish that old rag would just wear out so I could get something more glamorous and colorful. But I know God has fashioned even this to enhance my life.

Bearing with others and forgiveness are the outerwear of God's designs. They are the last things we pull on over everything else before we go out into the world.

Above all else, Paul says, put on love. Without this, we are never fully dressed.

AWAY—OR UP?
Ruth Bell Graham

I remember once when troubles descended like a sudden storm that dumps ten inches of rain in twenty-four hours. But why is it that way? Why do troubles so often come in bunches or in such rapid succession that we barely have time to catch our breath before another downpour?

I'm glad the psalmist did not live on a perpetual high. David once longed for wings of a dove so that he might fly away and be at rest. We would settle for the wings of a Concorde or a 747—even a Piper Cub!!

Then I discovered God's promise in Isaiah 40:31. There, those who "wait upon the Lord shall renew their strength; they shall mount up with wings as eagles; they shall run, and not be weary; and they shall walk, and not faint."

So it boils down to: "Away—or up"? The key seems to be "waiting on the Lord."

In this "instant" generation, most of us don't wait easily. But we can learn. F. B. Meyer once wrote: "Not always talking to Him or about Him but waiting before Him till all the stream runs clear, till the cream rises to the top; till the mists part and the soul regains its equilibrium."

The Lord is good unto them that wait for him, to the soul that seeketh him.
LAMENTATIONS 3:25

Hospitality Begins At Home

Karen Mains

*Use hospitality one to another
without grudging.*
1 Peter 4:9

Why is it always easier to extend the courtesies of hospitality to those outside our immediate families? Husbands, relatives, children, or strangely enough their friends often receive short shrift of our kind attention. This point was brought forcibly home to me by my daughter, who cleverly exclaimed before a roomful of guests, "Mommy, why aren't you this nice to us when people aren't here?"

Hospitality, like charity, in order to be true, has to begin at home. The Lord has humiliated me enough through the comments of my own children that I have been forced to examine my attitudes toward them. Did it count, all this gracious open-house business, if I acted like a hellion the hour before company arrived? Wasn't there something hypocritical about receiving laurels for my church work if my own children's friends were neglected? Wasn't there a glaring inconsistency if I really treated my children differently when outsiders were around? Through the years I had come to an understanding of the use of hospitality as a gift of the Holy Spirit for ministry. But was I really ministering to my own?

A woman can't be perfect in everything, can she? Yet telltale marks had been imprinted on my own heart by the timely reading of the Scriptures: If you give even a cup of cold water to a little child. . .anyone who takes care of a little child is caring for God who sent Me.

SOUL FOOD

Hannah Whitall Smith

"Give us this day our daily bread," is a prayer that includes the soul as well as the body, and unless the religion of Christ contains this necessary food for our weekday lives, as well as for our Sunday lives, it is a grievous failure. But this it does. It is full of principles that fit into human life, as it is in its ordinary commonplace aspects; and the soul that would grow strong must feed itself on these, as well as on the more dainty fare of sermons and services and weekly celebrations.

Does not plain common sense teach us that, when people feed their souls upon a diet of gossip or of frivolities of any kind, they must necessarily suffer from languor of spiritual life, debility of spiritual digestion, failure of vitality, and a creeping moral paralysis?

"But lusted exceedingly in the wilderness, and tempted God in the desert. And he gave them their request; but sent leanness into their soul" (Psalm 106:14–15).

"Leanness of soul" arises far more often than we think from the indigestible nature of the spiritual food we have been feeding upon.

Wherefore do ye spend money for that which is not bread? and your labour for that which satisfieth not? hearken diligently unto me, and eat ye that which is good, and let your soul delight itself in fatness.

ISAIAH 55:2

BLESSED ARE THE MEEK

Eileen Egan and Kathleen Egan, O.S.B.

*"Blessed are the meek,
for they shall inherit the earth."*
MATTHEW 5:5 RSV

Other words for "meek" are lowly or gentle. In a competitive world, these words hardly express prized qualities. The aim of Mother Teresa's Sisters, "to remain right on the ground" and never to desert the lowliest is lived out with spectacular fidelity. This fidelity stops people short and even stuns them.

Their actions present a mystery that only the Gospel can clarify. Their actions, performed with alacrity and joy, are understood in the light of the Gospel. It is Jesus who told us, "Take my yoke upon your shoulders and learn from me, for I am gentle and humble of heart. Your souls will find rest, for my yoke is easy, and my burden light" (see Matthew 11:29–30).

Of course, there are times when faith falters. One becomes sad at the powerlessness of our small actions, lowly things, done for lowly people. Mother Teresa reminds us of this, saying, "Do the small things with great love."

*Lord Jesus,
We want to imitate You, who told us, "I am meek and humble of heart." We ask You that, day by day, You lead us in this path. We wish to bring You, dear Christ, to others, in Your freedom, in Your liberations. Help us overcome our impatience, our anger, our tendency to manipulate others. Help us daily to cultivate meekness, humility, and nonviolence.*

RESURRECTED LIVES
Judy Reamer with Donna Arthur

All of us were created sexual beings, and sexual stimuli surrounds us daily. But not every woman, thank God, becomes a victim to an affair.

Why? She has learned the secret of knowing herself and preparing herself by putting on the full armor of God.

If we truly desire to have resurrected lives, we cannot rationalize sin in any area. My close friend and confidante, Jo Anderson, put it this way: "Because we know our needs, we cannot bend the Word of God to meet those needs. We cannot rationalize sin by saying, 'God wants my needs met; I want my needs met; so I'll bend God's Word, and He won't mind.' What God wants is for death to work in us. He wants us to apply the cross. What is the cross? It's the point where my will crosses His will."

God wants to resurrect new life in us.

While only God knows what is in each woman's heart, we, when we are made aware of our own special problem areas, can and must allow God to replace those potentially sinful ways with wholesome and holy character traits.

For this is the will of God, even your sanctification, that ye should abstain from fornication.
1 THESSALONIANS 4:3

PRAYING PATIENTLY

Mrs. Charles E. Cowman

Rest in the Lord,
and wait patiently for him.
PSALM 37:7

Have you prayed and prayed and waited and waited, and still there is no manifestation? Are you tired of seeing nothing move? Are you just at the point of giving it all up? Perhaps you have not waited in the right way.

"With patience wait" (Romans 8:25). Patience takes away worry. He said He would come, and His promise is equal to His presence. Patience takes away your weeping. Why feel sad and despondent? He knows your need better than you do, and His purpose in waiting is to bring more glory out of it all. Patience takes away self-works. The work He desires is that you "believe" (John 6:29), and when you believe, you may then know that all is well. Patience takes away all want. Your desire for the thing you wish is perhaps stronger than your desire for the will of God to be fulfilled in its arrival.

Patience takes away all weakening. Instead of having the delaying time, a time of letting go, know that God is getting a larger supply ready and must get you ready, too. Patience takes away all wobbling. "Made me stand upon my standing" (Daniel 8:18, margin). God's foundations are steady; and when His patience is within, we are steady while we wait. Patience gives worship. A praiseful patience sometimes "longsuffering with joyfulness" (Colossians 1:11) is the best part of it all. "Let (all these phases of) patience have her perfect work" (James 1:4), while you wait, and you will find great enrichment.

LEAVE HIM TO ME

Elisabeth Elliot

There is a deep misunderstanding which has led to the erection of barriers between two who once were close; every day brings the strengthening of those barriers if they are not, by God's grace, breached. One prays and finds no way at all to break through. Love seems to "backfire" every time. Explanations become impossible. New accusations arise, it seems, from nowhere (though it is well to recall who is named the Accuser of the brethren). The situation becomes ever more complex and insoluble, and the mind goes round and round, seeking the place where things went wrong, brooding over the words which were like daggers, regretting the failures and mistakes, wondering (most painfully) how it could have been different. Much spiritual and emotional energy is drained in this way, but the Lord wants to teach us to commit, trust, and rest.

"Leave him to Me this afternoon," is what His word is. "There is nothing else that I am asking of you this afternoon but that: Leave him to Me. You cannot fathom all that is taking place. You don't need to. I am at work in you, in him. Leave him to Me. Someday it will come clear. Trust Me."

"Humble yourselves then under God's mighty hand, and he will lift you up in due time. Cast all your cares on him, for you [and the other] are his charge" (1 Peter 5:6–7 NEB).

At that day ye shall know that I am in my Father, and ye in me, and I in you.
JOHN 14:20

SPIRITUAL MAPS
Millie Stamm

Thy Word is a lamp unto my feet, and a light unto my path.
PSALM 119:105

My husband and I traveled a great deal. Before we took a trip, we always secured maps and studied them thoroughly to know the best route to take.

On one trip I had been informed that a certain highway was the best route. We came to a turnoff which I thought was the highway we were to take. However, I didn't check the map. Soon we discovered we were not on the right road. Instead of a wide paved road we were on a narrow, dusty road winding through the mountains. Not only did it take us longer, but it was a rough road. I should have checked the map. Official maps are wonderful guides, saving time and gasoline, if we use them and follow them.

We need spiritual illumination for our walk through life and God has provided it. The Bible is God's "official map" for our daily travel to show us the right way.

Foot lamps used to be worn at night. They were fastened on the toes, and as the person walked, the lamp cast a light on the next step ahead. So God's Word is a lamp for our way, lighting our feet step by step for our immediate needs just ahead. We can be assured of its light on our path through life.

Spurgeon said, "The Word of God is a lamp by night, a light by day, and a delight at all times."

PRINCIPLES ALONE ARE NOT ENOUGH
Jean Fleming

When the principles are clear, there is still the need to make personal application.

A young Christian from a Hindu family faced a dilemma. His neighbors considered him a disrespectful son because he no longer walked with his family to the marketplace to receive ashes on his forehead and then return home to worship the family idols. He consulted with a mature Christian friend who asked him, "What are the principles involved?"

"I must worship the Lord alone. And I must honor my parents."

"That's right. Now spend time alone with the Lord to see how He wants you to apply them."

After prayer, the young Christian decided to walk with his parents to the marketplace, but when they worshipped the idols, he would step back and pray to the Lord.

Sometime later, another new Christian approached the young believer with the same problem. Then wisely he advised, "Get alone with God and see how He wants you to apply them."

Each person must relate personally with Christ in applying His principles.

Man shall not live by bread alone, but by every word that proceedeth out of the mouth of God.
MATTHEW 4:4

OBEDIENCE
Martha Thatcher

He that hath my commandments,
and keepeth them, he it is that loveth me.
JOHN 14:21

To draw nearer to God and to show Him our love, we are to keep His Word.

This truth was my first discovery in the search for a biblical understanding of obedience: We love God by obeying God. In asking people, "How can we show our love to God?" I have received many imaginative answers, mostly reflecting a vague, rather ethereal, perspective: "by giving Him my whole heart"; "by being who He wants me to be"; "by living a praiseful life"; "by making Him Number One." These are great ideas, but they are still in the realm of a nebulous heart experience, devoid of specifics to act on.

Obeying God, on the other hand, is thought of as something that "dedicated" Christians and missionaries and pastors do well, while the rest of us just try! Thinking that separates loving God and obeying God is a trap of Satan, designed to discourage and frustrate sincere Christians through misunderstanding. As long as we do not understand that we love God by keeping His Word, we will not be deliberately carrying out the greatest commandment.

Loving God is not a nebulous heart experience, but a concrete and active expression of commitment through obedience. This is so exciting: I can learn to express love to God in the way He wants me to, by learning how to be actively obedient to Him.

SARAH'S BEAUTY REGIMEN

Lisa Bevere

It is obvious from these accounts that Sarah was a woman of exceptional beauty. So let's see what her beauty regimen consisted of.

1. She left all that was comfortable and familiar.
2. She followed her husband to a strange land.
3. She lived in a tent in the desert.
4. She trusted God and did not fear or worry.

This was not the life of a pampered queen in a palace. It was a life of constant transition and faith. She would settle (if you call living in a tent "settling") in one place for a while, then travel across the desert to another. She was always waiting for the fulfillment of God's promise and trusting the guidance of her husband. She honored and obeyed her husband, and he honored and obeyed God. There is no record that she complained. Abraham, the father of faith, and his princess, Sarah, are an example and pattern of Christ and His bride, the church.

We are called to adapt ourselves as dependent and secondary to Christ. He is our Head, and all who believe are subject to His lordship, leadership, and authority. But we have no reason to fear. He is our Maker-Husband. He has forged us with His love.

Even as Sarah obeyed Abraham, calling him lord: whose daughters ye are, as long as ye do well, and are not afraid with any amazement.
1 PETER 3:6

JESUS CARES ABOUT CHILDREN
Quin Sherrer and Laura Watson

"Whoever welcomes this little child in my name welcomes me."
LUKE 9:48 NIV

Once when His disciples argued over who would be the greatest, Jesus stood a little child beside Himself and said, "Whoever welcomes this little child in my name welcomes me; and whoever welcomes me welcomes the one who sent me. For he who is least among you all— he is the greatest" (Luke 9:48 NIV).

Some years ago author Pat King wrote me about her own hospitality lessons. Mother of ten youngsters herself, she never knew when she would have an extra child to feed.

One morning I stopped in to see my friend Julie, who has four children under the age of five. Remembering my own days of little children, my heart often went out to her. I peered in the doorway; there were Julie and her three oldest children sitting in a circle of the floor with a dish towel spread out in the middle as a tablecloth. The baby watched from his bed as Julie poured water into the children's teacups and divided up the raisins and graham crackers. "Now, Mrs. Jones," she asked her three-year-old, "would you like milk or sugar in your tea?"

Julie's smile acknowledged me in the doorway, but she went on with her tea party as if she were entertaining the most important people in the world. I watched for a few moments, then slipped out the back door. Driving home, I thought about the women that day who would serve the Lord by entertaining those around them.

KEEP YOUR EYES ON THE ROSE
Peggy Benson

I once read an article in which a young man was describing his mother. He said, "She is the kind of person who doesn't notice the dust on the table, but instead, looks at the rose in the vase."

My friend Karen is that kind of person. She immediately sees the flower; she'd never notice the dust in my friendship garden. Karen belongs in a sunny flower bed. Bright, cheerful, and fun-loving, she tolerates warm summer breezes and demands little upkeep. By nature, she is a nurturer, a motivator, an encourager, so that as a result of her example, they begin to realize their own potential.

When I think of her, I am thankful that she listened to the lessons taught by the Master Gardener. She has discovered His secrets about seeds and knows that those that He plants within each of us will do their work—even without human intervention. But Karen has allowed God to use her to inspire others, encouraging them to open themselves to the energy of the Creator so that they may become exactly and completely what He intended for each of them.

I pray that I may follow Karen's example— looking for the rose, guarding my eyes from seeing only the dusty dry places, being a model for others, claiming for myself the promises of Philippians 1:6.

Being confident of this, that he who began a good work in you will carry it on to completion until the day of Christ Jesus.
PHILIPPIANS 1:6 NIV

No Unforgiveness
Betty Malz

And the Lord said unto Moses,
Thus thou shalt say unto the children
of Israel, Ye have seen that
I have talked with you from heaven.
Exodus 20:22

Heaven is a place of no more unforgiveness.

A young couple brought their seven-year-old daughter, Heather, to meet me and sent her out to play while they told me an amazing story.

The little girl had dived into the deep end of their backyard swimming pool, and they found her drowned, floating facedown. The paramedics arrived in three or four minutes. In the emergency room of the hospital, after a miraculous recovery from death, Heather gave her mother a curious message. She looked at her mother and said, "Grandma says she forgives you." Heather had never seen even a photograph of her grandmother, but was able to describe her—her size, her hair, the mole near her left ear.

This young woman, Heather's mother, was able to put her heart at rest because of the unusual message her daughter brought back from heaven.

Forgiveness is the order of the day in heaven. Perhaps we will understand as never before the enormous gift of forgiveness that God has given us through His son, Jesus Christ, and our own grievances will seem petty in the light of that love.

EMPTY NEST
Ruth Bell Graham

It comes sooner or later to us all. All who have nests.

You have never seen a bird hanging onto her babies' tail feathers, with her beak herding them back into the nest when they would fly away. Quite the opposite: If the fledgling is reluctant, he is gently nudged out.

I had left Ned at a boarding school in England. The other children by now were either married or away in college. Bill was off on a crusade. I dreaded returning to that now empty house.

But as I entered the front door and looked down the length of the hall and up the steps leading to the children's now vacant rooms, suddenly it wasn't empty. I was greeted by a living Presence, and I realized anew how true His last words were: "Lo, I am with you" (Matthew 28:20).

So home is where I hope to stay for the most part. I hope to be here when any of the children or grandchildren need me. From my vantage point, I can look back on circumstances involving our children, situations I once felt were hopeless, only to see in disbelief and amazement as God brought order out of chaos, light out of darkness.

As each little family builds its nest, I shall be watching with interest and love, concern at times, but concern undergirded with confidence, knowing God is in control.

As an eagle stirreth up her nest, fluttereth over her young, spreadeth abroad her wings, taketh them, beareth them on her wings: So the Lord alone did lead him.
DEUTERONOMY 32:11–12

THE VASE
Gigi Graham Tchividjian

And that repentance and remission of sins should be preached in his name among all nations.
LUKE 24:47

I could hear the screaming and arguing all the way to my bedroom. It sounded serious, so I ran to investigate. I arrived just in time to see one son throw a flower vase at another. The vase flew past his head and exploded on the brick terrace. A hush fell as they looked up and found me standing in the doorway, staring at the fragments of broken pottery. After a scolding in which I expressed my disappointment at their behavior and my regret over the shattered vase, I returned to my room, leaving them silent and subdued.

Later as I passed the terrace, I saw the two culprits, their heads bent together over what had once been the vase. With a large pot of glue on the floor beside them, the two little fellows were patiently trying to piece it back together. They had made a mistake, but they were sorry and were doing their best to repair the damage.

I stood there for a moment thinking of all the times that I, too, have caused damage. How often has my insensitivity shattered someone's self-esteem? How often have I crushed a child's will? How often have I damaged self-confidence and caused discouragement by harping on faults instead of praising a job well done?

Never let the sense of the irreparable cause you to despair. Give your mistakes to the Lord and allow Him to "make all things new."

Boost Yoour Teen's Esteem
Bonnie Bruno

What frustrates many of us is that the method we use on our teens today may fall flat tomorrow. However, because adolescents can be unpredictable, we must handle them lovingly and cautiously.

Listen to their music. . . . Imagine their shock when you take the time to ask the name of their favorite musical group, whether or not they write their own lyrics, and what makes them unique.

Ask your teen for advice. . . . Teenagers, who so often feel trapped between childhood and adulthood, will jump at the chance to express their ideas. Showing you value their input and respect their opinions raises their self-esteem a notch or two.

Look for ways to compliment them. Many times our natural instinct is to correct. Our teens experience days when they thirst like a droopy, neglected ivy. A single compliment will work wonders at such moments.

Control your shock. Whether the topic is who's doing drugs at school or the latest rumored pregnancy, practice listening to your teen with your mouth shut. If you must speak, it's better to ask questions than sermonize.

When your teen comes to you and admits a personal mistake, how do you react? Did you ever consider the courage it takes for him to ask for forgiveness?

A man hath joy by the answer of his mouth: and a word spoken in due season, how good is it!
PROVERBS 15:23

Focusing Your Heart

Cheryl Biehl

And we know that all things work together for good to them that love God.
Romans 8:28

I was totally overwhelmed by my friend's situation.

Then I remembered the Old Testament prophet Elisha's prayer to open the eyes of his servant. Do you remember the story? It's found in 2 Kings 6. Elisha was an old, blind prophet, who had "eyes" to see what his young servant couldn't. Elisha apprised the Israelite king of war plans being made by the enemy, the king of Aram. After losing a string of battles, the king of Aram thought there was treason among his troops. But upon thorough investigation, he discovered that Elisha was the informant.

So Aram's king sent soldiers to destroy the old man. When Elisha's servant looked out and saw an army with horses and chariots surrounding the city, he assumed the odds against Elisha and himself were overwhelming.

I love Elisha's reply: "Don't be afraid. Those who are with us are more than those who are with them." I can picture the servant smiling over Elisha's obvious blindness. And then Elisha prayed: "O Lord, open his eyes so he may see." Miraculously, God allowed the servant to see what He already had shown Elisha—"hills full of horses and chariots of fire all around."

Remembering the story, my heart relaxed. I realized that this same Sovereign God had sent His angels to surround my friend, even as He had Elisha. Who was I to worry?

FAILURE OR SUCCESS IS OPTIONAL
Lilian Whiting

Failure or success is optional with the individual, for each lies in character and is not a matter of possessions or external conditions. To become cynical, despondent, indifferent is failure, and one has no moral right to fall to that level. The happy conditions of life are to be had on the same terms. The fretful, the ill-tempered, the selfish, the exacting must somewhere and some way learn their lesson and grow toward the light; but their influence should not be allowed to poison the spiritual atmosphere. It is neither a moral duty nor is it even true sympathy to share the gloom and depression generated by these qualities. The inward whisper of the Spirit is the summons to a nobler plane on which all the higher powers find their expression. It is a fatal mistake to enter into the dark and unreasoning moods of every unfortunately constituted person. To do this habitually is to so deplete the forces of the spirit that one has nothing left. Let one keep his heart and mind in the currents of the Divine Power; let him actively follow the vision that is revealed to him, and he shall achieve and realize his ideals. It is the law and the prophets. A force as resistless as that of the attraction that holds the stars in their courses will lead him on. The love of God accomplishes all things quietly and completely.

This book of the law shall not depart out of thy mouth; but thou shalt meditate therein day and night. . . and then thou shalt have good success.
JOSHUA 1:8

WORST THINGS FIRST
Marabel Morgan

If ye know these things,
happy are ye if ye do them.
JOHN 13:17

I find that it helps to prepare your list for tomorrow's jobs tonight. This way your subconscious mind is preparing for action even while you sleep.

Defuse the pressure spots by tackling worst things first, early in the day when you're fresh. Delaying action on those worst things only increases your tension and makes the problems loom larger. Sometimes facing a problem squarely makes it diminish in size or even disappear altogether.

The secret of attaining goals is working a little bit on it each day. You can't move a mountain in a day, even if you work until you're exhausted. Pace yourself. Exhaustion inhibits your work. Don't stay on the goal until you're bleary. Break down your big projects into little projects.

I wish young mothers with babies could realize that those hectic demanding days and nights will pass. When you think you are going under for the third time, remember that your babies and your schedule will improve. Soon the children will learn to dress themselves, feed and entertain themselves, and within a few years, go off to school.

As they grow older, you can then exchange ideas adult-to-adult. One day you will desire their companionship above all others. But now, while they are in your hands, you are building the very foundation of their lives.

You haven't much time.

A Very Present Help

Amy Carmichael

Which is harder: to do or to endure?

I think to endure is much harder, and our Father loves us too much to let us pass through life without learning to endure. So I want you to welcome the difficult little things, the tiny pricks and ruffles that are sure to come almost every day. For they give you a chance to say "No" to yourself, and by doing so you will become strong not only to do but also to endure.

I know that each one of you is in need of continual help if you are continually to conquer. I have splendid words to give you; they are from the first verse of Psalm 46: "a very present help."

Our loving Lord is not just present, but nearer than thought can imagine—so near that a whisper can reach Him. You know the story of the man who had a quick temper and had no time to go away and pray for help. His habit was to send up a little telegraph prayer. "Thy sweetness, Lord!"—and sweetness came.

Do you need courage? "Thy courage, Lord!" Patience? "Thy patience, Lord!" Love? "Thy love, Lord!" A quiet mind? "Thy quietness, Lord!"

Shall we all practice this swift and simple way of prayer more and more? If we do, our Very Present Help will not disappoint us. For Thou, Lord, hast never failed them that see Thee.

God is our refuge and strength, a very present help in trouble.

PSALM 46:1

DRAWN TO OBEY
Hannah Whitall Smith

For it is God which worketh in you both to will and to do of his good pleasure.
PHILIPPIANS 2:13

God's promise is that He will work in us to will as well as to do of His good pleasure. This means, of course, that He will take possession of our will and work it for us and that His suggestions will come to us, not so much commands from the outside as desires springing up within. They will originate in our will; we shall feel as though we desired to do so and so, not as though we must. And this makes it a service of perfect liberty; for it is always easy to do what we desire to do, let the accompanying circumstances be as difficult as they may. Every mother knows that she could secure perfect and easy obedience in her child if she could only get into that child's will and work it for him, making him want himself to do the things she willed he should. And this is what our Father, in the new dispensation, does for His children; He "writes his laws on our hearts and on our minds," so that our affection and our understanding embrace them, and we are drawn to obey instead of being driven to it.

PRACTICE MAKES PERFECT PEACE
Sheila Walsh

Solitude is a gift.

Discipline is required in solitude. It is learned discipline. Our environment offers any number of noisy options to keep us constantly entertained. We have forgotten how to be quiet. When I first began to give myself to the discipline of solitude, I despaired of ever being able to quiet my mind. I would turn the radio or TV off and sit for a while. My mind would wander all over the place. I was repeatedly discouraged, wanting to quit, reasoning that this was simply not the way for me to fellowship with God. But I didn't give up. I kept trying. After a while I began to relax into being alone with God. I left all my lists and requests behind. This was time for quiet, not for petition.

My times of silence before God are very important to me now. I put everything else down, every word away, and I am with the Lord. When I'm quiet, life falls into perspective for me. I have a very active mind and I'm a worrier, but in those moments when I choose to put that away, I rest beside the Shepherd in still places.

Why don't you give yourself a gift today? Turn off the television or the car stereo, put down the newspaper or the business plan, and in the quietness, rest for a while beside the Shepherd of your soul.

The Lord is my shepherd, I shall not be in want. He makes me lie down in green pastures, he leads me beside quiet waters.
PSALM 23:1–2 NIV

PACING
Susan L. Lenzkes

My soul, wait thou only upon God.
PSALM 62:5

The doctor's office is not my favorite spot to spend a sunny spring morning. But that's exactly where I spent this one. It helped, though, that there was a sunny-faced little boy to watch. This blond, wide-eyed preschooler completely captivated me and everyone else with his eagerness to experience everything a doctor's waiting room could offer.

He checked out the chairs and their occupants. He covered his baby sister with her checked blanket and tenderly explained that there was no need to be afraid. He marched down the hall to explore the bathroom, and a roomful of weary patients' eyes lit with amusement as his giggle echoed from behind the door. Perhaps he'd discovered he was finally tall enough.

Eventually, when he'd exhausted the room's possibilities, he announced with finality, "I'm tired of this place now. Let's go, Mommy."

"We have to wait, honey," she said.

"But I'm ready to go. Let's get out of here!"

He didn't really understand that he was waiting there for a purpose, his good health.

Lord, sometimes You put me in Your waiting rooms. Help me to be patient with Your schedule. I need to learn all I can from those waiting rooms, but I should never forget that I must remain there until I see You. It's absolutely essential to my health.

SORROWS AND HOLY LIVING
Elizabeth Prentiss

"Doesn't it seem hard when you think of the many there are in the world, that you should be singled out for such bereavement and loneliness?"

She replied with a smile: "I am not singled out, dear. There are thousands of God's own dear children scattered over the world suffering far more than I do. And I do not think there are many persons in it who are happier than I am. I was bound to my God and Savior before I knew a sorrow, it is true. But it was by a chain of many links; and every link that dropped away brought me closer to Him, till at last, having nothing left, I was shut up to Him and learned fully what I had only learned partially, how soul-satisfying He is."

"You think, then," I said while my heart died within me, "that husband and children are obstacles in our way and hinder our getting nearer to Christ?"

"Oh no!" she cried. "God never gives us hindrances. On the contrary, He means, in making us wives and mothers, to put us into the very conditions of holy living."

For godly sorrow worketh repentance to salvation not to be repented of: but the sorrow of the world worketh death.
2 CORINTHIANS 7:10

TRUST AND WORRY
Hannah Whitall Smith

I will put my trust in him.
HEBREWS 2:13

Remember always that there are two things that are more utterly incompatible even than oil and water, and these two are trust and worry. Can you call it trust, when you have given the saving and keeping of your soul into the hands of the Lord, if day after day you are spending hours of anxious thought and questionings about the matter? When a believer really trusts anything, he ceases to worry about the thing he has trusted. And when he worries, it is a plain proof that he does not trust. Tested by this rule, how little real trust there is in the Church of Christ! No wonder our Lord asked the pathetic question, "When the Son of man cometh, shall he find faith on the earth?" He will find plenty of work, a great deal of earnestness, and doubtless many consecrated hearts; but shall He find faith, the one thing He values more than all the rest? Every child of God, in his own case, will know how to answer this question. Should the answer, for any of you, be a sorrowful No, let me entreat you to let this be the last time for such an answer; and if you have ever known anything of the trustworthiness of our Lord, may you henceforth set to your seal that He is true, by the generous recklessness of your trust in Him!

LOWLY WORK
Mary W. Tileston

A lowlier task on them is laid,
With love to make the labor light;
And there their beauty they must shed
On quiet homes, and lost to sight.
Changed are their visions high and fair,
Yet, calm and still, they labor there
—Hymns of the Ages

These were the potters, and those that
dwelt among plants and hedges: there
they dwelt with the king for his work.
1 CHRONICLES 4:23

Anywhere and everywhere we may dwell "with the King for His work." We may be in a very unlikely or unfavorable place for this; it may be in a literal country life, with little enough to be seen of the "goings" of the King around us; it may be among hedges of all sorts, hindrances in all directions; it may be furthermore, with our hands full of all manner of pottery for our daily task. No matter! The King who placed us "there" will come and dwell there with us; the hedges are all right, or He would soon do away with them; and it does not follow that what seems to hinder our way may not be for its very protection; and as for the pottery, why, that is just exactly what he has seen fit to put into our hands, and therefore it is, for the present, "His work."

—Frances Ridley Havergal

ARE YOU LISTENING?
Linda Dillow

Wherefore, my beloved brethren, let every man be swift to hear, slow to speak, slow to wrath.
JAMES 1:19

Are you listening? Can your husband talk to you and not be ridiculed? Can he confide in you and know his confidences will be safely guarded? Do you create a climate in which he feels safe to voice his fears because you believe in him? Do you treat your husband as the most special person in the world or are you more polite to the neighbors? We teach our children to be polite, yet how polite are we to their fathers?

Wives often complain their husbands won't talk, but many times we fail to encourage them to talk. Draw him out. Set aside time each day to talk to him. Often I take an index card and write down all Jody is doing that day. As I pray for him, I refer to the card and feel like I'm vitally involved in each thing he does. At the end of the day, I am full of knowledge-able questions.

We have found that we talk better away from home. There are always interruptions: two phones ringing, three precious children needing attention, paper boys at the door to be paid, and many more. On our "dates," we go to a restaurant and sit and talk. We always find that we talk on a deeper level and communicate better away from the distractions of home. This technique may not be everybody's bag, so find something that works for you and do it!

A Firm Grasp of the Hand

Amy Carmichael

I found that Rotherham sometimes translates [trust] lean on, as in, "On Thee do we lean?" (2 Chronicles 14:11), and "Because thou has not leaned" (2 Chronicles 16:7).

"I have trusted in Thy mercy [leaned on Thy mercy]" (Psalm 13:5 Rotherham), that mercy which has loved us with an everlasting love, which pardons and cleanses and will never tire of us. "He that trusteth in the Lord [leaneth on the Lord], mercy shall compass him about" (Psalm 32:10 Rotherham).

"Now there was leaning on Jesus' bosom one of His disciples, whom Jesus loved" (John 13:23 Rotherham). It was when John was leaning, that he heard his Lord's answer to a question which puzzled the others.

"Whoso leaneth on the Lord, happy is he" (Proverbs 16:20 Rotherham). He is indeed.

"What time I am afraid, I will lean on Thee" (Psalm 56:3 Rotherham).

"The Lord is my strength and my shield; my heart leaned on Him, and I am helped: therefore my heart greatly rejoiceth; and with my song I will praise Him" (Psalm 28:7 Rotherham).

May the Lord of love make this word of His to be "like a firm grasp of the hand" to teach each one of us.

For the Lord spake thus to me with a strong hand, and instructed me that I should not walk in the way of this people.
Isaiah 8:11

THE BEST FAMILY TRADITION: PRAYER

Quin Sherrer and Laura Watson

The sacrifice of the wicked is an abomination to the Lord: but the prayer of the upright is his delight.
PROVERBS 15:8

Recently Laura came across a letter her uncle Ted, a missionary, had written to his mother on her eighty-first birthday:

Thank God that our every memory of you is one of beauty and holy living and rare parental guidance. Every one of us will be able to remember our family prayers morning and night. And how you taught us the Scriptures.

Laura's grandmother went to heaven just three months after receiving that letter. But her prayers and the influence of her godly life are still an active blessing for her children, grandchildren, great-grandchildren, and a fast-growing number of great-great-grandchildren. Following a family reunion several years ago, Laura realized that all her grandmother's descendants were Christians.

What a heritage to ponder. What a tradition for all mothers (and all of us) to follow: Pray for our children (and others in our extended family), pray with our children (and others), and live a godly life before them. The results are always far-reaching. Heaven will be full of the evidence.

REMEMBER YOUR POSITION
Ruth Bell Graham

The local sheriff had decided to tighten the requirements for his deputies. Each man had to qualify on the firing range, and the distance had been extended from fifteen yards to twenty-five yards. So the deputies gathered to try their hand at hitting the target at the increased distance. Each man had eighteen seconds to get off twelve shots.

The best shot in the area is also a personal friend. When his time came to shoot, he drew a bead on the target.

"Suddenly," as he told me later, "I began to perspire. And when I perspire, my glasses fog up. There I was with a bead drawn on the target, and all I could see was fog.

"Then I remembered what our old navy instructor had taught us: 'If (for some reason) you ever lose sight of the target,' he said, 'just remember your position.'

"So," our friend said, "I just held my position and pulled the trigger as fast as I could. When I took off my glasses and wiped them, I had hit the bull's-eye every time."

There are times when we, for some reason, lose sight of our target—which is to glorify our Lord. The world is too much with us. Tears blur our vision. Unexplained tragedy raises questions that cannot be answered and shakes our faith to its foundations.

Then we must remember our position, for the Christian's position is "in Christ."

I will praise thee, O Lord my God, with all my heart: and I will glorify thy name for evermore.
PSALM 86:12

HELPING HANDS

Jill Briscoe

Our soul waiteth for the Lord: he is our help and our shield.
PSALM 33:20

Ken had no funds for Bible school tuitition. The youth group of which he was a part was made aware of the problem. One girl began to work overtime "laboring with her hands that which was good that she might have to give"— to Ken. Others sold precious items and gave to the "common cause."

And what did I do? Well, I was faced with a real dilemma. At that time I literally had no extra cash.

One night a friend came down to my house in order for me to cut her hair. To my amazement she gave me a thank you note with ten pounds inside. I knew it was for Ken. The next day as I scribbled him a little note, I opened our mail. Inside was a bill for ten pounds! Now I was in a quandary. Apart from the money my friend had given me, I had absolutely no funds to pay that bill!

Eventually I put the ten pounds in Ken's card and posted it. That very afternoon a neighbor stopped by and told me she loved the way I had fixed my friend's hair and asked me if I would fix hers and her kids' for ten pounds! What joy! It isn't a question of giving only if I am so rich it won't hurt. It is a question of realizing nothing I have is my own.

MY BODY, MY HOUSE
Marabel Morgan

Every woman knows she must someday grow old and lose the bloom of youth. Yet when it begins to happen, she registers shock. Wrinkles appear overnight. She sees the law of gravity pulling on her underarms and chin and everything below the chin. Who would have ever thought it could happen to her?

Proverbs 31 describes God's Total Woman. One of her chief characteristics is "no fear of old age," because she follows His plan for her, day-by-day. He makes life so great there's not much time to fret about the bags and sags, much less time to fear them.

While my girls and I were talking about life one day, I told them, "Your body is actually a shell, a 'house' you wear. The real you which is inside your body will someday leave. So if anything happens to your body, it won't affect the real you. Even if you were in an accident and your arms or legs were cut off, the real you would still be intact inside."

To me, that's very comforting. Knowing that God designed my house takes great pressure off me. I am not going to fight His design. Someday we'll be free of these bodies and their diseases and limitations, but for now we're stuck inside. I'll change what I can and accept what I can't.

Now also when I am old and greyheaded, O God, forsake me not.
PSALM 71:18

CALLED TO GREATER SEPARATION

Cora Harris MacIlravy

Thou hast ravished my heart, my sister, my spouse; thou hast ravished my heart with one of thine eyes, with one chain of thy neck.
SONG OF SOLOMON 4:9

Precious Savior! How oft have we heard Thee knocking at the doors of our hearts; not only when we were sinners, but even after we had tasted and knew that the Lord was good and had proved Thine infinite love.

How dull we are when it comes to a realization of the love of Christ. We are like little children who watch the beautiful colors and dazzling lights in a priceless diamond, but know not its value. We have no conception of what it cost our Lord to purchase redemption for mankind; we know not His suffering. We shall never know the anguish that broke His heart as He hung on the cross, deserted by all who had claimed to love Him.

Oh, that we might love Him more! It seems that He demands so little from us in comparison with what He has given us. Even a little turning of our love toward Him, and His heart responds to us, and the warmth of His love sweeps over us like flaming billows. Even a little turning of our faces toward Him with determination to go on into all He has bought for us, and He hastens to meet us.

NECESSITY OR LUXURY?

Ruth Youngdahl Nelson

The crowd that followed Jesus to the lakeside was so large that He had to get into the boat on the lake, and as the gospel writer records, "There he sat, with the whole crowd on the beach right down to the water's edge!" Many in that crowd earned their livelihood by sowing and reaping, so they could well envision the parable.

What were the worldly cares and false glamour of wealth in that day, we wonder. Surely according to our standards, we would have considered them minimal. No indoor plumbing, no car (very few had even a donkey), no TV, no boat, and no snowmobile.

We need to take inventory of our possessions. Which are necessities? which luxuries? Next time we go shopping, we would do well to pause and hear the Lord say, "Do we really need that?"

Take inventory!

My home is filled with things I don't really need, Lord, and yet I go out and buy more. I haven't even cupboard space enough. Help me not to get caught up in the rash of compulsive buying. Weed out the thistles that would choke out the Word! Amen.

And these are they which are sown among thorns; such as hear the word, and the cares of this world, and the deceitfulness of riches, and the lusts of other things entering in, choke the word, and it becometh unfruitful.
MARK 4:18–19

IF I BELITTLE
Amy Carmichael

Consider what a great forest is set on fire by a small spark. The tongue also is a fire.
JAMES 3:5–6 NIV

[Jesus said], Anyone who says [to his brother or sister], 'You fool!' will be in danger of the fire.
Matthew 5:22 NIV

If, in any way, I belittle those who I am called to serve. . .

if I talk of their weak points in contrast, perhaps, with what I think of as my stronger points. . .

if I adopt a superior attitude, forgetting to consider the wisdom of the voice that asks me, inwardly, "Who made you different from the one you are criticizing—and what do you have that you have not been given?"

If I can easily discuss the shortcomings of the sins of any man or woman. . .

if I can speak in an offhanded way, even of a child's wrongdoing. . .then I know nothing of Calvary love.

My Father, how often do my words "singe" someone else? (And how much time do I spend thinking critically about another—so that nothing but words that singe come out?)

Today, Lord, work in me. Change the thought-life in me when I strip others of dignity. . . or reduce them point by point. . .in order to build myself up.

And give me your voice, to speak words of value. . .admiration. . .encouragement. . .compassion. . .true kindness.

THROUGH LIFE'S CHANGES
Anita Corrine Donihue

Everything that is good and perfect comes from You, O Lord and Creator. How great are Your fullness and wonder. You shine on my life day and night with no shadow of turning away. Thank You for keeping the promises You gave in Your Word. You never forsake, You never fail. You are truth, You are life.

When I go through life's changes, I sometimes find myself getting way off base. But You snatch me from destructive situations. Thank You for being here. At times I can't see why things happen the way they do. But You know, and You are still here. Thank You for being patient with me. Thank You for how Your compassion and love never fail.

I'm growing in my walk with You. Because of all You teach me, I'm learning to give my joys, my worries, my disappointments, my goals, and dreams. They are all in Your sure hands. Lord, You are first now in everything I do and plan.

What a comfort to know You will live forever and ever and that I can always be with You. You have promised to always be my God and keep me Your child. Through eternity, I cling to You, the Rock of my salvation. I shall never fear, for You are with me. You are first, last, always, my God and my dearest Friend.

But I trusted in thee, O Lord: I said,
Thou art my God.
My times are in thy hand.
PSALM 31:14–15

August 14

RECEIVING GOD'S THOUGHTS
Lyn Klug

*For My thoughts are not your thoughts,
neither are your ways My ways,
declares the Lord.*
ISAIAH 55:8 NASB

A mother was tucking her young son into bed. "Have you said your prayers?" she asked. "No," the boy replied. "Why not?" the mother asked. "Because there was nothing I wanted."

We may smile at that story, but children aren't the only ones to treat prayer as primarily a way of getting what they want. God does want us to bring our needs to him in prayer, but prayer is more than that. We come in prayer not to get God to do our will, but to open ourselves to doing His will.

Our time of reflecting on God's Word is a chance to get away from our own words and thoughts to receive God's thoughts, to learn from Him.

In prayer we open ourselves "to a transformation of conscience and consciousness with all that can lead to. One's life will never be the same again" (Basil Pennington). Our time of prayer may lead us to see ourselves or others in a new light. We may receive a new insight, or peace of mind, or a call to a specific action.

Sometimes it may seem that we receive nothing from our time of prayer. That's all right, too. Sometimes it's enough just to be close to God, just because we love Him.

MIND GAMES

Gail MacDonald, Karen Mains, Kathy Peel

One trap that's easy to fall into is expecting our husbands to be mind readers. Let's face it, if we want them to do something, we need to let them know what it is we need their help with. Be specific. Ask, "Honey, could you call out spelling words for Junior at 7:30?" or "After the rest of the kids go to bed, could you talk to Julie about the struggle she's having with her history teacher?" Asking for his help with specific tasks may get a better response than just asking for "a little help around here."

If your husband has been pretty much uninvolved up to this point, it's probably unrealistic to expect him to take over all responsibility for the children when he gets home, even though you've had the kids all day or have been working outside the home yourself. It would be worthwhile to write down exactly what and how much work you expect your husband to do and then discuss your expectations with him. Work out a compromise that reflects your hope and his willingness to participate.

Perhaps the most important factor in getting our husbands more involved in parenting is to show genuine gratitude for the effort they do make in taking on more responsibility. We can offer support, instruction, and encouragement, each family member doing his part to help the others toward the goal—becoming more like Christ.

Wives, submit yourselves unto your own husbands, as it is fit in the Lord. Husbands, love your wives, and be not bitter against them.
COLOSSIANS 3:18–19

PERSONALITY PLUS POWER PRODUCES POSITIVE PEOPLE

Florence Littauer

*But now hath God set the members
every one of them in the body,
as it hath pleased him.*
1 CORINTHIANS 12:18

God made each one of us different so we could function in our own role.

I learned this principle personally through the experience with my two brain-damaged sons. Each one was beautiful to look at. They had bright blue eyes, blond hair, turned-up noses, dimpled chins. They had normal arms and legs that moved, but they did not have normal brains. They looked all right on the outside, but without a brain, nothing worked.

A lot of us are like my boys—we look all right on the outside, but without Christ as our head, nothing much is working.

Have you ever had a friend whom you loved so much that you wanted to be with him all the time and get to know him better every day? Has his presence lit up your life so you felt energized, just being close? Have you watched him so closely and followed him so much that you've almost become like him? Jesus wants that kind of relationship with you. He wants you to get to know Him better by reading His words and talking to Him; He wants you to feel His power in your life so you can overcome your weakness. He wants you to spend so much time together that you become like Him.

YOUR FAITH
Hannah Whitall Smith

Let your faith now lay hold of a new power in Christ. You have trusted Him as your dying Saviour; now trust Him as your living Saviour. Just as much as He came to deliver you from future punishment did He also come to deliver you from present bondage. Just as truly as He came to bear your stripes for you has He come to live your life for you. You are as utterly powerless in the one case as in the other. You could as easily have gotten yourself rid of your own sins, as you could now accomplish for yourself practical righteousness. Christ, and Christ only, must do both for you; and your part in both cases is simply to give the thing to Him to do and then believe that He does it.

Lord Jesus, I believe Thou art stronger than sin and that Thou canst keep me, even me, in my extreme of weakness, from falling into its snares or yielding obedience to its commands. And, Lord, I am going to trust Thee to keep me. I have tried keeping myself, and have failed, and failed most grievously. I am absolutely helpless. So now I will trust Thee. I give myself to Thee. I keep back no reserves. Body, soul, and spirit, I present myself to Thee as a piece of clay to be fashioned into anything Thy love and Thy wisdom shall choose.

And David said to Solomon his son,
Be strong and of good courage,
and do it: fear not, nor be dismayed:
for the Lord God,
even my God, will be with thee.
1 CHRONICLES 28:20

WORSHIP IN YOUR SANCTUARY

Twila Paris with Robert Webber

O come, let us worship and bow down:
let us kneel before the Lord our maker.
PSALM 95:6

The word *sanctuary* brings thoughts of a safe place, a hiding place. For all of us, that safe place is in the Lord. We must turn to Him for refuge because the Lord is a strong and mighty tower.

The sanctuary is also the place where we worship. The smallest sanctuary is our own heart, that private place where we meet God all alone, hear the voice of God, and respond. The sanctuary is also the gathering of believers for worship, whether it is a small gathering of five or six in a home or a larger gathering in the local church.

What happens when people gather for corporate worship reminds me of going to my grandmother's house for Christmas. My grandmother's house had this special, wonderful, inviting smell to it. I get nostalgic when I think of that smell and of the whole atmosphere of being with my family at my grandparents.

For me, corporate worship is like going to Grandma's house. There is something really special about going to God's house with the family of God and meeting together to worship.

When we gather together, the thoughts of our hearts and the words of our mouth proclaim that God's name, God's throne, and God's love is above all names, all thrones, and all loves.

TO PRAY IN THE NAME OF JESUS
Mrs. Charles E. Cowman

What is it to pray in Christ's name? There is nothing mystical or mysterious about this expression. If one will go through the Bible and examine all passages in which the expression "in My name" or "in His name" or synonymous expressions are used, he will find that it means just about what it does in modern usage. If I go to a bank and hand in a check with my name signed to it, I ask of that bank in my own name. If I have money deposited in that bank, the check will be cashed; if not, it will not be. If, however, I go to the bank with somebody else's name signed to the check, I am asking in his name, and it does not matter whether I have money in that bank or any other; if the person whose name is signed to the check has money there, the check will be cashed. So it is when I go to the bank of heaven, when I go to God in prayer. I have nothing deposited there, I have absolutely no credit there, and if I go in my own name I will get absolutely nothing; but Jesus has unlimited credit in heaven, and He has granted to me the privilege of going to the bank with His name on my checks; and when I thus go my prayers will be honored to any extent."

—R. A. Torrey

And whatsoever ye shall ask in my name, that will I do, that the Father may be glorified in the Son.
JOHN 14:13

THE BRIDE AWAKENED
Cora Harris MacIlravy

I have put off my coat;
how shall I put it on?
I have washed my feet;
how shall I defile them?
SONG OF SOLOMON 5:3

She does not see what it means to refuse to open the door to Him, for she is so nearly asleep that her senses and discernment are clouded. Her own trouble, and what it will mean for her to rise and let Him in, are filling her mind, crowding out the apprehension of the sin she is committing. Her delay in opening the door does not look so heinous to her, for she knows that she loves Him; she would rejoice if He were within. She really desires to have Him within and longs to enter into that closer communion to which He is inviting and urging her.

Dear child of God, for what trifles have you and I repulsed our Lord when He has knocked upon our door and called us to rise up to higher ground? When He has called us to wait upon Him and we found that it was hard to enter in, how quickly have we left our knees and gone away. We do not apprehend that He is calling us to get into the place where He can do something for us.

It only needs a few repulses through some trifle or selfish reason, and sleep will prevail. In the end, the bride loses what God is offering her and misses the blessing and the revelation that He is waiting to bring her. The best God has for her, she carelessly lets fall from her indolent and powerless fingers.

DISCOVERING GOD'S WILL

Carole Mayhall

Before we can address the questions we have about God's specific will, we must look at how we are leading our lives in light of His revealed will. Take God's command that we walk in love. If, after a tough day, I snap at my family and take out my frustration on them in a hateful way, I'm obviously not living in God's will.

If I'm not obeying the revealed will of God, it isn't likely that I will receive further instruction on the specific choices I face in my life. That would be like asking for directions when I hold a road map in my hands.

Once we've made a concentrated effort to know and follow God's revealed will, we can ask for His direction on the specifics in our life—those forks in the road. Fortunately, we can relax a little on knowing God's specific will for one simple reason—one many of us overlook. Discerning God's specific will is not a mystery game where He's trying to hold something back from us. Often we feel we must go through layers and layers, all the time wondering, "Will God really let me know about this?" when all along God is saying, "I'll show you." He is a God who loves us and wants us to find His will. We just need to have an open heart to His leading.

Wherefore be ye not unwise, but understanding what the will of the Lord is.
EPHESIANS 5:17

THINKING BIBLICALLY

Linda R. McGinn

*And these words, which I command
thee this day, shall be in thine heart:
And thou shalt teach them
diligently unto thy children.*
DEUTERONOMY 6:6–7

Personal choices encompass every aspect of life. When these reflect the secure absolutes of truth found in God's Word, stability is ensured. Confusion, instability, despair, and hopelessness flow from building one's life on anything other than God's Word. Even good things we cherish, like church and family traditions, the wise sayings of respected persons, or the practical insights of leaders, cannot supply the foundation or substitute for the security that only God's Word can provide.

So how can we help? By evaluating our thoughts, considerations, and decisions against the truth of God's Word and by helping those with whom we are in contact, both Christian and non-Christian, to begin to search God's Word and "think biblically." We don't need to impose our thinking upon them or attempt to force them to agree with our conclusions of faith. We simply lead them to our Teacher. The Holy Spirit will teach them His truth. They need only seek Him.

Our role is to guide, leading them to the One who holds all truth: Jesus. Truly He is "the way, the truth, and the life." So the next time you're unsure of God's will in light of decisions you must make or actions you must take, seek God in the Word. He never contradicts His Word, and His ways are always without error.

THE DIVINE IDEAL
Linda Dillow

In the biblical view of marriage, the submission of the wife is always set in the context of the total love of the husband.

"Husbands, love your wives, just as Christ also loved the church and gave Himself up for her. . . . So husbands ought also to love their own wives as their own bodies. He who loves his own wife loves himself; for no one ever hated his own flesh, but nourishes and cherishes it, just as Christ also does the church" (Ephesians 5:25, 28–29 NASB).

The husband is to love his wife as Christ loved the church. (Right on, Paul. Preach it!) No one would ever measure a love that great. I'm ready for it—how about you? I can hear many of you saying, "This commandment wouldn't be so bad if my husband would love me as Christ loved the church and if he loved me as his own body. Maybe then submission would be a natural thing."

I personally believe it would become more natural. No woman will have difficulty with submission if she is being loved like that. I am blessed to have a godly husband who seeks to obey God and love me totally! You're right in thinking I have it easier than many of you. But at the same time, God requires more of me in my response to Jody. To whom much is given, the Bible says, much will be required.

Submitting yourselves one to
another in the fear of God.
EPHESIANS 5:21

GOLD BY MOONLIGHT
Amy Carmichael

For I know the thoughts that I think
toward you, saith the Lord,
thoughts of peace, and not of evil,
to give you an expected end.
JEREMIAH 29:11

When heaven is about to confer a great office on a man, it always first exercises his mind and soul with suffering, and his body with hunger, and exposes him to extreme poverty, and boggles all his undertakings. By these means it stimulates his mind, hardens his nature, and enables him to acts otherwise not possible to him," wrote Mencius, the Chinese sage, two thousand years ago.

Suffering, hunger, poverty, boggling circumstances cannot of themselves make anything but confusion. But if there be the touch of the Hand, all these things work together for good, for something like the harmony of music.

Hammer this truth out on the anvil of experience—this truth that the loving thoughts of God direct and perfect all that concerns us.

I have been told, "It is possible to gather gold, where it may be had, with moonlight."

By moonlight, then, let us gather our gold.

BOUNDARIES

Susan L. Lenzkes

The morning had been fairly routine—until I discovered the bird trapped in the family room.

Perched quivering on the arm of the couch, the pathetic little bird splattered pale droplets of fear on the upholstery. At my startled sound, he took flight, crashing first into one window and then another. Finally, exhausted, he clutched a ledge for a brief and trembling rest before trying to break free again.

Then a surprising thing happened. From outside, another sparrow hopped toward the open door. He moved right up to the doorjamb, loudly chirping the way to freedom. And it worked.

As his trapped friend paused, he heard and cocked his feathered head, riveting his attention to the liberating call. He jumped from the couch arm, to the cushion, to the floor. He listened, not yet seeing, but following the call closer and closer. Then one more hop and he was out with his friend, flying free.

Sometimes I feel trapped. It's those times I need to be reminded that You, Lord, are the only Way out. Thank You for brothers and sisters who care enough to sound the call to freedom in Christ.

For you were called to freedom, brethren; only do not use your freedom as an opportunity for the flesh, but through love be servants of one another.
GALATIANS 5:13 RSV

LET ME SEE YOUR FACE

Doris Coffin Aldrich

Beloved, now are we the sons of God, and it doth not yet appear what we shall be: but we know that, when he shall appear, we shall be like him; for we shall see him as he is.
1 JOHN 3:2

Becky had been naughty, and now in the quiet of her room she was tearfully repentant.

Mommie went in and sat on the edge of bed. It was dark, but the light from the hallway streamed across the rug. Becky's arms reached up to pull Mommie down to the pillow. There were several quick hugs, one last sob, and a sigh of satisfaction.

"Let me see your face, Mommie. Put on the light; I want to see your face." And so Mother reached over and switched on the light.

Becky looked carefully and then smiled and wriggled all over. The love she saw there—and "nothing between"—satisfied her heart. She had known that she was forgiven, but she had to see it in Mommie's face.

We, too, have known the joy of forgiveness. Time and again we have come to the Lord to have things made right. He has forgiven us, that we know, for "If we confess our sins, he is faithful and just to forgive us our sins, and to cleanse us from all unrighteousness" (1 John 1:9).

With the eye of faith we look into His face and know that nothing stands between us.

REJOICE IN THE LORD
Hannah Whitall Smith

The only thing that can bring unfailing joy to the soul is to understand and know God. This is only plain common sense. Everything for us depends upon what He is. He has created us and put us in our present environment, and we are absolutely in His power. If He is good and kind, we shall be well cared for and happy; if He is cruel and wicked, we must necessarily be miserable. Just as the welfare of any possession depends upon the character and temper and knowledge of its owner, so does our welfare depend upon the character and temper and knowledge of God. The child of a drunken father can never find any lasting joy in its poor little possessions, for at any minute the wicked father may destroy them all. A good father would be infinitely more to the child than the most costly possessions. And, similarly, none of our possessions could be of the slightest worth to us if we were under the dominion of a cruel and wicked God. Therefore, for us to have any lasting joy, we must come to the place where we understand and know "the Lord which exercises loving-kindness, judgment, and righteousness in the earth."

When all else is gone, God is still left. Nothing changes Him. He is the same yesterday, today, and forever, and in Him is no variableness, neither shadow of turning. And the soul that finds its joy in Him alone can suffer no wavering.

Finally, my brethren, rejoice in the Lord.
PHILIPPIANS 3:1

WORKING WOMEN
Elizabeth Cody Newenhuyse

And whatsoever ye do, do it heartily, as to the Lord, and not unto men.
COLOSSIANS 3:23

A few months ago, I was in a group with Beth, talking about some of the struggles Christian families face today. Beth led off the discussion: "My greatest problem is that I'm a working mom, and I have to deal with people's attitudes toward that. I sense criticism. So I always tell them, 'I have to work. My husband's income just doesn't cover our needs.'"

As she spoke so candidly, I felt my face redden in anger at the judgments some cast at the working woman. I had to speak up: "You know, Beth, why is it we always feel compelled to add the I-have-to-work apology? Why can't we Christian women be honest about enjoying our work? Talk about what we do?"

"You're right," Beth said with surprise. "I enjoy my work, and I think I'm good at it. But somehow, that isn't enough for some people."

Beth is not driven by me-first ambition—if anything, like most of us, she could use more self-esteem. She does not need darts of judgment shot her way.

IS THE LORD LISTENING?

Evelyn Christenson

Lorna and Signe and I began to pray together.
Everything seemed to be going great in our
church. In four years our membership had
almost doubled, a building program was in
progress, and we had a full schedule of activities to meet the needs of our congregation. Yet,
the three of us sensed that there was a missing
dimension. We decided to meet once a week to
pray for our church—a very noble idea, we
thought.

We agreed at the start to base our praying
on a verse of Scripture (a good rule to follow),
and right away God gave us Psalm 66:18: "If I
regard iniquity in my heart, the Lord will not
hear me."

"Lord, what do You mean?" we asked.
"We're going to pray for our church." But He
continued to apply the pressure gently: "If I
regard iniquity in my heart, the Lord will not
hear me." Wow! I, the pastor's wife? Lorna and
Signe? Uh, huh.

God didn't release us to pray for other
needs until we had cleaned up our own lives by
confessing our sins. It took us, oh, so long. We
prayed and prayed, and God kept bringing sins
to our minds. As our first prayer meeting came
to a close, we thought, Phew! We got that one
over with; next week we can start praying for
the needs of the church. But when we met the
following week, we still couldn't get beyond
Psalm 66:18 and into effectual, fervent praying.

*If I regard iniquity in my heart,
the Lord will not hear me.*
PSALM 66:18

WISING UP ABOUT MONEY
Jo Berry

He that trusteth in his riches shall fall:
but the righteous shall flourish as a branch.
PROVERBS 11:28

Just as there is nothing wrong with sex when it is used properly, there is nothing wrong with money or material possessions. Actually, God in His sovereignty decides who gets what. "The rich and the poor have a common bond, the Lord is the maker of them all" (Proverbs 22:2 NASB). In some instances financial prosperity is a reward for righteous behavior. "The reward of humility and the fear of the Lord are riches, honor and life" (Proverbs 22:4 NASB).

Money and possessions are not problems; our attitude toward them is. When we get "things," too often we lose our sense of value. We start thinking how great we are to have acquired what we have. We take pride in our belongings and focus onto transitory, temporal possessions, forgetting that God is the source of all we have.

Eventually, if they become too important to us, we depend on material goods for happiness. That is the height of foolishness because, as an old proverb muses, "Money cannot buy happiness."

Most important, we need to remember that "it is the blessing of the Lord that makes rich, and He adds no sorrow to it" (Proverbs 10:22 NASB). Blessing, a state of well-being where we rest in God's grace, is true, lasting wealth. That is what we should seek after and desire.

THE BLAME GAME
Eugenia Price

We women are blamed for many things which we do not do.

We women are praised for being what we certainly are not. Mothers are extolled in the wordy stanzas of the Mother's Day greeting card versifiers as being so nearly perfect no one but God could possibly live up to them!

When mother love is of the quality God intended it to be, it is probably closest to the love of God of all the kinds of human love which exist. But, it is a little considered fact that simply in the process of becoming a mother, one does not automatically become a saint.

Over and over, as I travel about the country and speak woman to woman with women in all walks of life, I hear the wail, "Why are we blamed for everything that goes wrong with our children? We're doing the best we know to do. Why doesn't someone tell us how to anticipate our teenagers instead of pointing out, when the damage is done, what we did that was wrong? Isn't it ever just a little bit someone else's fault? Are we always to blame?"

Take, therefore, no thought for the morrow: for the morrow shall take thought for the things of itself. Sufficient unto the day is the evil thereof.
MATTHEW 6:34

A MOTHER'S DISCIPLINE
Ellyn Sanna

Provoke not your children to wrath: but bring them up in the nurture and admonition of the Lord.
EPHESIANS 6:4

As mothers, all of us cling to the same burden. We feel we ought to manage our children's lives, and both our interior discipline of our own hearts and our exterior discipline of our children become a source of pride and fear.

The only solution is to let go of our children, to let go of our own need to be in control. "One cannot love God," Mother Teresa says, "except at the cost of oneself." In fact, we can't love anyone without this same cost. Loving means you give yourself away. This self-giving love disciplines our own hearts, and it's also necessary for our children's discipline. The best discipline is built not on anger, but on loving affirmation.

This will not weaken our discipline. It will not turn us into wishy-washy mothers who allow our children to trample us. The word *affirmation* comes from the Latin *to make firm*. It's not a namby-pamby sort of word. Instead, its demands are rigorous and astringent. When we affirm our children we give them strong, definite outlines. We impose boundaries on their worlds. We allow them to separate from us. We show them who they are in God's eyes.

And in the process, we as mothers are also both disciplined and affirmed. We become more whole even as we let go.

THAT YE MAY KNOW
Hannah Whitall Smith

Uncertainties are fatal to all true progress and are utterly destructive of comfort or peace. And yet it has somehow become the fashion among Christians to encourage uncertainties in the spiritual life as being an indication of the truest form of piety. There is a great deal of longing and hoping among Christians, but there is not much knowing. And yet the whole Bible was written for the purpose of making us know. The object of a revelation is to reveal. If nothing has been revealed to us by the Bible beyond longings and hopes, it has failed its purpose. But I fear a large proportion of God's children never get beyond these hopes and longings. "I hope my sins will be forgiven someday"; "I hope I may be favored to reach heaven at last"; "I hope God loves me"; "I hope Christ died for me." These are samples of the style of much Christian testimony in the present day. Indeed, I have even known Christians who could never get further than to say, "I hope that I have a hope." If this word were used in the sense that the Bible always uses it, that is, in the sense of firm expectation, it might be all right; but in the use of it which I have described, there is so great an element of doubt, that it does not amount to a Bible hope at all.

These things have I written unto you that believe on the name of the Son of God; that ye may know that ye have eternal life, and that ye may believe on the name of the Son of God.
1 JOHN 5:13

LEARNING TO SPEAK LIFE
Stormie Omartian

He that keepeth his mouth keepeth his life: but he that openeth wide his lips shall have destruction.
PROVERBS 13:3

We create a world for ourselves by what we speak. Words have power, and we can either speak life or death into a situation. The Bible says that what we say can get us into trouble or keep us away from it. It can even save our lives. "He who guards his mouth preserves his life, But he who opens wide his lips shall have destruction" (Proverbs 13:3 NKJV). We need to ask God to put a guard over our own mouth as well as the mouth of our child.

Speech that is not godly or not of the Lord, such as, "I'm no good," "I wish I was dead," "Life is terrible," "People are horrible," "I'll never be anything special," does not reflect a heart filled with the Holy Spirit. It reflects the work of darkness. And that is exactly what will play itself out on the stage of your child's life if you don't help him monitor what he says.

The Bible says that when we go to be with the Lord we will have to account for every careless word we have spoken. We pay for them here on earth also. I believe the price is too high to pay for something that can easily be controlled by our own will. We can speak love, joy, and peace into our world, or we can speak strife, hatred, deception, and all other manifestations of evil.

A Bruised Reed He Will Not Break

Amy Carmichael

To what end is pain? I do not clearly know. But I have noticed that when one who has not suffered draws near to one in pain, there is rarely much power to help. There is not the understanding that leaves the suffering thing comforted, though perhaps not a word was spoken. I have wondered if it can be the same in the sphere of prayer.

Does pain accepted and endured give some quality that would otherwise be lacking in prayer? Does it create sympathy which can lay itself alongside the need, feeling it as though it were personal, so that it is possible to do just what the writer of Hebrews meant when he said, "Remember them that are in bonds, as bound with them; and them which suffer adversity, as being yourselves also in the body" (Hebrews 13:3)?

"A bruised reed shall he not break" (Isaiah 42:3). The poorest shepherd boy on our South Indian hills is careful to choose, for the making of his flute, a reed that is straight and fine and quite unbruised. But our heavenly Shepherd often takes the broken and the bruised, and of such He makes His flutes.

A bruised reed shall he not break, and the smoking flax shall he not quench: he shall bring forth judgment unto truth.
ISAIAH 42:3

September 5

GIVE GOD TIME
Ann Kiemel Anderson

When I am afraid,
I will put my trust in Thee.
PSALM 56:3 NASB

Frankly, I thought God would instantly and easily give me children because I had waited so long for His man. At thirty-five, I figured there was not much time left for motherhood. Again, however, God wanted me to learn more about this significant issue of life: giving God time.

When a beautiful birth mother flew into Idaho Falls for us to be with her in labor and delivery and handed us our firstborn son, I wept. All the losses and waiting became so important because they brought us Taylor, and now we could not imagine life without him.

When Taylor was eight months old, I became pregnant with twins. We could not love a child of our own flesh and blood more than Taylor, but he was going to have siblings. We were ecstatic.

On a frozen, dreary night, with Will out of town on business, I miscarried the twins. Will flew home the next day to remind me, "Ann, Jesus never takes away except to give back something better. Give Him time."

Yes, written across my forehead and my heart, and tested by years of perseverance and determination, is the greatest lesson I have ever learned. . .and the hardest: Give Jesus time.

COMFORTER
Anita Corrine Donihue

Thank You, Father, for Your Holy Spirit, Your Comforter. What peace it gives me to know You are with me throughout my day. The world can't see Your comfort unless they choose to accept Jesus Christ as their Savior. Otherwise, they can never recognize Your sustaining power and grace.

I have so many questions to ask You about things I can't understand. I realize some answers may not come until I see You face-to-face. This is where I learn to trust You and depend upon Your Word. Guide me into truth and knowledge, so I can make right decisions. Let me learn from Your stories of old so I may grow in You.

I wonder what it was like that evening long ago when Your disciples hid in fear behind bolted doors, not knowing what to do next. Would I have been so fearful? I think so.

Past the bolted doors You came and stood before them. "Peace be with you!" You assured them.

I would have been thrilled and frightened at the same time if I could have seen Your hands and feet and side.

"Peace be with you," again You charged. "As the Father has sent me, so send I you." You breathed on them, and they received Your Comforter, Your Holy Spirit!

Breathe on me now, I pray. Fill me with Your Spirit. Grant me Your Comforter. Give me Your power so I may share the gospel in my life to everyone around me.

And I will pray the Father, and he shall give you another Comforter, that he may abide with you for ever.
JOHN 14:16

September 7

INTERRUPTIONS
Mary W. Tileston

The Lord thy God shall bless thee in all thy works, and in all that thou puttest thine hand unto.
DEUTERONOMY 15:10

My place of lowly service, too,
Beneath Thy sheltering wings I see;
For all the work I have to do
Is done through sheltering rest in Thee.
—A. L. Waring

I think I find most help in trying to look on all interruptions and hindrances to work that one has planned out for oneself as discipline, trials sent by God to help one against getting selfish over one's work. Then one can feel that perhaps one's true work—one's work for God—consists in doing some trifling haphazard thing that has been thrown into one's day. It is not a waste of time, as one is tempted to think. It is the most important part of the work of the day—the part one can best offer to God. After such as hindrance, do not rush after the planned work; trust that the time to finish it will be given sometime, and keep a quiet heart about it.

—Annie Keary

THE DOVE OF FAITH
Mrs. Charles E. Cowman

A visitor at a school for the deaf and dumb was writing questions on the blackboard for the children. By and by he wrote this sentence: "Why has God made me to hear and speak, and made you deaf and dumb?"

The awful sentence fell upon the little ones like a fierce blow in the face. They sat palsied before that dreadful "Why?" And then a little girl arose.

Her lip was trembling. Her eyes were swimming with tears. Straight to the board she walked, and, picking up the crayon, wrote with firm hand these precious words: "Even so, Father: for so it seemed good in thy sight" (Matthew 11:26). What a reply! It reaches up and lays hold of an eternal truth upon which the maturest believer as well as the youngest child of God may alike securely rest—the truth that God is your Father.

Do you mean that? Do you really and fully believe that? When you do, then your dove of faith will no longer wander in weary unrest, but will settle down forever in its eternal resting place of peace. "Your Father!"

I can still believe that a day comes for all of us, however far off it may be, when we shall understand; when these tragedies that now blacken and darken the very air of heaven for us, will sink into their places in a scheme so august, so magnificent, so joyful, that we shall laugh for wonder and delight.

—Arthur Christopher Bacon

Your heavenly Father knoweth.
MATTHEW 6:32

September 9

PRAY WITH YOUR MATE
Susan Alexander Yates

This is the confidence we have in approaching God: that if we ask anything according to his will, he hears us.
1 JOHN 5:14 NIV

In our careers we set up times to discuss how to handle thorny problems, yet we often fail to do this in our marriages. As we meet to discuss the "sore subject," we should keep several things in mind. Before beginning our discussion, we should pray together, asking for God's leading in the conversation. The most precious and the most powerful form of communication with our mates occurs when we pray together. God has promised to hear our prayers and to answer them (1 John 5:14; Matthew 18:19). As we go to God together, we are reminded that His power holds our marriages together. Praying together also has a wonderful way of dissolving tensions. It enables us together to seek God's wisdom about family decisions. Our relationship is more important than the "sore subject," so as we talk we must attack the problem rather than each other. We must be willing to give all of our rights away, to sacrifice, to hurt, to work for the sake of the relationship. Sometimes we may have to ask forgiveness of our mate. Perhaps we must forgive them.

GROUCH TIMES FOUR
Marabel Morgan

Most mornings when I awake, I am pleasantly surprised to find I'm still alive. On occasion I have been known to wake up mean and irritable, but even then I can choose not to stay that way. Yesterday is gone, and tomorrow may not come. Today is the only slot of time I really have. What a shame to blow it. I want to make today the very best possible.

Ultimate freedom, according to Dr. Viktor E. Frankl, is man's right to choose his own attitude in a given set of circumstances. Before I crawl out of bed, I thank the Lord for another day and ask for strength. Maybe I'm to clean the house, or work at the office, or talk with a friend over lunch. The tasks aren't the issue; my attitude is.

Sometimes I may choose to just pout or withdraw from the human race for a day, and there's a certain sadistic satisfaction in doing that, too. But it doesn't compare with the exhilarating joy that comes when I fall into bed at night thinking, "What a day! I did well. I feel good. Thank You, Lord."

Wait on the Lord: be of good courage, and he shall strengthen thine heart: wait, I say, on the Lord.
PSALM 27:14

ENCOURAGING HONEST OPINION
Florence Littauer

Whoso loveth instruction loveth knowledge: but he that hateth reproof is brutish.
PROVERBS 12:1

When any of us take the time to think about our interchanges with other people, we realize how little honest opinion we encourage. We build our boxes around us, people learn how near they dare come to our fence, and they develop a working relationship with us that may be utterly phony. Does your family have to humor you to keep peace? Do your coworkers know how close they can come before you get mad or moody? If people are having to handle you with kid gloves, maybe it's time you got honest with them and allowed them to be honest with you.

Some people build their walls so thick no one ever gets to know the real person inside. This is often their reason for doing so: "If you really knew what I'm like inside, you wouldn't care for me." Let's come out from behind our masks and dare to change. We don't need to be fenced in by our failures of the past; we need to step out into the fields of future potential.

CONCERNING FAITH
Hannah Whitall Smith

The subject of faith is very generally misunderstood; for, in reality, faith is the simplest and plainest thing in the world, and the most easy of exercise.

Your idea of faith, I suppose, has been something like this. You have looked upon it as in some way a sort of thing—either a religious exercise of soul, or an inward, gracious disposition of heart; something tangible, in fact, which, when you have secured it, you can look at and rejoice over, and use as a passport to God's favor, or a coin with which to purchase His gifts. Now, faith, in fact, is not in the least like this. It is nothing at all tangible. It is simply believing God; and, like sight, it is nothing apart from its object. You might as well shut your eyes and look inside and see whether you have faith. You see something and thus know that you have sight; you believe something and thus know that you have faith. For as sight is only seeing, so faith is only believing. And as the only necessary thing about sight is that you see the thing as it is, so the only necessary thing about belief is that you believe the thing as it is. The virtue does not lie in your believing, but in the thing you believe. Your salvation comes, not because your faith saves you, but because it links you to the Saviour who saves; and your believing is really nothing but the link.

But without faith it is impossible to please him: for he that cometh to God must believe that he is, and that he is a rewarder of them that diligently seek him.
HEBREWS 11:6

September 13

YOU ARE SOMEBODY
Alma Kern

For whom he did foreknow, he also did predestinate to be conformed to the image of his Son, that he might be the firstborn among many brethren.
ROMANS 8:29

Some of us were born to parents who wanted us and rejoiced at our birth. They received us joyfully as precious gifts from God. They raised us as best they could.

Others seem to have been biological accidents, arriving unplanned, unexpected, unwelcomed, and unloved.

No matter what the circumstances of your birth, you are not just a happenstance of nature. God made you! God uses the best intentions of people. He can also overrule the worst intentions to accomplish His purpose.

God once used a condemned child of a slave woman. By a remarkable twist of events the Lord not only preserved the life of that boy but also gave him the advantages of growing up in a palace. God used strange circumstances to raise up a leader for His ancient people. Yet, when God finally called Moses into special service, Moses asked, "Who am I?" (Exodus 3:11). He had self-doubts, felt unfit.

It didn't matter who Moses was or who he had been. What did matter was that God had called him. God wanted to make somebody special out of him.

When you ask, "How come I am what I am?" assure yourself: "By the grace of God I am what I am" (1 Corinthians 15:10).

You are special. God made you.

OPENING THE DOOR OF YOUR HEART
Cora Harris MacIlravy

Christ never forces any door open, He only comes in when we have opened the door. There is no power in hell or upon earth that can prevent us getting all God has for us. Only one person can do this, and that is you or I. He does not force anyone against his will to turn to Him and be saved. He does not force any child of His against his will to press on into His best.

If we would be refreshed by heavenly showers, we must take the steps that will bring us where they are falling. Though the droppings of God's mercy and grace, of His dealings and revelation, have their source in Him and come from Him alone; though they are ever falling with copious blessings upon all who are where they can receive; only those who go where they are falling receive refreshment and have their prayers answered. We pray that the Holy Spirit may fully control us.

I opened to my beloved; but my beloved had withdrawn himself, and was gone: my soul failed when he spake: I sought him, but I could not find him; I called him, but he gave me no answer.
SONG OF SOLOMON 5:6

PREPARED FOR SERVICE
Mary W. Tileston

And as many as walk according to this rule, peace be on them, and mercy, and upon the Israel of God.
GALATIANS 6:16

Lord, I have given my life to Thee,
And every day and hour is Thine—
What Thou appointest let them be;
Thy will is better, Lord, than mine.
—A. Warner

Begin at once; before you venture away from this quiet moment, ask your King to take you wholly into His service, and place all the hours of this day quite simply at His disposal, and ask Him to make and keep you ready to do just exactly what He appoints. Never mind about tomorrow; one day at a time is enough. Try it today, and see if it is not a day of strange, almost curious peace, so sweet that you will be only too thankful, when tomorrow comes, to ask Him to take it also—till it will become a blessed habit to hold yourself simply and "wholly at Thy commandment for any manner of service." The "whatsoever" is not necessarily active work. It may be waiting (whether half an hour or half a lifetime), learning, suffering, sitting still. But shall we be less ready for these if any of them are His appointments for today? Let us ask Him to prepare us for all that He is preparing for us.
—Frances Ridley Havergal

SALTY CHRISTIANS
Ruth Bell Graham

It happened in one of those countries whose leaders deny the existence of God but allow the church to exist under a secretary for church affairs. In this case, the secretary was not only a brilliant pastor, he was a medical doctor as well.

One day he was called on the carpet by the authorities. Knowing there would be a new crackdown on the Christians, he started right in: "I know you gentlemen wish to interrogate me," he began. "But first, may I say something?"

Permission granted, he continued. "You know I am a medical doctor. I know the importance of salt in the human body: it should be maintained at about two percent. If it is less, a person gets sick. If it is eliminated altogether, he will die.

"Now, Jesus Christ has said Christians are the salt of the earth." Then he paused. "That is all. And now, gentlemen, what is it that you wish to say to me?"

"Oh nothing, nothing," they agreed. And he was dismissed.

Salt is indispensable to man's health and is fed to livestock for the same reason (see the *Encyclopaedia Britannica*). It is also used as a preservative and for seasoning, as well as in curing hides and as brine for refrigeration. But there is another fact about salt that is worth considering: Salt makes a person thirsty.

Do we as Christians make people thirsty for the Water of Life?

Ye are the salt of the earth.
MATTHEW 5:13

LATCHKEY KIDS
Jill Briscoe

She is like the merchants' ships;
she bringeth her food from afar. . . .
She perceiveth that her merchandise is good:
her candle goeth not out by night.
PROVERBS 31:14, 18

As I talk to women, I find no lack of caring concern for the little ones, but there certainly seems to be a huge struggle with conscience. Mother is wondering, "What am I doing to my child, to my relationship with my husband, to myself and to my God? If I have a choice about the matter, should I be working at all?" Those women who economically have no choice wrestle with disturbing guilt as to what long-term effects their absence from home will have upon their children.

Here in Proverbs 31 we find the model of a godly working woman, and that from a passage of Scripture used in the past to point out the traditional domestic duties of the docile spouse. Our Queen of Hearts was a working woman, seemingly, coping with many of the challenges of our modern-day world. She had no mechanical helps around as we have, and yet she managed to do it all and finish up with children that adored her, a husband who praised her, servants that obeyed her, and traders that appreciated her. Yes, she was even queen of the merchants' hearts!

IS TEMPTATION SIN?
Hannah Whitall Smith

Temptation cannot be sin; and the truth is, it is no more a sin to hear these whispers and suggestions of evil in our souls than it is for us to hear the wicked talk of bad men as we pass along the street. The sin comes, in either case, only by our stopping and joining in with them. If, when the wicked suggestions come, we turn from them at once, as we would from wicked talk, and pay no more attention to them than we would to the talk, we do not sin. But, if we carry them on our minds, and roll them under our tongues, and dwell on them with a half consent of our will to them as true, then we sin. We may be enticed by temptations a thousand times a day without sin, and we cannot help these enticings and are not to blame for them. But if we begin to think that these enticings are actual sin on our part, then the battle is half lost already, and the sin can hardly fail to gain a complete victory.

Blessed is the man that endureth temptation: for when he is tried, he shall receive the crown of life, which the Lord hath promised to them that love him.
JAMES 1:12

THE DIFFERENCE CHRIST MAKES IN YOUR MARRIED LIFE

Eugenia Price

And the Lord God said, It is not good that the man should be alone; I will make him an help meet for him.
GENESIS 2:18

It would be a horrible and chaotic world if honeymoons did last. On honeymoons, I am told, the lovers have only eyes and ears and minds for each other. If all married people remained in this introverted state, who would keep the stores open, who would preach the sermons, who would run the banks, who would operate the bakeries and the beauty salons, and who would practice medicine, try legal cases, and repair automobiles? For that matter, not only the gentlemen would be immobilized where society is concerned, but so would the ladies. Who would wash the dishes and type the letters and mend the clothes and teach politeness and instill emotional stability in the little tousled dears who would keep resulting from the perpetual honeymoon?

If God created the marriage relationship, certainly He is capable of making it work. Provided at least someone involved is willing to live a Christ-controlled life. The statistics on the divorce rate among active Christians are low. This would indicate that Christian couples have a way of meeting and solving their difficulties. They still have them, but they have a way out, too.

DAYDREAMING
Jean Lush with Pam Vredevelt

Successful stress managers have the ability to create for themselves periodic islands of peace. Whether we are behind our desk at work or ironing six baskets of laundry, daydreaming can break the cycle of chronic tension. On your island of peace you can build the residence of your dreams—a castle, a log cabin, or a Victorian house. Perhaps it's a little farm like the one where you spent summers with your grandparents. It can be as plush as a modern penthouse flat or as simple as a little grass hut.

A simple five-minute imaginary game can bring emotional relief. Some people may call this splitting, or an irresponsible way to check out of reality. I call it dilly-dallying or mental play for the purpose of reducing tension.

If it's hard for you to daydream, hang around children and ask them to tell you stories. They are experts at using their imagination. Boys and girls freely use fantasy to cope with the pressures of life. Unfortunately, many of us take ourselves much too seriously and, in the name of maturity and responsibility, work too hard. Take time for make-believe. Abandon yourself in play. I think God gives us an imagination for a reason. Christ knows the pressures we endure. Perhaps this is one reason He encourages us to "become as little children."

Come, ye children, hearken unto me: I will teach you the fear of the Lord.
PSALM 34:11

THE GREAT COMMISSION
Anita Corrine Donihue

Go ye therefore, and teach all nations,
baptizing them in the name of the Father,
and of the Son, and of the Holy Ghost.
MATTHEW 28:19

We, as part of the church, must step forth and share the good news of what God has done for us with everyone and anyone who will listen. There is an urgency in this, for life here on earth is short. This is our commandment: to tell the world about the love of Jesus.

When you feel reserved or frightened about testifying of Jesus, think how you would feel if you inherited a million dollars. Could you keep quiet? Or would you shout for joy and tell all your friends the good news?

Christ paid our debt of sin and gave all who accept Him the most valuable gift of all: an abundant, joyful life on earth and eternal life with God in heaven. And it didn't cost a thing except submitting to His will and accepting His gift. Most incredible is that we can share this wonderful gift with those around us, so they may also receive Him. Our friends, our family, the hairdresser, the store clerk, our coworkers, the gas station attendant —the list goes on and on.

Stand up for Jesus. Use the Word of God for your guide. Help lead others to Christ. If you need assistance, call on a Christian friend or your pastor to help. But, you can also pray with someone all by yourself. What a thrill it is to watch a baby soul be born in the Lord!

IT'S LATER THAN YOU THINK

Luci Swindoll

Many of us cannot grasp the truth that the time allotted to us on this earth is sufficient for all the Lord has planned for us to do. We don't need one minute more or one minute less to get the job done: Our greatest fear is running out of time. So we hurry through life trying desperately to get everything done: working overtime, eating fast food in the car, and racing down the freeway.

In our quest to save time, we're losing something. I thought the other day about how my grandparents valued time. They always had time for my parents and my brothers and me; they had time for music in their home; they emphasized beautifully served meals, family reunions, and long conversations. It seemed they had time for everything in life that was important because they took time to live. They treasured the biblical injunction that proclaims, "This is the day the Lord has made; let us rejoice and be glad in it" (Psalm 118:24 NIV).

Today, this very day, why don't you think of something that takes a bit of extra time to do and do it. . . . Maybe it will be an act of generosity or a moment of kindness directed toward a loved one or a stranger. Perhaps it will be simply singing a hymn of praise and thanksgiving because your heart is so full of gratitude.

Don't wait for another time. Rejoice in this day and be glad.

What I mean. . .is that the time is short. . . .
For this world in its present form
is passing away.
1 CORINTHIANS 7:29, 31 NIV

SUFFICIENT SUPPLY
Corrie ten Boom

But my God shall supply all your need.
PHILIPPIANS 4:19

I was at the end of my first week in America and practically at the end of my money. The clerk at the YWCA had told me I could not stay there another week. Where should she forward my mail?

"I don't know yet. God has a room for me but He has not told me where yet."

I could see by the look on her face that she was concerned about me. Then she handed me a piece of mail which she had overlooked. The letter was from a woman who heard me speak in New York. She was offering me the use of her son's room.

I gave the amazed clerk my new address after thanking God for His care.

Thank You, Lord, that we may know that our need is never greater than the Helper.

ALL THINGS SERVE THEE

Elisabeth Elliot

The Lord's decrees (His promises, His plans, His every word) stand fast, no matter what news we receive. A child has run away. A mother has cancer. A business has failed. The events in our lives and the great catastrophes in the world do not budge the solid ground on which the Christian takes his position. How can this be? Are there not conditions which harm and hinder and destroy? Not in the end. There is nothing on earth or in hell or heaven, in time or in eternity, which can alter in any final sense what God has promised—because all things serve Him.

A word in the Book of Revelation shows this truth most gloriously. Ten great kings will join their powers with an enormously powerful beast to wage war on the Lamb. God does not intervene to prevent that war.

"But the Lamb will defeat them, for he is Lord of lords and King of kings, and his victory will be shared by his followers, called and chosen and faithful" (Revelation 17:14 NEB).

All things serve Him. That is, everything will at last be seen to be under his control, contributing to his eternal purposes—and the Lamb's victory will be ours as well.

But thanks be to God, which giveth us the victory through our Lord Jesus Christ. Therefore, my beloved brethren, be ye stedfast, unmoveable, always abounding in the work of the Lord, forasmuch as ye know that your labour is not in vain in the Lord.
1 CORINTHIANS 15:57–58

BLESSED ARE THE PEACEMAKERS
Eileen Egan and Kathleen Egan, O.S.B.

Blessed are the peacemakers:
for they shall be called the children of God.
MATTHEW 5:9

Let us thank God for this gift of peace that reminds us that we have been created to live that peace, and that Jesus became man to bring that good news to the poor. The good news was peace to all of good will, and this is something that we all want—peace of heart.

When the Virgin Mary discovered that He had come into her life, she went in haste to give that good news to her cousin, Elizabeth. The child in the womb of Elizabeth leaped with joy. That little unborn child recognized the Prince of Peace. He recognized that Christ had come to bring the good news for you and for me.

Christ died on the Cross to show that greater love. He died for you and for me and that leper, and for that man dying of hunger, and for that naked person lying in the streets, not only of Calcutta, but of Africa and New York, London and Oslo.

He insisted that we love one another as He loves each of us. We read that in the Gospel. As the Father loved Him and He loved us, so we must love one another until it hurts. It isn't enough for us to say, "I love God, but I do not love my neighbor." How can you love God, whom you do not see, if you do not love your neighbor whom you see, whom you touch, with whom you live?
—Acceptance Speech, Nobel Peace Prize, December 10, 1979

THE LITTLE THINGS
Ruth Youngdahl Nelson

A news item reported that many pending trials could not be held in Salonika, Greece, because mice had devoured files in the civil court archives.

It called to mind a novel, *Quiet Street,* by Ossorgin. Skillfully the writer depicted generation after generation of mice in a certain home, gnawing away at the joists, until one day the floor caved in. Until then life had gone on as if nothing were happening. No one seemed aware of the rodents at work.

What a telling parable this is of our lives! Unless our ears are opened to the Lord; unless our eyes see beyond the obvious; unless we seek grace to discern the things that are eternal; WHAM! Our house caves in!

What could be the "little mice" in your life? Could they be frittering away your time on nonessentials? Could they be anxieties that you haven't turned over to the Lord? Could they be "harmless" indulgences of the flesh that seem to be so inconsequential?

The way to defeat the mice is to build on the Solid Rock. And in this building, little things are very important. Little deeds of kindness, a passing encouraging word, a cup of cold water, in His name.

Little things can destroy, but little things can also build.

Take us the foxes, the little foxes, that spoil the vines: for our vines have tender grapes.
SONG OF SOLOMON 2:15

FINDING YOUR MINISTRY
Melinda Fish

A man's gift makes room for him,
And brings him before great men.
PROVERBS 18:16 NKJV

Timothy was young when he was set in charge of the church at Ephesus, particularly in comparison to the apostle Paul, whose reputation preceded him everywhere. Following in Paul's footsteps was not easy, especially for a meek young man raised by a godly mother and grandmother. A father's influence in Timothy's life is not mentioned in the Bible. Perhaps that is why Paul took such an interest in him.

Pastoring in Ephesus brought out the best and worst in Paul's young protégé. False teachers, silly women, contentious people, and those who mocked his youth rose up against him, intimidating him out of the place God had given him.

Paul knew what he needed: "Kindle afresh the gift of God which is in you through the laying on of my hands. For God has not given us a spirit of timidity, but of power and love and discipline [sensibility]" (2 Timothy 1:6–7 NASB). To drive out the giants of timidity that threatened him, Timothy needed to stir up the gift of the Holy Spirit he had received when Paul had ordained him.

The Holy Spirit within is equal to the task without when you are living in the boundaries of the inheritance God has given you. Just stir up the Holy Spirit within you, seek to edify the Church, and the power of God will make a path for you.

THAT YOUR JOY MIGHT BE FULL

Joy MacKenzie

If therefore there is any encouragement in Christ. . . make my joy complete by being of the same mind, maintaining the same love, united in spirit, intent on one purpose.
PHILIPPIANS 2:1–2 NASB

*L*oving and being loved—being connected, valued, befriended, cherished by another—is a compelling need that permeates the life of every human being on God's earth. Yet how are such relationships to come about?

I teach creative writing. The first several weeks, my young students spend most of their time learning to use words that show rather than tell. Creating a visual image of an object or idea precipitates a much stronger response than just telling about it. Brilliant as I may seem (ha!), this is not a concept I just happened to dream up—it's been around a couple of thousand years. The model, again, is Jesus. When Jesus talked to His disciples, He didn't give long discourses on friendship. He demonstrated friendship by being available, compassionate, self-sacrificing, and tender. His chosen friends responded! Yes, He called them to accountability; He rebuked them when they were wrong. But when He was finished, they still felt cherished by Him. What a picture—another of His gifts to us—to be treasured, to be emulated.

We need not set out in search for a friend. Rather, we must simply set out to be the friend Christ modeled—anticipating the needs of others, wearing ourselves out at giving. Jesus died doing it. The rewards are infinite and joyous!

THE POWER IN THANKS

Lynne Ricart

Be anxious for nothing, but in everything by prayer and supplication with thanksgiving let your requests be made known to God. And the peace of God, which surpasses all comprehension, will guard your hearts and your minds in Christ Jesus.
PHILIPPIANS 4:6–7 NASB

Inoperable! The words echoed again and again as I lay cold and alone in the special testing area of my local hospital. The radiologist was referring to the arteriovenous malformation (AVM) in my brain, a spider-web-like section of blood vessels that did not belong there.

As I lay there trying to absorb the frightening turn my life was taking, I clung to Paul's words to the Philippians that had ministered to me so many times in the past. However, I stopped short at the "with thanksgiving" part. I knew God told us to be thankful in all things, but surely He didn't include AVMs in that. Or did He? OK, He did! So reluctantly, but honestly, I began to pray, "God, You said to be thankful in all things, and even though I don't feel very thankful, I'm thanking You for this AVM." As I continued praying this prayer, guess what happened? In a few days, I was praising God for the very thing that threatened my life! As I thanked God for the most difficult obstacle I had ever faced, He unleashed His power and brought His perfect peace, healing, and wholeness into my heart and into my life.

Today, I am still living with the AVM, but I am giving thanks for it in a new light. I use it as a reminder that every day is a gift from God and that I need to make each day count for Him and live it as though it may be my last!

A "Fragrant" Home

Susan Alexander Yates

Our homes will never be a perfect place. However, the atmosphere that marks the home will determine whether it is a positive happy place, a place that offers shelter from the world, a place where we can have our batteries recharged to go out again. Our homes should encourage humor, appreciation, forgiveness, and a sense of belonging, where we are believed in and accepted. Creating a home with such an atmosphere of love, forgiveness, and laughter brings healing into a broken world.

As mothers we have the major responsibility of creating the atmosphere in the home. Just as we often assume the initiative in planning the decor of our homes, we also have the opportunity to determine what kind of atmosphere we want in our homes. Often we fail to realize that creating a loving atmosphere in the home takes work. It does not just happen. We must have a vision of the atmosphere we desire, goals to work toward and a plan of action. In 2 Corinthians 2:14–16, Paul refers to us as a "fragrance" through whom God will manifest the "sweet aroma" of Himself in every place. How wonderful it would be if the "sweet aroma" of God Himself would permeate our homes! What sweet joy and peace would then characterize our homes.

But thanks be to God, who always leads us in triumphal procession in Christ and through us spreads everywhere the fragrance of the knowledge of him.
2 Corinthians 2:14 NIV

PERFECTION IS GOD'S GIFT
Elizabeth Prentiss

*In all thy ways acknowledge him,
and he shall direct thy paths.*
PROVERBS 3:6

You have forgotten that body of yours and you have been trying to live as if you were all soul and spirit. You have been straining every nerve to acquire perfection, whereas this is God's gift and one that He is willing to give you, fully and freely."

"You rush from one extreme to another. The only true way to live in this world, constituted just as we are, is to make all our employments subserve the one great end and aim of existence, namely, to glorify God and to enjoy Him forever. But in order to do this we must be wise taskmasters and not require of ourselves what we cannot possibly perform. Recreation we must have. Otherwise, the strings of our soul, wound up to an unnatural tension, will break."

"Some liberty of action He must leave us or we should become mere machines. I think that those who love Him and wait upon Him day by day learn His will almost imperceptibly and need not go astray if we only consent to let Him work in us of His own good pleasure."

MELODY IN OUR HEAVINESS

Amy Carmichael

Sometimes we cannot sing much, but we can look up to our God and say a word or two. I did not know till one day last week that He calls that little word a song. In the Revised Version of Psalm 42:8 we have this: "In the night his song shall be with me, even a prayer unto the God of my life." Other versions have the same thought: Prayer is song to God.

"If thou be tempted, rise thou on the wings of prayer to thy beloved," and He will take that poor little prayer and turn it into a song.

From the midst of frustrations in Central Africa, Fred Arnot, who was the Livingstone of those regions, wrote, "I am learning never to be disappointed, but to praise."

I read that journal letter of his when it came home—it must be more than forty years ago—but that vital word in an ordinary letter remained with me, ready for a moment of need. I am learning never to be disappointed, but to praise.

God keeps us so near to Himself that there will be little shining seeds like that scattered about our letters—seeds that will bear a harvest of joy somewhere, sometime, and be melody to others in their heaviness.

For there they that carried us away captive required of us a song; and they that wasted us required of us mirth, saying, Sing us one of the songs of Zion.

PSALM 137:3

October 3

Restoring Men and Women
Jane Hansen

So God created man in his own image, in the image of God created he him; male and female created he them.
Genesis 1:27

The man and woman were the beginning place, the foundation of the House of the Lord—the place where He would dwell and begin to reveal Himself on earth.

He specifically fashioned this union, this relationship, to vividly and accurately display His image, His heart, His character on earth.

Satan endeavored to rise up against God, to exalt his throne, his rule, above the throne of God, and he knew right where to strike (see Isaiah 14:13–14). He knew it was essential to bring separation, distrust, fear, and suspicion between male and female, the image bearers God purposed to use for His unfolding plan on earth. The strength of the man and woman was in their union. Without unity, without oneness, God's plan would fail.

Satan struck, and his strategy worked. In shame, blame, and distrust, Adam and Eve covered themselves from each other even before they hid from God. God's original design was broken. His image was corrupted.

Today, the Holy Spirit is working to open our eyes so that we might open our hearts to one another. He is bringing restoration to this first relationship between man and woman— the image bearers of God.

Through the man and woman together, God is fully revealed.

THE RECORD
Hannah Whitall Smith

The "record" God has given us of His Son has been given for the express purpose of making us know that in His Son we have eternal life. "This is the record," i.e., that God hath given to us eternal life in Christ, and whoever believes in Christ has this life, and, of course, ought to know it. If we do not believe this record and consequently do not know that we have eternal life, we are "making God a liar." These are solemn words, and yet, taking the commonsense view of things, what is a doubt of God's record but the making a liar of God? If I doubt the record of one of my friends, I do in effect make that friend a liar, although I may never dare to use the word.

The flood of doubt and questioning that so often overwhelms Christian hearts in these days was apparently never so much as conceived of in Bible times nor by Bible Christians, and consequently it was nowhere definitely provided against. The one uniform foundation upon which were based all commands and all exhortations was the fact, taken for granted, that of course those to whom the commands and exhortations were addressed knew that they were God's children and that He was their Father.

He that believeth on the Son of God hath the witness in himself: he that believeth not God hath made him a liar; because he believeth not the record that God gave of his Son. And this is the record, that God hath given to us eternal life, and this life is in his Son.
1 JOHN 5:10–11

PACKED MAN
Ruth Bell Graham

But the God of all grace, who hath called us unto his eternal glory by Christ Jesus, after that ye have suffered a while, make you perfect, stablish, strengthen, settle you.
1 PETER 5:10

The man, asleep in the trash bin, was awakened with a jolt.

He had been scooped up along with the trash by a twenty-one-ton Indianapolis garbage truck.

Knocked unconscious, he came to upside-down and squeezed into an area where, as the driver later put it, "a human being shouldn't fit."

When the driver stopped, he heard some hollering. Getting out, the driver looked around. The voice sounded far away, and he could see no one. Then, he later reported, he "heard a voice saying he sure would like to get out of wherever he was." Fortunately, the driver saw to it that he did.

This was the way I have felt at times: too much to do, too far to go, and not enough time or strength to do it all, so that "you would like to get out of wherever you were."

Perhaps you're attempting things He hasn't commanded. When I began to feel compacted and cried for help, God showed me my priorities had gotten distorted. He was to come first. Then I realized I needed to be "liberated" from wherever I was: getting off boards and committees, attending no unnecessary meetings, and accepting fewer outside responsibilities.

This was God's answer for me.

LONGING FOR THE HOLY SPIRIT
Ruth Youngdahl Nelson

I believe there is a yearning for God in every heart. In the time of the psalmist's writing, there were underground watercourses that the deer could hear and smell but not see or reach. Often he would frantically follow this sound, hoping to find its source. The King James version reads, "As the hart panteth after the water brooks, so panteth my soul after thee, O God." Often people do weird things and follow strange paths in their effort to assuage this thirst.

These are the nudgings of the Spirit. God in His infinite love has taken the first step to us, long before we inch our way to Him. Somewhere in the depth of every living soul there is this longing.

After Miss Sullivan had established a means of communication with Helen Keller, she felt she wanted to tell her about God. The young girl's spirit rose as she said, "I know Him! I know Him! I didn't know His name."

In everyone you see or meet today, you look beyond the exteriors of appearance, of status, of intellect, of age, of race, or nationality and see a soul longing for God. The Holy Spirit will help you.

Open my heart to Your Spirit, O Lord, that I may accept all others as people whom You created and redeemed. Amen.

As a hind longs for the running streams, so do I long for thee, O God. With my whole being I thirst for God, the living God.
PSALM 42:1–2 NEB

SETTING PRIORITIES
Jean Fleming

*Set your affection on things above,
not on things on the earth.*
COLOSSIANS 3:2

I view my life as a tree. The trunk represents my relationship to Christ; the limbs represent major areas of God-given responsibility such as family, job, ministry, and personal development; and the branches represent the activities and opportunities of life. Even without special care, activity branches multiply. Soon the profusion of branches becomes more prominent than the trunk and limbs. When this happens, I feel trapped, frustrated, and empty. Why? Because my life is shaped and drained by activities that have lost their pertinence to Christ.

For example, the activities expected of a mother multiply conspiratorially: supervising a school field trip, organizing a car pool for soccer games, baking for the fourth-grade bake sale, helping a child with fractions.

To "sacrifice" for my family is a sincere veneer that wears thin in time. I must go beyond defining life by activities. I must focus not on the branches, but on the trunk and limbs. I do what I do because of Jesus and His claim on my life. I don't do what I don't do for the same reason.

On a finely pruned tree, the trunk and limbs are prominent. The limbs grow out of my relationship with Christ and sprout many new branches each year. I must examine my tree and determine which branches need to be pruned back or hacked off at the base. Life is always changing. My tree must undergo changes, too.

APPROACH OF THE BRIDEGROOM
Cora Harris MacIlravy

When God sees us in danger of treasuring His gifts rather than Himself, or when He is preparing us for the walk of naked faith, into which very few of His children ever enter, He often withdraws from the open window, and we only see Him as He glances through the lattice. His apparent withdrawal brings a great distress, for in such dealing there is nothing between Him and us that has made Him withdraw. As our faith increases, we comfort ourselves with the assurance of God's faithfulness and unchangeableness; and we begin to discern Him as clearly through the lattice as we had before seen Him through the window.

But the Lord finally withdraws behind an apparent wall, which our eyes cannot pierce, though His eyes are ever upon us. Again we are distressed and dismayed, but as faith disperses the clouds of doubt and fear, He gives us "Songs in the night." We are able to say: "I know Him whom I have believed." And the eye of faith is strengthened, that He begins to reveal Himself to our chastened vision; and we catch glimpses of Him through the lattice—passing visions of His beauty which we have never before beheld. If He hides Himself, we press on with our eyes more and more toward Him, and we endure as beholding Him who is invisible.

My beloved is like a roe or a young hart: behold, he standeth behind our wall, he looketh forth at the windows, shewing himself through the lattice.
SONG OF SOLOMON 2:9

CONCENTRATE ON THANKS
Corrie ten Boom

*Always and for everything giving thanks
in the name of our Lord Jesus Christ
to God the Father.*
EPHESIANS 5:20 RSV

Conditions in our barracks in the concentration camp at Ravensbruck were terrible. When we first arrived, I told Betsie I could not bear the lice that lived in our filthy blankets and mattresses. She replied, "You must thank God for everything, even for lice."

Betsie was right. Because of the bugs which infested our barrack, the women guards and officers kept their distance, and we were able to hold our Bible studies without fear. God has a use for the vermin, after all!

Sometimes what we see as a curse one day becomes a blessing the next day. How much more simple it would be if we would learn to thank God for everything instead of using our own judgment.

Lord, I need a miracle by Your Holy Spirit to thank You for my problem of today. Thank You that You are willing to make me willing.

LOVE
Helen Roseveare

How can we measure what we "give" to God to show Him our love? I think of an African parent who brought a chicken to me two weeks after I had done a lifesaving operation on his little child. Some might say that the value of a chicken hardly equaled the value of all the training that had been necessary to enable me to undertake that delicate operation and that therefore the gift was inadequate as a thank-offering.

If that were so, then there is no way that I can show God the thankfulness of my heart for His great gift to me of redemption: Anything I offered would be inadequate! But I believe, in God's eyes, the two acts, my operating and their chicken, were of comparable value. We had each given ALL we had. In evaluating the two gifts, the attitude of heart was the important factor.

"God so loved the world that He gave"—no end, no time limit, no measure, no calculation. His giving could only be called a reckless abandonment of love. Do I love Him in like measure, and am I willing to show it by a similar reckless abandonment?

For God so loved the world, that he gave his only begotten Son, that whosoever believeth in him should not perish, but have everlasting life.
JOHN 3:16

October 11

DELIVERANCE COMES IN GOD'S TIME
Stormie Omartian

Many are the afflictions of the righteous: but the Lord delivereth him out of them all.
PSALM 34:19

Deliverance is the severing of anything that holds you other than God. It could be a spirit of fear, of anger, of lying, of depression, or of lust. It could be a behavior you've acquired for self-defense, like compulsive overeating or a habitual withdrawal from people. Being born again delivers us from death, but we need to be delivered from dead places in our lives as well.

If you sat in a dark closet all your life and suddenly hundreds of high wattage floodlights were turned on you, you would be blinded. It's the same with deliverance. Too much light all at once would be too difficult to manage. That's why deliverance must take place a layer at a time to match your growth in the Lord.

You don't have to be a spiritual power-house to be delivered. If that were so, few people would be. But you can't be delivered from a problem you aren't ready to let go of, nor can deliverance be forced on you if you don't fully desire it. Also, learning to walk in the freedom you've been given takes time, and if God freed you of everything at once, you couldn't do it. Continued deliverance comes after you have lived in what you've received already.

It's never too late for God's presence to make a difference.

God's Love
Ney Bailey

I had always heard that I was supposed to love other people with a First Corinthians 13 kind of love. Someone suggested that I test my love for others by putting my name in wherever the chapter mentions "love." Then I remembered 1 John 4:16 says that God is love. And since 1 Corinthians 13 explains what love is, I decided to put God's name beside the word love and relate it to myself:

God's love toward me is kind,
God's love toward me is patient,
God's love toward me is not provoked,
God's love toward me does not take into
account a wrong suffered,
God's love toward me would bear all things,
believe all things,
hope all things,
endure all things.
God's love toward me would never fail.

It was overwhelming to think that He loved me in that way.

Heaven and earth shall pass away, but my words shall not pass away.
MATTHEW 24:35

YIELD, TRUST, OBEY

Hannah Whitall Smith

Neither yield ye your members as instruments of unrighteousness unto sin: but yield yourselves unto God.
ROMANS 6:13

To yield anything means simply to give that thing to the care and keeping of another. To yield ourselves to the Lord, therefore, is to give ourselves to Him, giving Him the entire possession and control of our whole being. It means to abandon ourselves, to take hands off of ourselves. The word *consecration* is often used to express this yielding, but I hardly think it is a good substitute. With many people, to consecrate themselves seems to convey the idea of doing something very self-sacrificing and very good and grand; and it therefore admits of a subtle form of self-glorification. But "yielding" conveys a far more humbling idea; it implies helplessness and weakness and the glorification of another rather than of ourselves.

Yielding is not the idea of sacrifice, in the sense we usually give to that word, namely, as of a great cross taken up; but it is the sense of surrender, of abandonment, of giving up the control and keeping and use of ourselves unto the Lord. To yield to God means to belong to God, and to belong to God means to have all His infinite power and infinite love engaged on our side. Therefore, when I invite you to yield yourselves to Him, I am inviting you to avail yourselves of an inexpressible and most amazing privilege.

VOLUNTEER SLAVES
Elisabeth Elliot

"Slave" is not a word most of us nowadays "feel comfortable" with. It is significant that most modern Bible translations use "servant" instead. For a slave is not his own, has no rights whatsoever, is not in charge of what happens to him, makes no choices about what he will do or how he is to serve, is not recognized, appreciated, thanked, or even (except by his absence) noticed at all.

Once we give up our slavery to the world, which is a cruel master indeed, to become Christ's bondslave, we live out our servitude to Him by glad service to others. This volunteer slavery cannot be taken advantage of—we have chosen to surrender everything for love. It is a wholly different thing from forced labor. It is in fact the purest joy when it is most unobserved, most unself-conscious, most simple, most freely offered.

Lord, break the chains that hold me to myself; free me to be Your happy slave—that is, to be the happy foot-washer of anyone today who needs his feet washed, his supper cooked, his faults overlooked, his work commended, or his button sewed on. Let me not imagine that my love for You is very great if I am unwilling to do for a human being something very small.

But God be thanked, that ye were the servants of sin, but ye have obeyed from the heart that form of doctrine which was delivered you. Being then made free from sin, ye became the servants of righteousness.
ROMANS 6:17–18

October 15

THE NIGHT WATCH
Evelyn Christenson

*Bear ye one another's burdens,
and so fulfil the law of Christ.*
GALATIANS 6:2

Are you one of these people whom God can awaken in the middle of the night to pray for one of His needs down here on Planet Earth? "But I need my sleep," you say. So did I, or at least I thought I did. For many years I was strictly hung up on sleeping pills. I thought I had to have eight solid hours of sleep or I'd never make it the next day. Then one summer day, I very undramatically tossed those pills into the toilet, flushed it, and said, "Lord, I'm not going to worry if I'm awake at night, because if You awaken me, there's a reason for it. I'll just ask You, 'For whom should I be praying?'"

God knows when I'm finished praying and ready to go back to sleep. And somehow there's no frustration, and I never miss the sleep when God needs me to pray. It's a very beautiful, exciting thing.

One night the Lord woke me and said, "Pray for Jacque" (a long-time prayer partner). At that time she was in San Francisco, and I learned later that she was going through a very deep spiritual battle, seemingly surrounded by forces of Satan. A letter Jacque wrote to me the next morning confirmed the reason God had awakened me. As I prayed in St. Paul, great peace had flooded her in San Francisco.

"If at night you can't sleep, don't count sheep—talk to the Shepherd!"

Know When to Say No

Gail MacDonald, Karen Mains, Kathy Peel

I believe my role as a parent is to help my children reach their full potential. There is, however, a tension between allowing them to cut back busy schedules if they realize they've overextended themselves and teaching them to stick with their commitments. Somehow we need to communicate two seemingly contradictory truths to our children: One, we live up to our commitments, and two, sometimes it's okay to quit. The deciding factor should be the reasons for wanting to quit.

Inconvenience is not a valid reason. If we aren't willing to work hard to see something through to completion, then it may be time to encourage a child to stick it out. The reward will be a job well done and a new sense of determination. But if a commitment is affecting out child's emotional or physical well-being, it should be looked at in a different light.

By watching our children's physical and emotional health, we should be able to gauge whether they are taking on too many commitments. As we come to know their limitations, we can effectively encourage them to grow in ways that use their talents for God's glory.

But let your communication be, Yea, yea; Nay, nay: for whatsoever is more than these cometh of evil.
Matthew 5:37

October 17

ARE YOU NEEDED?
Mary Hollingsworth

For as we have many members in one body, and all members have not the same office: So we, being many, are one body in Christ, and every one members one of another.
ROMANS 12:4–5

Those who love you need you in so many different ways, in every area of their lives in which you play a role.

How are you needed?

Your parents need you as a daughter, as a support, as a source of joy. Your siblings need you as a sister, a correspondent, and a partner in family matters.

Your best friend needs you as a listener, as a funmate, as a burden sharer, as an encourager and helper.

If you are married, your husband needs you as a loving wife. He may also need you as a tennis partner, bill payer, confidante, and secret keeper. Your children need you as a mother, as a teacher, as a guide, and as a counselor.

Your church family needs you as a spiritual light, a fellow traveler along the Way, a prayer partner, a spring of hope and faith.

God needs you, too. Whatever gifts and abilities He gave you, He needs you to be at work in His world and His kingdom. No one else can do what He designed you for in the same way you can.

No one else can play your role. No one else knows your lines. You are uniquely created to fit in the special you-shaped space God formed in His world.

THE GROANING OF THE SPIRIT

Joni Eareckson Tada

Immediately after church, a young woman with cerebral palsy approached me in her wheelchair.

CP is usually characterized by paralysis, weakness, or loss of coordination due to brain damage. Sometimes there are uncontrolled movements and slurred speech. This woman's speaking was especially difficult to grasp. She kept groaning a certain sentence over and over again.

Finally, after many attempts, I was able to piece her sentence together. She was asking me to help her find someone who could assist her into the restroom!

Can you imagine the hardship of not even being able to make your needs known? Ah, and yet that is the very predicament you and I find ourselves in.

There are times we want to talk to God but somehow can't manage it. The hurt goes too deep. Fear locks our thoughts. Confusion scatters our words. Depression grips our emotions.

I'm so glad God can read my heart and understand what's going on even when I am handicapped by my own weakness for words. As it says in Hebrews 4:13 (NIV), "Nothing. . . is hidden from God's sight. Everything is uncovered and laid bare before the eyes of him to whom we must give account."

Our heavenward groans have a voice before God.

The Spirit himself intercedes for us with groans that words cannot express.
Romans 8:26, NIV

DIFFICULTIES CONCERNING THE WILL
Hannah Whitall Smith

For that ye ought to say, If the Lord will, we shall live, and do this, or that.
JAMES 4:15

There was a lady who had a besetting sin, which in her emotions she dearly loved, but which in her will she hated. Believing herself to be necessarily under the control of her emotions, she had fully supposed she was unable to conquer it, unless her emotions should first be changed. But she learned this secret concerning the will, and going to her closet she said, "Lord, Thou seest that with my emotions I love this sin, but in my real central self I hate it. Until now my emotions have had the mastery; but now I put my will into Thy hands and give it up to Thy working. I will never again consent in my will to yield to this sin. Take possession of my will, and work in me to will and to do of Thy good pleasure."

Immediately she began to find deliverance. The Lord took possession of the will thus surrendered to Himself and began to work in her by His own power, so that His will in the matter gained the mastery over her emotions, and she found herself delivered, not by the power of an outward commandment, but by the inward power of the Spirit of God, "working in her that which was well pleasing in his sight."

THE COMPUTER AND ME
Ruthe White

"Am I anything more than a number on the computer of life?" Sometimes I wonder!

The computer is not the final authority of my life. There is another machine working. One that counts the very hairs on my head. (Someone once told me I have ninety thousand. Had I been born a blond or redhead, they say the count would have been different.)

I speak of the "Master Computer," the one that records my thought patterns: Each word, deed, goes down on its pages of time. This is the recording device I am most concerned about!

Someday, I know, I will walk up to the counter of life and try to cash a check on the reserve of my past. When that happens, I hope some good data is fed back from the management of heaven and that God okays the transaction.

For we must all appear before the judgment seat of Christ; that every one may receive the things done in his body, according to that he hath done, whether it be good or bad.
2 CORINTHIANS 5:10

A Colony of Caring

Arvella Schuller

But let the righteous be glad; let them rejoice before God: yea, let them exceedingly rejoice.
PSALM 68:3

What a precious treasure the Almighty created when He planned the human family—sharing together, loving together, growing together, building together.

What is a family? To the positive believer, it is a colony of caring—two or more individuals caring very deeply for each other. A family, then, is a group of people who, when you hurt, show that they care. You know they care!

Belonging to a family assures that we need never be lonely or lost, for we are surrounded by those who love us and care deeply for us. I like to call this our "treasure of assurance."

"Home is the place where, when you have to go there, they have to take you in." Through the years, these words from the beloved poet Robert Frost have sparked in me an amused and understanding attitude—as I have watched the family come home, one by one—happy or sad, angry or "hyper," fighting or withdrawn. Anyone who lives in a family knows the many moods that cross the thresholds of our homes each day, but because we are a "colony of caring," we open the door, hold out our arms, and love!

I'll See You at the Banquet
Betty Malz

A few years ago, Mary Pallesen came over for a cup of tea. We sat on the sundeck overlooking the Red River Valley area of the prairies of the Dakotas and decided to walk out to Clark's Corner. We didn't contemplate the fact that it was eight miles out—and the same distance back!

The last mile we were sliding our feet along the ground, dragging them in order to move. My left hip felt out of place, my back hurt, we were dehydrated, nearly faint, and my heels had bled so much my shoes were red in the back.

But our pride would not let us quit and our silly sense of humor volleyed back and forth, encouraging us to make it. Suddenly we caught sight of the old, brown farmhouse with the white gingerbread trim and window boxes blooming with pink and white petunias! We had made it home! We had succeeded in our venture! We smiled ridiculously between long, gasping drinks of water and collapsed into chairs.

If we took the happiness we felt at that moment of homecoming and magnified it a million times, it still could not compare with the exhilaration each of us will feel upon entering the gates of heaven. It seems too good to be true—but it is!

What a homecoming awaits us!

I'll see you at the banquet.

For who in heaven can be compared unto the Lord?
PSALM 89:6

HANDLING POWER
Jill Briscoe

And he sat down, and called the twelve, and saith unto them, If any man desire to be first, the same shall be last of all, and servant of all.
MARK 9:35

How do you handle power? How do I? All of us have some power and authority over other people. Every mother inherits her home and rules there. How does a mother handle the authority she has over her children, for example. Does she deal with it with strength and dignity like a true Queen of Hearts? The word *meekness* has the connotation of something totally wild that has been tamed. The meaning of the word is something akin to a wild horse that has been bridled—a harnessed horse, in fact. There has to be a sense of control about our lives if we are to win the respect of those we expect to follow our orders.

When I think of Jesus, I think of His strong dignity, of eternal power wrapped in earthly gentleness. When faced with man's inhumanity to man—even in His own servants, as was the case when James and John demanded He call down fire from heaven and burn up some discourteous people who wouldn't give them hospitality—Jesus responded with meekness. He simply rebuked His men for their lack of understanding and compassion, reminded them the Son of Man had come to save men's lives and not destroy them—and moved on (Luke 9:52–56). This was not weakness, as some have supposed; rather, this heavenly meekness illustrates for us the power to control anger and respond with grace.

OUR ASSIGNED WORK
Mary W. Tileston

Thou know'st not what is good for thee,
But God doth know—
Let Him thy strong reliance be,
And rest thee so.

—C. F. Gellert

I will surely do thee good.
GENESIS 32:12

Let us be very careful of thinking, on the one hand, that we have no work assigned us to do, or, on the other hand, that what we have assigned to us is not the right thing for us. If ever we can say in our hearts to God, in reference to any daily duty, "This is not my place; I would choose something dearer; I am capable of something higher," we are guilty not only of rebellion, but of blasphemy. It is equivalent to saying, not only, "My heart revolts against Thy commands," but "Thy commands are unwise; Thine Almighty guidance is unskillful; Thine omniscient eye has mistaken the capacities of Thy creature; Thine infinite love is indifferent to the welfare of Thy child."

—Elizabeth Charles

THE SPIRIT OF HAPPINESS

Amy Carmichael

Finally, brethren, whatsoever things are true, whatsoever things are honest, whatsoever things are just, whatsoever things are pure, whatsoever things are lovely, whatsoever things are of good report; if there be any virtue, and if there be any praise, think on these things.
PHILIPPIANS 4:8

The spirit of happiness is sheer miracle. It is the gift of the happy God, as Paul names our heavenly Father in writing to Timothy. It is the gift of the God of love. He pours it out of His own fountains, through unseen channels, as He poured it upon Paul and Silas before their feet were taken out of the stocks and their stripes washed; for "no created power in hell, or out of hell, can mar the music of our Lord Jesus, nor spoil our song of joy."

One of the great secrets of happiness is to think of happy things. There were many unhappy things in Philippi, things false, dishonorable, unjust, impure, hideous and of very bad report; the air of Philippi was darkened by these things. The Christians of that town might easily have had their lives stained by continually letting their thoughts dwell on what they could not help seeing and hearing and feeling, that evil they must often have met and fought in their striving together for the faith of the gospel.

But they were definitely told to think of things true, honorable, just, pure, lovely, and of good report. "If there be any virtue, and if there be any praise, think on these things" (Philippians 4:8).

FEAR NOT

Mrs. Charles E. Cowman

Stormy wind fulfilling his word.
PSALM 148:8

Is there no music in the heart of sorrow that the Lord of all has chosen for His own? Are you not nearer to the Master, have you not grown in faith, in patience, in prayerfulness, in thankful hope, since the time the storm winds first sighed across your life?

It is no small matter to grow nearer to God; it is worth all the tempest your soul has known. The heart of the Lord was yearning over you, and could not be satisfied till His winds had driven your soul entirely into the refuge and protection of His love.

Do not tremble because of the winds of the future; your Lord will be living and loving tomorrow, even as He lives and loves today and no storm waits in your path but shall leave behind another record that your Heavenly Father is stronger than the tempest, nearer than the grief.

We are traveling home to that beauteous shore where the chill winds never sweep, the hurricane makes no moan; yet, amid the rest of the painless Homeland, shall we not love the Lord a thousandfold more for every storm of earth in which He drew near to us, saying, "Fear not," and held us by the hand, and tenderly bore us through the hour that seemed the darkest?

Set your thoughts, not on the storm, but on the Love that rules the storm.

—*In Rainbow Weather*

SERVICE
Helen Roseveare

I beseech you therefore, brethren, by the mercies of God, that ye present your bodies a living sacrifice, holy, acceptable unto God, which is your reasonable service.
ROMANS 12:1

God wants to fit us perfectly in His plan, if we will allow Him to do so. He is willing to bring all circumstances to bear to that end. Ephesians 2:10 tells us that God had already prepared, before the creation of the world, the "good works" that He wants us to do, when He planned our salvation. He doesn't have to look around to see if He can find a job to fit my qualifications when I decide to apply to Him for employment! No. All is prepared. The only problem is my unwillingness to obey and take my part in the predetermined plan.

Hatred of sin and love for the Saviour must lead, first and foremost, to obedience. Obedience to the Word of God will show itself in service. This will be true godly service, a giving without any thought of gaining.

Not only must there have been a decisive act in the past when I committed my life to Christ, being identified with Him in His death, but there must also be a continual daily identifying of myself with that death, in putting aside my own will and self-pleasing, in order to live according to His will and good pleasure. This is the deliberate daily choosing to "die" to self in order to allow the Spirit of Christ to indwell me and to rule my choices.

EXPECTATIONS
Ruth Bell Graham

It is a foolish woman who expects her husband to be to her that which only Jesus Christ Himself can be: always ready to forgive, totally understanding, unendingly patient, invariably tender and loving, unfailing in every area, anticipating every need, and making more than adequate provision. Such expectations put a man under an impossible strain.

The same goes for the man who expects too much from his wife.

Ellen de Kroon Stamps commented about husbands playing a significant role in the family.

> Bob often talks about a sense in his life that God has called him to be a priest over our household—an awesome but precious responsibility. I've been very thankful of late that he has interpreted his priesthood to include taking the garbage out, changing diapers, cleaning bathtubs, and being up with the children during the night, in addition to helping to draw us ever closer to our Lord!

We have often said we would not choose to go back to some of those early days of our marriage. Too often, early love is a mirage built on daydreams. Love deepens with understanding, and varying viewpoints expand and challenge one another. So many things improve with age. So it is with marriage.

I will make him an help meet for him.
GENESIS 2:18

October 29

No Need to Be an Orphaned Christian

Catherine Marshall

I will not leave you comfortless:
I will come to you.
JOHN 14:18

An orphan is one who has known the warmth of a father's and mother's love, the security of home and hearthside, and is then deprived of these gifts.

Jesus' apostles were fearful of being in exactly that position. For three years the Master had been everything to them—beloved Companion, staunch Friend, never-failing Guide, provocative, exciting Teacher. When they wanted to know how to pray with results, they had but to ask Him. When Peter daringly tried to walk on the water, then became fearful and began to sink, he had but to stretch out his hand to have Jesus rescue him.

But lately, more and more often their Master had been speaking of His own death. "The time is at hand," He now told them. With dismay the apostles heard His soft "I go away."

Then Jesus, seeing their anxious faces, noting Thomas's fearful question, "Lord, I don't understand. Where are you going?" hastened to reassure them. "I will not leave you orphans," He promised the little group. "I will not leave you comfortless. I will manifest Myself to you."

Jesus' promise to you and me is that the Helper will be with us always, standing by for any protection we need and for every emergency. Our only part is to recognize His presence and to call upon Him in joyous faith.

THE MEANING OF TROUBLE
Hannah Whitall Smith

Many times in my life in practical affairs I have had my "mourning turned into dancing," because I have found that the trial I mourned was really a gateway into the good things I longed for. And I cannot help suspecting that this is far more often the case than we are inclined to think. I knew a man who had both his feet frozen off and was thwarted in all his plans by the lameness that ensued. He thought his life was ruined and mourned with unspeakable anguish. But this very trial opened out for him another career, which proved finally to be the thing of all others he would have chosen and which brought him a success far beyond the wildest dreams of his early aspirations. His greatest trouble became his greatest triumph. Instances of this are innumerable. Every life has some.

Since we have so often experienced our deserts to be turned into the garden of the Lord and have found fir trees and myrtle trees coming up where we thought there were only thorns and briers, the marvelous thing is that we should ever let ourselves be so utterly cast down and overwhelmed when fresh trouble comes. I think it would be a good exercise of soul for us to write out a little record for our own use of all the times when this marvelous transformation has happened in our experience. It might make us less ready to despair under our next trial.

Thou hast turned for me my mourning into dancing: thou hast put off my sackcloth, and girded me with gladness.
PSALM 30:11; see also ISAIAH 35:6–7

THE COAT

Anita Corrine Donihue and Colleen Reece

He that hath two coats,
let him impart to him that hath none.
LUKE 3:11

After Fran's older sister died, Fran donated most of her clothing to charity. One of the few items she kept was The Coat.

Just touching The Coat brought memories of Joy's laughing face. Fran wore The Coat after Joy died.

A year later, Fran thought of a teacher going through hard times. Would Susan feel insulted if she offered her the rest of Joy's clothing?

A startling thought came: Give Susan Joy's coat. "What?" she protested. Susan needs it more than you do, the small inner voice whispered.

"Offering Susan an old coat might hurt her feelings, Lord." A bright idea came. "How about a test? If I'm supposed to give Susan The Coat, help me find a replacement for. . ." (She named a ridiculously low figure.) A few hours later, she found a coat far below her stated limit.

That evening Susan dropped by Fran's house. Fran brought out two almost-new sweatshirts. "Can you use a few things?" Susan's face lit up, so Fran added, "There's one more thing." She took The Coat from a closet.

Susan swallowed hard and bowed her head.

When she looked up, her lips quivered. "For weeks I've been praying for a winter coat, but didn't know how it was possible."

May we always appreciate our blessings as much as Susan appreciated The Coat.

EVALUATING MY LIFE
Jean Fleming

Three or four times a year, I spend half a day with the Lord to evaluate my life, to examine my schedule, and to set some new directions for the months ahead. . . . I pray, "At this point in my life, Lord, what is it You want me to do? What must I do to keep my relationship to You vital? What do You want me to say yes and no to?"

Looking at life this way helps me ensure that I don't become too busy or fragmented to maintain my relationship to the Lord, to have vital time with my family, or to have a part in influencing the world for Christ.

As I evaluate my life before the Lord every three or four months, I remind myself that life is seasonal. There is a time and a season for everything (see Ecclesiastes 3:1). I can't do everything at once, nor should I. The question is, At this point in my life—what should I be doing?

Jesus did not heal everyone. He did not meet the needs of all the poor or cast out all demons. I cannot meet every need I'm aware of. I cannot exploit every opportunity.

The goal of much that is written about life management is to enable us to do more in less time. But is this necessarily a desirable goal? Perhaps we need to get less done, but the right things.

Shew me thy ways, O Lord;
teach me thy paths.
PSALM 25:4

November 2

THE PROBLEM OF SIN
Martha Peace

The Spirit of truth; whom the world cannot receive, because it seeth him not, neither knoweth him: but ye know him; for he dwelleth with you, and shall be in you.
JOHN 14:17

Sin is the only thing that will keep a woman from becoming a godly wife. Sin is lawlessness, a transgression from any of God's standards (1 John 3:4). The bad news is that there are a number of ways to sin. The good news is that God Himself has provided a remedy for sin. "He [God] made Him [Jesus Christ] who knew no sin to be sin on our behalf, that we might become the righteousness of God in Him" (2 Corinthians 5:21 NASB).

When a wife trusts in Jesus Christ as her Savior and Lord, she is no longer a slave to sin. "Knowing this, that our old self was crucified with Him, that our body of sin might be done away with [rendered powerless], that we should no longer be slaves to sin" (Romans 6:6 NASB). The Lord Jesus put it this way, "Truly, truly, I say to you, everyone who commits sin is the slave of sin. . . . If, therefore, the Son shall make you free, you shall be free indeed" (John 8:34, 36 NASB). There is help available for every wife's struggle against sin.

If a wife truly is a Christian, God has provided everything she needs "pertaining to life and godliness." God has broken the grip of sin in her life, and He has given her the supernatural power of the indwelling Holy Spirit to enable her to obey His Word and submit to His way and His will.

IF ONLY THERE WERE MOUNTAINS

Amy Carmichael

I stand, on this dreary seashore of my life, looking over this dreary backwash bay. Nothing invigorating or inspiring. Nothing hard enough to inspire anyone.

"The whole of my life is like that these days—not hard, just dull. I would have chosen challenging over dull. A challenge that would make me want to achieve at any cost. It's this useless feeling that's so devastating.

"I must confess, my spiritual vision has failed, what with waiting so long upon my God."

"So long? You need to grow in patience. For after you have done the will of God, you must learn to wait to receive the full extent of His promise.

"It is written: 'As for me, when I am poor and feeling heavy, your help, O God, will lift me up. I wait patiently, trusting that you will lift me up.'

"So I ask: Have you tried to face your life—those dull, dreary days—with the lifting power of praise?"

Lift my sights, Lord. Let me see today, and each duty in this day, as You see it.

Teach us to number our days aright, that we may gain a heart of wisdom. . . . Satisfy us in the morning with your unfailing love, that we may sing for joy and be glad all our days.
PSALM 90:12, 14 NIV

DAILY BREAD
Hannah Whitall Smith

Thy words were found, and I did eat them; and thy word was unto me the joy and rejoicing of mine heart: for I am called by thy name,
O Lord God of hosts.
JEREMIAH 15:16

Very few persons realize the effect of thought upon the condition of the soul, that it is in fact its food, the substance from which it evolves its strength and health and beauty, or upon which it may become weak and unhealthy and deformed. If we think low and corrupt thoughts, we bring diseases upon our soul, just as really as we bring diseases upon our body by eating corrupt and improper food. The man who thinks about self, feeds on self, just in proportion to the amount of thought he gives to self, and may at last become puffed up with self, and suffer from the dreadful disease of self-conceit and self-importance. On the other hand, if we think of Christ, we feed on Christ. We eat His flesh and blood practically, by filling our souls with believing thoughts of Him. He tells us this when He says, "It is the spirit that quickeneth; the flesh profiteth nothing: the words that I speak unto you, they are spirit, and they are life." If we will take the words of God, that is, His revealed truth, into our lips and eat it; that is, if we will dwell upon His words and say them over and over to ourselves, and thoroughly take in and assimilate their meaning in a commonsense sort of way, we shall find that our soul-life is fed and nourished by them and is made strong and vigorous in consequence.

DEPRESSION
Anita Corrine Donihue

My nights are sleepless again, dear Lord. Shadows creep around my room. I toss and turn in anguish. When I finally do sleep, I bolt up in bed, frightened that something or someone is after me.

I realize I need Your help more than ever. Life is too tough for me to handle. Lead me to people who can help. Open my mind to ways for me to overcome this terrible depression.

At times I am so distraught I can't even pray. Yet Your Holy Spirit knows my heart. I know You are lifting my needs to my Heavenly Father in words that can never be expressed by any human. I take comfort in that.

Let me give my burdens all to You, my Lord. I must let You carry them for me. Most of all, help me be willing not to take them back.

I know You watch over me and will help me through this. I put my trust in You. I won't depend on my own understanding. I purpose to acknowledge You in every way and be alert to Your direction. Let me not worry. Help me do my best to solve each problem as it comes along and pray about everything, large and small. Here are my anxieties and my problems. I thank You for your answers, given according to Your will. You know my needs before I ask.

*The peace of God,
which passeth all understanding.*
PHILIPPIANS 4:7

GRACEFUL LIVING
Gail MacDonald

But exhort one another daily, while it is called To day.
HEBREWS 3:13

I was stimulated to do some important thinking one day when I picked up a book that presented the opinions of several wives of famous men.

One woman said that the only worthwhile pursuit she could think of was the acquisition of money. Another, the victim of a tragic divorce, said, "I never want to be in a supportive role again." But then sandwiched between such opinions was the answer of Mrs. Billy Graham. When asked what she would like to do with the last third of her life, Ruth responded, "Help Bill."

I was stimulated by the answer Mrs. Graham gave to the question that was addressed to her: "What will you do with the rest of your life?"

I saw that for nearly thirty years I had worked from a "relational perspective"—the notion that relationships are the most important thing.

I saw that I am a home-oriented person, one who is striving to be a homemaker, a people-builder, a steward of things in whatever place people come together as family and friends.

If I cannot be at the locality we normally call home, then I find I instinctively try to make a home wherever I am. I find tremendous satisfaction when I am able to create pockets of safety and encouragement for those who are close to me at any given time. A place of grace, if you please.

MATURITY IN THE LORD
Hannah Whitall Smith

I knew a lady who had entered into this life of faith with a great outpouring of the Spirit. She expected to be put forth immediately into the Lord's harvest field. Instead of this, almost at once her husband lost all his money, and she was shut up in her own house to attend to all sorts of domestic duties, with no time or strength left for any Gospel work at all. She accepted the discipline. And the result was that, through this very training, He made her into a vessel "meet for the master's use, and prepared unto every good work."

Another lady, who had entered this life of faith under similar circumstances, was shut up with two peevish invalid children to nurse, and humor, and amuse all day long. Unlike the first one, this lady did not accept the training and went back into a state of sad coldness and misery. She had understood her part of trusting to begin with, but she took herself out of the hands of the Heavenly Potter, and the vessel was marred on the wheel.

The maturity of a Christian experience cannot be reached in a moment, but is the result of the work of God's Holy Spirit. And we cannot hope to reach this maturity in any way other than by yielding ourselves up, utterly and willingly, to His mighty working.

For unto the angels hath he not put in subjection the world to come, whereof we speak.
HEBREWS 2:5

Do It Now!

Alma Kern

A man's heart deviseth his way: but the LORD directeth his steps.
PROVERBS 16:9

"Never put off till tomorrow what can be done today." We've heard that since childhood. But too often we make exceptions to that old rule.

Of course, some actions must be postponed for good reason. Many actions, however, are put off for poor reasons. Our excuses?

Maybe we feel too tired. As a matter of fact, we feel less tired on busy, well-planned days. Boring, aimless days make us more tired and listless.

We may think we don't have time. Most of us need more character, not more time. If we set goals and program ourselves, we get the necessary things done. We also have time to help others and to do things we like to do.

Once in a while we just can't make up our minds. So we delay decisions. We wait and wait. We should wait on the Lord; trust Him to guide us; be alert to His direction through people and circumstances; then forge ahead.

Procrastination is an enemy. It is the thief of time. It causes anxiety, stress, frustration. We weary ourselves thinking about what ought to be done. We condemn ourselves for not doing it.

What have you been putting off? Do it now. You'll feel better about yourself.

STEPPING INTO GOD'S HAND

Linda R. McGinn

Walking with God is risky business. The study of His Word and fellowship with Him demonstrates that He orchestrates every event, circumstance, and experience of life. He transforms life in a way that enables us to take the risks necessary to follow Him.

Risking is stepping into the unknown, but that which is completely known by God. Stepping into the unknown does not mean stepping into oblivion. It means stepping into the known will of God—something you may not see right now as tangible but something more real than life itself. It requires stepping into His hand—the trusted hand of a faithful friend.

Why does the Christian life involve risk? Because everything seems risky when our natural instincts are opposed. God's ways and thoughts are not our own. Often, the directions of His will seem unnatural and uncomfortable. That's because they are supernatural. The Spirit of God is the only one who can give us the power to complete them.

The more we rely on God alone in every aspect of life, the more we experience His power.

I, even I, am he that comforteth you: who art thou, that thou shouldest be afraid of a man that shall die, and of the son of man which shall be made as grass?

ISAIAH 51:12

CREATING A GODLY ATMOSPHERE IN THE HOME
Martha Peace

*She looketh well to the ways
of her household,
and eateth not the bread of idleness.*
PROVERBS 31:27

"If Mama ain't happy, ain't nobody happy!" We smile as we read the plaque in the novelty store. But our smile quickly turns to a frown if truly "Mama ain't happy." This is because the wife and mother in a family often "sets the tone" in the home. The "tone" God wants her to set is one of joy, optimism, and a delight in the Lord and in her family. Most assuredly she "smiles at the future" (Proverbs 31:25 NASB).

If your family were called upon to describe you, what would they say? Would they report that you are a godly, Christian woman who loves life and loves her Lord? Or would they report that you are an unhappy, complaining, bitter woman?

If you do not have the "joy of the Lord" (Nehemiah 8:10), you can begin now to cultivate a joyful attitude. Find Scriptures that point to the goodness and the works of God. Think about what the Scriptures mean and how you could actually incorporate them into your life. Meditate on them so often that you commit them to memory. Actually "[sing] with thankfulness in your heart to God" as you go about your daily chores (Colossians 3:16 NASB). Smile and share with the other family members what wonderful things God has done for you and for them that very day.

BEAUTY IN BLUNDERS
Corrie ten Boom

I once visited a weaver's school where the students were making beautiful patterns. I asked, "When you make a mistake, must you cut it out and start from the beginning?"

A student said, "No. Our teacher is such a great artist that when we make a mistake, he uses it to improve the beauty of the pattern."

That is what the Lord does with our mistakes. He is the greatest artist, but we must surrender. Surrender your blunders to the Lord. He can use them to make the pattern of your life more beautiful.

> *Faith came singing into my room,*
> *And other guests took flight.*
> *Sped out into the night.*
> *I wondered that such peace could be,*
> *But Faith said gently, "Don't you see,*
> *That they can never live with me?"*
> —Elizabeth Cheney

Lord, we can be so depressed when we blunder. It is wonderful to know that our mistakes can be useful to You, because You are our Master Artist.

Thy faith hath made thee whole.
MATTHEW 9:22

November 12

NURTURING INDEPENDENCE
Gail MacDonald, Karen Mains, Kathy Peel

And, ye fathers, provoke not your children to wrath: but bring them up in the nurture and admonition of the Lord.
EPHESIANS 6:4

Sometimes you don't know you've given a child too much freedom until he blows it. When a child does make a mistake, don't respond with blame or shame. Instead, ask, "What can we learn from this?" It's important to show sympathetic understanding, to treat our children the same way God treats us when we mess up. The reality is we learn by failure.

Along with helping my children become independent of me, I wanted them to become dependent upon their heavenly Father. When I began to see my children do that, I felt I had been a successful parent.

I think that's where a lot of Christian parents stumble. They set themselves up as "the last word." There were times when I'd think one way about a situation and, after we'd pray, my mind would be changed. The children saw that and learned God was the final authority.

As parents it's scary to let our children go, to give them the freedom to make their own choices. When we let our children see us relying on God's wisdom rather than our own, we paint the best picture of adulthood: independent of parents and dependent upon God.

SAFE IN HIS HANDS
Hannah Whitall Smith

It is of course evident that everything in one's religious life depends upon the sort of God one worships. The character of the worshiper must necessarily be molded by the character of the object worshipped. If it is a cruel and revengeful God, or a selfish and unjust God, the worshiper will be cruel, and revengeful, and selfish, and unjust, also. If it is a loving, tender, forgiving, unselfish God, the worshiper will be loving, and tender, and forgiving, and unselfish, as well.

The poorer and more imperfect is one's conception of God, the more fervent and intense will be one's efforts to propitiate Him and to put Him in a good humor; whereas on the other hand, the higher and truer is the knowledge of the goodness and unselfishness of God, the less anxiety, and fuss, and wrestling, and agonizing will there be in one's worship.

I have discovered therefore that the statement of the fact that "God is good" is really, if we only understand it, a sufficient and entirely satisfactory assurance that our interests will be safe in His hands. Since He is good, He cannot fail to do His duty by us, and, since He is unselfish, He must necessarily consider our interests before His own. When once we are assured of this, there can be nothing left to fear.

This then is the message which we have heard of him, and declare unto you, that God is light, and in him is no darkness at all.
1 JOHN 1:5

PRAY AND BELIEVE

Mrs. Charles E. Cowman

When ye pray, believe.
MARK 11:24

When there is a matter that requires definite prayer, pray till you believe God, until with unfeigned lips you can thank Him for the answer. If the answer still tarries outwardly, do not pray for it in such a way that it is evident that you are not definitely believing for it. Such a prayer, in place of being a help, will be a hindrance; and when you are finished praying, you will find that your faith has weakened or has entirely gone. Prayers that pray us out of faith deny both God's promise in His Word and also His whisper "Yes," that He gave us in our hearts. Such prayers are but the expression of the unrest of one's heart, and unrest implies unbelief in reference to the answer to prayer. This prayer that prays ourselves out of faith frequently arises from centering our thoughts on the difficulty rather than on God's promise.

You will never learn faith in comfortable surroundings. God gives us the promises in a quiet hour; God seals our covenants with great and gracious words, then He steps back and waits to see how much we believe; then He lets the tempter come, and the test seems to contradict all that He has spoken. It is then that faith wins its crown. That is the time to look up through the storm and among the trembling, frightened seamen cry, "I believe God that it shall be even as it was told me."

WHEN GOD SAYS, "THANK YOU"

Jill Briscoe

Most of our lives we concentrate on the fact that we must affirm our faith in God and appreciate Him. It's quite different to think of God affirming His faith in us and appreciating us. It's a new concept for many of us that He can be pleased with us at all! But it's a good concept! Once a human being has been on his knees and felt the hand of God upon his head in praise, he will never be the same again. There is nothing that makes you feel quite so loved, warm, and complete as when God says, "Thank you." No matter if all the world rejects you—His word of affirmation is enough. We must learn to live our lives looking for that word.

His lord said unto him,
Well done, thou good and faithful servant.
MATTHEW 25:21

GATHERED IN HIS ARMS

Amy Carmichael

I am Alpha and Omega,
the first and the last.
REVELATION 1:11

What must it have been like for the apostle John to hear the great voice, bold and musically clear as a trumpet, announcing these words?

This is the New Testament echo of that glorious word in the Old Testament:

"The Lord will go before you, the God of Israel will be your rear guard" (Isaiah 52:12 NIV).

In one translation of the Bible, it is: "For your Vanguard is the Lord, and your Rear-guard the God of Israel" (Rotherham).

Alpha and Omega.

Vanguard and Rear-guard.

No wonder that, over and over again, in one form or another, the Lord says to us: "Fear not!" and "Do not let your hearts be troubled" (John 14:1 NIV).

He who begins, finishes. He who leads us on, follows behind to deal in love with our poor attempts. He gathers up the things that we have dropped—our fallen resolutions, our mistakes. He makes His blessed pardon to flow over our sins till they are utterly washed away. And He turns to fight the Enemy, who would pursue after us, to destroy us from behind.

He is first, and He is last!

And we are gathered up in between, as in great arms of eternal lovingkindness.

WONDERFULLY MADE
Lyn Klug

Our culture bombards us with messages about fashion, glamour, exercise, nutrition, and care of the body. The Bible stresses inner beauty. "Your beauty should not come from outward adornment, such as braided hair and the wearing of gold jewelry and fine clothes. Instead, it should be that of your inner self, the unfading beauty of a gentle and quiet spirit" (1 Peter 3:3–4 NIV). This Christian principle is worth stressing again in a society that often measures women by how decorative they are.

Yet we recognize that our bodies are God's creation, "fearfully and wonderfully made." We know that body, mind, and spirit are closely interrelated. The way I exercise and eat and how I look can make a big difference in how I feel and how I relate to others.

While I do not have to buy into the current obsession with a "beautiful bod," I can make the most of God's work. I like the attitude of Pat's mother, who recently moved to a nursing home at age eighty-six. Pat got her all settled in. A few days later when she came back to visit, her mother appeared with hair combed, a new dress, and lots of makeup—one cheek considerably redder than the other. "You look so nice, Mom," Pat said. "Why are you all dressed up?"

"Well," her mother replied, "I don't want to make anyone here feel worse than they already do."

I praise you because I am
fearfully and wonderfully made.
PSALM 139:14 NIV

OVERCOMING YOUR DOUBTS
Hannah Whitall Smith

Trust in the Lord with all thine heart; and lean not unto thine own understanding.
PROVERBS 3:5

Do not give heed to your doubts for a moment. Turn from them with horror, as you would from blasphemy; for they are blasphemy. You cannot perhaps hinder the suggestions of doubt from coming to you any more than you can hinder the boys in the street from swearing as you go by; and consequently you are not sinning in the one case any more than in the other. But just as you can refuse to listen to the boys or join in their oaths, so can you also refuse to listen to the doubts or join in with them. They are not your doubts until you consent to them and adopt them as true.

Put your will in this matter over on the Lord's side, and trust Him to keep you from falling. Tell Him all about your utter weakness and your long-encouraged habits of doubt, and how helpless you are before it, and commit the whole battle to Him. Believe He is faithful, not because you feel it, or see it, but because He says He is. Believe it, whether you feel it or not. Cultivate a continuous habit of believing, and never let your faith waver for any [reason], however plausible it may be. The result will be that sooner or later you will come to know that it is true, and all doubts will vanish in the blaze of the glory of the absolute faithfulness of God!

The Golden Age Lies Onward

Lilian Whiting

The Life Radiant is that transfiguration of the ordinary daily events and circumstances which lifts them to the spiritual plane and sees them as the signs and the indications of the divine leading.

Life prefigures itself before us as a spiritual drama in which we are, at once, the actors and the spectators. The story of living goes on perpetually. The days and the years inevitably turn the pages and open new chapters. Nothing is ever hopeless, because new combinations and groupings create new results. The forces that determine his daily life are partly with man and partly with God. They lie in both the Seen and the Unseen. We are always an inhabitant of both realms, and to recognize either alone and be blind to the other is to deprive ourselves of the great sources of energy. The divine aid, infinite and all-potent as it is, capable at any moment of utterly transforming all the conditions and transferring them to a higher plane, is yet limited by the degree of spiritual receptivity in the individual. As one may have all the air that he is able to breathe, so may one have all the aid of the Holy Spirit which he is capable of receiving. Man can never accept so gladly and so freely as God offers; but in just the proportion to which he can, increasingly, lift up his heart in response, to that degree God fills his life with a glory not of earth.

Even there shall thy hand lead me, and thy right hand shall hold me.
PSALM 139:10

PRAISE YOU, BECAUSE OF. . .

Anita Corrine Donihue

"Who of you by worrying can add a single hour to his life?"
MATTHEW 6:27 NIV

To whom or what could I compare You, O Lord? Can any begin to measure the waters with the palm of a hand as You can? Is there one who is able to know the breadth and height of the heavens or earth's contents? Where is one who can weigh and balance the mountains, the foothills? There is no one.

Who knows all the movements of God's Spirit other than You? Can any see what all Your plans are for our future? Does one person know the day of Your return? There is no one.

The earth, these tiny nations, are less than a drop in the bucket or a speck of dust in Your immense vision. So with all this, how are You mindful of me? How do you know me by name? My joys? My heart-cries? How is it that You love me?

I cannot fathom it, Father. I only know You are my everlasting God. You never grow faint or weary in caring for me. Your strength goes beyond all other means I depend upon. Even with all our technology, You are even greater. You control the balance of it all. Because of this, why should I fear?

CLOGGED PENS
Ruth Bell Graham

I shook it. I knocked it gently, sideways, on the top of the desk. I licked a piece of paper and wrote carefully in the moisture. (I can't tell you why this works, but it usually does.) I repeated each procedure without results. Then I carried the pen to the sink, took it apart, and carefully flushed out the point. Refilling it, I sat down to write.

How like me, I thought with exasperation.

I have mugs full of pens on my desk: ball-points, felt tips, ink pens—even pencils. But for very fine writing, such as notes in the margins of my Bible, I need a Rapidograph pen. This pen has a needle-fine point and uses India ink, which will not seep through or smear on the thin India paper.

How often when God has needed me I have been clogged up (too busy or inundated with things—the necessary giving way to the unnecessary). Or I've gone dry.

When that happens, I need a "shaking up" or I need special cleansing. And I need to be filled and refilled and filled again. There have been times when God has patiently and carefully done just that. But unlike a pen, I do have a choice. I can decide whether or not I remain usable.

And to know the love of Christ, which passeth knowledge, that ye might be filled with all the fulness of God.
EPHESIANS 3:19

November 22

OUR WORK, WHAT IS IT?

Anna J. Lindgren

And in every work that he began in the service of the house of God, and in the law, and in the commandments, to seek his God, he did it with all his heart, and prospered.
2 CHRONICLES 31:21

The one thing that more than any other keeps men from the Cross is the fact that the Cross stands for man's complete failure both to be and to do. "Just as I am, without one plea," is not the natural tendency of the human heart. "A golden deed" a day, or salvation on the installment plan, appeals more.

God's great command is not do but be! "Be ye holy" rings through the Old Testament. And the whole Old Testament story bears out the evidence that man was not holy.

But "being justified freely," what is my work? Again, God's command is not do but be. "Be ye filled with the Spirit" is an all-inclusive New Testament command. "If any man have not the Spirit of Christ, he is none of his" (Romans 8:9). And—do I dare to write it—it seems such a daring thought: To have the Spirit of God is to have the character of God.

Why so troubled about your weakness? Does not the Master know how to use His tools? Why so disappointed in environments and people? Does He not know how best to bring out His likeness in you? Whatever your peculiar condition just now, God's eye is watching you. He is eagerly looking for His own likeness.

COST OF GOOD LIVING
Jo Berry

Security embodies peace of mind: freedom from fear and danger and agitating passions. Those who live according to God's righteous standards do not have to worry about what will happen to them because of wrongs they have done. An unrighteous person is constantly faced with reaping the results of his evil deeds, dreading the time when his sin will find him out.

Fear, another by-product of insecurity, is also negated by living according to God's standards. As you walk with the Lord in a trust relationship, "You will walk. . .securely, and your foot will not stumble. When you lie down, you will not be afraid. When you lie down, your sleep will be sweet" (Proverbs 3:23–24 NASB).

Righteous living also assures security because it keeps us from trouble. If we do the right thing, we will not get into trouble for doing what we should not. "The righteous is delivered from trouble." "The righteous will escape from trouble" (Proverbs 11:8; 12:13 NASB).

A final security factor in the low cost of good living is that it guarantees us freedom from want. "The Lord will not allow the righteous to hunger" (Proverbs 10:3 NASB) in either the physical or spiritual sense. He will supply our needs; He knows what they are.

But whoso hearkeneth unto me shall dwell safely, and shall be quiet from fear of evil. . . .He that walketh uprightly walketh surely: but he that perverteth his ways shall be known.
PROVERBS 1:33; 10:9

LET'S KEEP IN TOUCH—REALLY

Elizabeth Cody Newenhuyse

A friend loveth at all times,
and a brother is born for adversity.
PROVERBS 17:17

One of the truest pleasures of work is the companionship it provides. When professional paths cross regularly, these relationships are easier to maintain. Yet they also can be freighted with the baggage of envy, competitiveness, calculated networking. If a friend calls me to share news of a professional success, I rejoice sincerely—but the worm is in there, burrowing. So my joy is shaded with, Why can't it be me?

Working women can lead very crowded, very lonely lives—many acquaintances, few real friends. The office banter and camaraderie can mask a deeper hunger to reach out and know another human being—and be known in turn. And we can't go home and dump all this longing on our spouse, who has his own concerns to deal with.

Yet if I sometimes feel isolated and needy, I must share culpability. People have moved out of state, and I have not answered their letters. I say I am a person who values loyalty and affection; I do not always act like it.

Yes, some friendships are transitory; some connections are temporary. But a good friend is so hard to find that he or she is worth holding onto. And, as a woman who recently moved noted in a letter, "We've forgotten how much energy it takes to make new friends."

ME!

Hannah Whitall Smith

There is no subject more vital to an everyday religion than a clear understanding of the right relations of our own individuality to the rest of the world. To most people the greatest person in the universe is themselves. Their whole lives are made up of endless variations on the word ME.

Like Solomon in Ecclesiastes, we "commune with our own hearts" concerning our great possessions of various kinds, our wisdom, our knowledge, our righteousness, our good works; and we are profoundly impressed with their great value and importance; and naturally we desire to call the attention of those around us to their magnitude!

There is never any "profit" in it, but always a grievous loss, and it can never turn out to be anything but "vanity and vexation of spirit." Have we not all discovered something of this in our own experience? You have set your heart, perhaps, on procuring something for the benefit or pleasure of your own great big ME; but when you have secured it, this ungrateful ME has refused to be satisfied and has turned away from what it has cost you so much to procure, in weariness and disgust. Never, under any circumstances, has it really in the end paid you to try and exalt your great exacting ME, for always, sooner or later, it has all proved to be "nothing but vanity and vexation of spirit."

I communed with mine own heart, saying,
Lo, I am come to great estate.
ECCLESIASTES 1:16

November 26

THE THANKFUL LIST
Joyce Landorf

Though there are no sheep in the pen
and no cattle in the stalls, yet
I will rejoice in the Lord,
I will be joyful in God my Savior.
HABAKKUK 3:17–18 NIV

It's Thanksgiving time again. I know it because everyone is talking about it. If I were to write a list of the things I'm thankful for, I'd put down all the good things of life, like a loving marriage, great children, and our growth this year in the Lord.

But as I look over my list, I wonder about the difficult things of the year. Should they be on the list, too? Our Lord clearly reveals in His Word that we are to be thankful and grateful for all things.

My list does not include some suffering I had this year, yet in order for my patience to grow (the epistle of James tells us), I need problems, pain, and suffering. My list includes none of the past months' disappointment, yet it was exactly when my disappointment was greatest that Jesus was especially close and comforting to me.

It is not easy to make out a pain and disappointment list and then be thankful over it, yet the Old Testament prophet did such a thing (see Habakkuk 3:17–18).

The secret is in the fact that he did not make up his list of praise and thanksgiving by how he felt emotionally. He made it a matter of will. He, like the psalmist says, "I will praise." That's Thanksgiving!

I'm making out a new list.

Let Us Cherish Thankfulness

Amy Carmichael

"In every thing give thanks."

This is a constant word to me. It is so easy to give thanks for what one naturally chooses, but that does not cover the "every thing" of the text.

One morning lately, in speaking of some small trouble, I quoted, "In everything give thanks," and at once someone answered, "But I cannot give thanks for everything." Now, if our God tells us to do a thing and we say we cannot, there is something wrong somewhere, for we all know the words, "I can do all things through Christ which strengtheneth me" (Philippians 4:13). It is treason to say, "I cannot." But first we should make sure that we are commanded to do this that we feel we cannot do.

I do not think we are to give thanks for everything. To make sure of this verse, which is sometimes quoted with *for* instead of *in*, I looked it up in seven versions. In six of the seven it is *in*; only one version has *for*. So I take it that we may understand the word to mean, not "Give thanks for everything," but "Give thanks in everything," which is a different matter.

We can do that. We will do that.

I often think we must disappoint our kind Father by not noticing the little things (as well as the countless great things) that He does to give us pleasure.

In every thing give thanks.
1 Thessalonians 5:18

TAKE COMFORT
Anita Corrine Donihue

For our light affliction, which is but for a moment, worketh for us a far more exceeding and eternal weight of glory.
2 CORINTHIANS 4:17

Do you ever feel your trials are like wearing a crown of thorns? Be faithful. As you trust in God, your crown of thorns will be taken away and He will hand you a crown with stars instead. Remember to thank and praise Him.

Do you feel like you are overloaded, your hands filled with heavy cares? Be faithful. As you keep trusting in God, He will take away your heavy cares and place a harp in your grasp so you may sing glory and honor to God for all He has done. Remember to thank and praise Him.

Do your garments feel soiled with dirt and grime from struggling in a sin-sick world? Stay faithful. He will replace them with clothing that is shining white. Remember to thank and praise Him.

Hold on and do not despair. There will be a time when you look back and your trials will seem as nothing in light of the many answered prayers, miracles, and evidence of God's glory and grace.

When we meet in heaven, our adversities will become strangely dim in the shadows of God's unfailing love. Remember to thank and praise Him.

THE LIFE DEFINED
Hannah Whitall Smith

Take my yoke upon you, and learn of me;
for I am meek and lowly in heart:
and ye shall find rest unto your souls.
MATTHEW 11:29

Most Christians are like a man who was toiling along the road, bending under a heavy burden, when a wagon overtook him and the driver kindly offered to help him on his journey. He joyfully accepted the offer, but when seated in the wagon, continued to bend beneath his burden, which he still kept on his shoulders. "Why do you not lay down your burden?" asked the kind-hearted driver. "Oh!" replied the man, "I feel that it is almost too much to ask you to carry me, and I could not think of letting you carry my burden, too."

And so Christians, who have given themselves into the care and keeping of the Lord Jesus, still continue to bend beneath the weight of their burdens and often go weary and heavy-laden throughout the whole length of their journey.

When I speak of burdens, I mean everything that troubles us, whether spiritual or temporal.

I mean, first of all, ourselves. Our own daily living, our frames and feelings, our especial weaknesses and temptations, our peculiar temperaments, our inward affairs of every kind—these are the things that perplex and worry us more than anything else and that bring us most frequently into bondage and darkness. In laying off your burdens, therefore, the first one you must get rid of is yourself.

On Earth, As It Is in Heaven

Evelyn Christenson

Saying, Father, if thou be willing, remove this cup from me: nevertheless not my will, but thine, be done.
LUKE 22:42

For us to pray, "Lord, I want Your will down here on earth," is a tremendous prayer. There is a spot on earth, a sphere of influence that belongs only to you. It has been given to you by our heavenly Father. And it's possible for you to bring about God's complete will in your sphere of influence here on earth.

The disciples, whom Jesus taught to pray: "Our Father. . .Thy will be done on earth as it is in heaven," knew they couldn't change the whole Roman Empire, but they also knew it was possible for them to change the spheres of influence which were theirs.

The Lord's Prayer really comes into focus right where we are when we pray, "Thy will be done on earth as it is in heaven." Is there anything contrary to God's will in heaven? No! Think of what would happen if every Christian really brought God's will to the little sphere which is his.

The supreme example of praying in the will of God is that of Christ praying in the garden of Gethsemane. He prayed, "Father, if thou be willing, remove this cup from me: nevertheless not my will, but thine, be done" (Luke 22:42).

Have you come to the place in your life where you can say, "Lord, not my will, but thine, be done"?

Letting Go of Our Children

Ellyn Sanna

Like Abraham, we, too, are called to let go of our children, releasing them into God's hands. God's request to Abraham to sacrifice his son seems heartless to us, and when God asks us to allow our own children to suffer, the request feels just as harsh.

Mary, the mother of Jesus, is sometimes called the mater dolorosa, the sorrowing mother who allowed her child to suffer. And Christ had another Parent who watched from heaven as His child died in agony. In other words, we are not alone in our pain when we let go of our children. God has experienced this same pain, and He is here with us in it.

Sometimes, though, we find we can trust God for our own lives more easily than we can for our children's. To watch our children's gradual separation from our protection and care radically tests our faith. But if we truly believe that God's grace is real and active, then we must believe it is equally real and equally active in our children's lives.

Worrying comes easily to mothers, though. It's hard to let go, but the most often repeated commandment in the Bible is "Fear not!" Fear makes us cling. It weighs us down and slows our progress.

Faith lets go.

Fear not: peace be unto thee, be strong, yea, be strong.
DANIEL 10:19

NO JOKE!

Judy Reamer with Donna Arthur

Like a madman shooting firebrands or deadly arrows is a man who deceives his neighbor and says, I was only joking!
PROVERBS 26:18–19 NIV

This kind of casual joking gets around easily and frequently even in Christian circles. Many became used to using sexual humor before they were Christians, and the habit remained.

A friend told me of an incident that caused her to battle with sexual thoughts for many days after it happened. A male friend phoned her home and asked for her husband.

"He isn't here right now," she answered.

"Oh, good," he said to her. "I'll be right over." Uncomfortable and unclean thoughts began to cross my friend's mind. What if he does show up? Has he been thinking about me? Why would he say that if there isn't a thread of suggestive truth in it? This woman had to get alone and pray away these strange feelings she was experiencing.

Sexual humor and teasing cannot be excused. Careless words can cause an enormous amount of problems for another person.

Examine yourself in these areas. The Holy Spirit is ever ready to help us understand ourselves. If we ask for His help, He will convict us if we are flirting either consciously or subconsciously. We need to use our godly friendliness wisely.

BLESSED ARE THE PURE IN HEART

Eileen Egan and Kathleen Egan, O.S.B.

Blessed are the pure in heart:
for they shall see God.
MATTHEW 5:8

"Clean of heart" is also given as "pure in heart" or "single-hearted." In Scripture, the heart includes not only the emotions, but the mind and the will—in fact, the whole person.

Purity of heart means simply to will one thing. An old phrase, used less today, "the one thing necessary," is apt here. The one thing necessary is salvation, union with God forever.

The clean of heart move through life constantly choosing God so that as they leave life, they receive the promise of this beatitude: They enter the presence of the Creator.

St. Augustine pointed out that God "made His Son not only to show the way but to be the very Way Himself."

Jesus as the very Way is the way of the single-hearted, concentrating on doing the will of God. This implies a certain emptying of the self, a discarding of what does not lead to God. We remember that Jesus "emptied himself, and took the form of a slave" in obedience to the Father (see Philippians 2:7).

Those of us fortunate enough to know Mother Teresa marvel at this quality in her.

When some young people asked Mother Teresa how they could learn to see and serve Jesus in the poor, she replied, "You need a clean heart."

If Only
Amy Carmichael

And it shall come to pass, that before they call, I will answer; and while they are yet speaking, I will hear.
ISAIAH 65:24

There was a day for me when I stood outside the door of the house we'd rented for the missions work. The old man who had charge of the key was not there, and the key was not to be found.

Just then another old man hurried up, the huge key of his own courtyard door in hand. "This may open it," he said hopefully.

What if the old man had not rushed up at the last moment with a key? What if the key had not worked? There was a pit dug, where no pit was supposed to be. And for me, a crippling fall.

The Lord allowed it. So far as we are concerned, He did it: He, Himself. And all that He does is good.

Less than three weeks before, a member of our fellowship was suddenly caused to feel that danger was threatening me. He prayed. He continued on until peace came, and he knew that his prayer was heard.

Should we have said that prayer was not answered?

We see hardly one inch of the narrow lane of time. To our God, eternity lies open as a meadow. It must seem strange to the heavenly people that we ever call prayer "Unanswered" when it is not what we expect.

I Love Presents!

Marilyn Meberg

I have begun to enter into that customary pre-Christmas "I find the holidays especially poignant since Ken died" phase. What is embarrassing for me to admit is that I also really miss the fantastic presents he used to give me.

I receive daily at least four or five catalogs. And yesterday, I was sufficiently activated to come up with the plan I feared might label me as dangerously out of touch with reality.

There were two catalog offerings that not only appealed to my aesthetic side but my practical side as well. In other words, not only did I want them, I felt I needed them. But how could I justify ordering these two items for myself?

Why not order them, wrap them, and put them under the tree with a Christmas tag reading, "To Marilyn from Ken." After all, if Ken were still living, he would love to get those items for me.

Occasionally I must remind myself that all gifts are given to me, God's beloved child, with incomparable love and joy. For me to feel guilty about buying myself something is to forget the original Author of that gift. Everything good and loving in life has its source in God, including all gifts. Actually, if I were to be theologically sound, I'd write on the Christmas tag, "To Marilyn from God." I love that idea!

Every good and perfect gift is from above, coming down from the Father of the heavenly lights.
James 1:17 NIV

December 6

Pray First, Plan Afterward

Evelyn Christenson

Hearken unto the voice of my cry, my King, and my God: for unto thee will I pray.
PSALM 5:2

If we could learn to pray first and plan afterward, how different would be whatever we are doing for Christ. Maybe, just maybe, we are planning in one direction and God's will is in another direction.

Even if we are plugged into God's will, we may be going at a snail's pace. God says, "Look, you see only a tenth of what I have for you. There are nine-tenths that you're not seeing, that you don't know anything about."

God wants us to make ourselves available to Him. Then our omnipotent God will pour out His power upon us. Instead of following our tiny, tiny plans, God wants to open heaven and flood us. It's exciting.

Gail, our children's worker, came up with a fantastic idea after she witnessed some miraculous answers to prayer. Her suggestion, "Let's pray first and plan afterwards," became the slogan for our church. During Vacation Bible School that year we set up a prayer room and collected requests along with attendance sheets. Then teachers and helpers spent their break times in prayer.

An urgent request came from one department. Not one child had received Christ though the school had been in session for a week and a half. What a difference prayer made! I stepped into the department to see twenty-three hands raised to receive Christ. The spiritual ceiling of our church went straight up!

VISION
Sheila Walsh

One verse buried in the Acts of the Apostles refers to King David, who "served God's purpose in his own generation." Christ, too, was so clear in the purpose of His life. His mission statement was well defined. Do you know why we are here, what we have been made for, our purpose? Sometimes we live out what other people perceive as our vision and calling and never discover for ourselves what that really is. Sometimes we are afraid to reach out and live the life that we believe we have been called to. But fear is no friend. It may seem to protect, but it slowly suffocates.

Someone recently asked me if I could state in a sentence what my life is all about. I replied, "The purpose of my life is to learn to love God more and to communicate that love and grace to others." That is why I am on the planet. When you know what your mission statement is, life is so much easier; you become free to line up your activities, relationships, and goals with that stated intent. What is your place in the kingdom of God? If I were to ask you to give me a sentence that encapsulated your vision for your life, what would it be? David discovered his purpose and fulfilled it in his generation, and so must we.

For when David had served God's purpose in his own generation, he fell asleep.
ACTS 13:36 NIV

LOVE OF THE WORLD

Elisabeth Elliot

Love not the world, neither the things that are in the world. If any man love the world, the love of the Father is not in him.
1 JOHN 2:15

John tells us in his first letter that anyone who loves the world is a stranger to the Father's love. We are not to set our hearts on the world or anything in it. The word used in the original is *cosmos*, which means the whole created order. Is there nothing here that I am allowed to love? What about the thundering, flashing sea that I see from my window? What about the rose on my desk, or even this house where I live with its warmth and pleasantness? They are not going to last forever. If I love them, am I then a stranger to my heavenly Father's love?

It has helped me to think of John's words in this manner. To love the world in the wrong way is to love it without knowing the Father's love. When a man knows Him and receives everything from His hand, the world is redeemed for him, no longer a snare and in opposition to the love of God. We must love the world only through and because of the Father, not instead of. Our ultimate concern must be God Himself. He is eternal, His gifts are not always so.

Lord, may no gift of Yours ever take Your place in my heart. Help me to hold them lightly in an open palm, that the supreme object of my desire may always be You and You alone.

GOSSIP (WATCH WHAT YOU SAY!)

Jo Berry

Another, and probably the most common, speech problem is gossip. Would you call yourself a gossip? A look in the dictionary reveals the many faces of gossip. The dictionary defines gossip as groundless rumor, hearsay, idle talk, prating and chatting needlessly.

The book of Proverbs refines the meaning further by showing that gossip is talebearing—repeating stories, rumors, or secrets—and also slandering and talking too much. To overcome the problem of gossip you must recognize how insidious and harmful it is and what it involves.

One thing gossip embodies is bearing tales. "He who goes about as a talebearer reveals secrets" (Proverbs 11:13 NASB). So gossip is running around telling stories, "going about" hearing something and purposely choosing to spread it. It is betraying both implied and stated confidences.

Gossip also involves revealing secrets; and whether they are betrayed accidentally or on purpose is irrelevant.

Along with bearing tales—going about repeating matters and revealing secrets—gossip incorporates slander: purposely and maliciously speaking against others. We should not even expose ourselves to such people lest we be judged guilty by association or pick up their unseemly behavior patterns.

A talebearer revealeth secrets: but he that is of a faithful spirit concealeth the matter.
PROVERBS 11:13

The Unselfishness of God
Hannah Whitall Smith

For God so loved the world,
that he gave his only begotten Son.
John 3:16

On the fly leaf of my Bible I find the following words, taken from I know not where: "This generation has rediscovered the unselfishness of God."

If I am not mistaken, the generation before mine knew very little of the unselfishness of God; and, even of my own generation, there are I fear many good and earnest Christians who do not know it yet. Without putting it into such words as to shock themselves or others, many Christians still at bottom look upon God as one of the most selfish, self-absorbed Beings in the universe, far more selfish than they could think it right to be themselves, intent only upon His own honor and glory, looking out continually that His own rights are never trampled on, and so absorbed in thoughts of Himself and of His own righteousness as to have no love or pity to spare for the poor sinners who have offended Him.

To discover that He is not the selfish Being we are so often apt to think Him, but is instead really and fundamentally unselfish, caring not at all for Himself, but only and always for us and for our welfare, is to have found the answer to every human question, and the cure for every human ill.

HONORING HEART'S DESIRES
Martha Peace

Where does such a heart come from? It is a grace gift from God to the believer (Jeremiah 31:33; Ezekiel 36:26). Scripture says, "Delight yourself in the Lord; and He will give you the desires of your heart" (Psalm 37:4 NASB). This means God will put the desires in a wife's heart that He wants to be there. In other words, God places that kind of passion within the deepest longings of a person. The wife's responsibility is to ask God for that passion and then diligently to seek God through His written Word. She also has a responsibility to cultivate a grateful attitude and thankfulness to God regardless of her circumstances (1 Thessalonians 5:18). To cultivate a grateful attitude, she will have to deliberately think grateful thoughts to God even though she may not feel like it. God will do the rest.

How should her desires change? Of what should the new desires consist? What a wife desires is what she spends time thinking about, daydreaming about, planning for, and longing after. What is your heart set on? What is really important to you? What you have your heart set on will make all the difference in the world in your fulfillment and your joy. Ask God to give you new heart's desires. Then proceed to seek after God with the same passion and energy that you are currently expending on idolatrous desires (1 John 2:15–17).

I have longed for thy salvation, O Lord; and thy law is my delight.
PSALM 119:174

December 12
LIFE HAS A TENDENCY TO BECOME FAR TOO STRENUOUS
Lilian Whiting

*And the Lord God formed man of
the dust of the ground, and breathed
into his nostrils the breath of life;
and man became a living soul.*
GENESIS 2:7

_____
_____
_____
_____
_____
_____
_____
_____
_____
_____
_____
_____
_____
_____
_____
_____
_____
_____
_____
_____
_____

The joy of faith in its inspiration and emotion is wonderfully renewed from the Divine Word. "The Lord shall be unto thee an everlasting light, and thy God thy glory" (Isaiah 60:19). The gospels are full of these positive and radiant assurances that invest faith with the most absolute joy of confidence and positiveness of trust. The human soul is stifled in the "strenuous" lower life, its energies are paralyzed unless it seek renewal at the divine springs. It is this strenuousness of latter-day life, unrelieved by love and by prayer; unrelieved by the spiritual luxury of loving service and outgoing thought; this strenuous attitude, intent on getting and greed and gain and personal advantage, that, at last, ends in the discords and the crimes, the despair and the suicides, whose records fill the daily press. The cure for all these ills is to be found only in the higher life of conduct and of beauty. "Thou shalt show me the way of life: Thou shalt make me full of joy with thy countenance." Here, and here alone, is the cure, the relief, the leading into peace and serenity and exaltation. It is in the serene and joyous exaltation of life alone that one truly lives; in that sweetness of mutual trust and generous aims and overflowing love that radiates its joy and beauty to all.

LET GOD USE YOU
Alma Kern

I gave my neighbor a ride today. It was only a few minutes out of my way. When I dropped her off at her house, she thanked me and added, "God sent you." Her bag of groceries was heavier than she had expected, and she had murmured, "O Lord, how will I ever make it home!"

It had seemed so casual an incident to me. I just happened to need a few things from the store. I just happened to have the car. Both of us just happened to be checking out at the same time.

Did God know her problem even before she did? Did He arrange my schedule so that I would be at the right place at the right time?

I didn't hear any special voice. No unusual prodding moved me. And yet there was a phone call just as I was ready to leave for the store. I was annoyed. It seemed a poor time to listen for ten minutes to the problems of a friend. Was that also part of His plan? Was that delay meant to put me on schedule to meet my neighbor at the moment of her need?

O Lord, thank You for using me today to share Jesus' love—as a listening post for my friend and a lift for my neighbor. Those were small favors to ask of me, those few moments of my time.

Be ready to [do] every good work.
TITUS 3:1

December 14
THE LIFE DEFINED (AS A LITTLE CHILD)
Hannah Whitall Smith

And Jesus called a little child unto him,
and set him in the midst of them,
And said, Verily I say unto you, Except
ye be converted, and become as little
children, ye shall not enter into
the kingdom of heaven.
MATTHEW 18:2–3

Now, what are the characteristics of a little child, and how does it live? It lives by faith, and its chief characteristic is freedom from care. Its life is one long trust from year's end to year's end. It trusts its parents, it trusts its caretakers, it trusts its teachers; it even trusts people sometimes who are utterly unworthy of trust, out of the abounding trustfulness of its nature. And this trust is abundantly answered. The child provides nothing for itself, and yet everything is provided. It lives in the present moment and receives its life unquestioningly as it comes to it day by day from its father's hands.

Who is the best cared for in every household? Is it not the little children? And does not the least of all, the helpless baby, receive the largest share? We all know that the baby toils not, neither does it spin; and yet it is fed, and clothed, and loved, and rejoiced in more tenderly than the hardest worker of them all.

This life of faith, then, about which I am writing, consists in just this—being a child in the Father's house. And when this is said, enough is said to transform every weary, burdened life into one of blessedness and rest.

TRUST AND FEAR NOT

Amy Carmichael

Let us listen to simple words; our Lord speaks simply: "Trust Me, My child." He says, "Trust Me with a humbler heart and a fuller abandon to My will than ever thou didst before.

"Trust Me to pour My love through thee, as minute succeeds minute. And if thou shouldst be conscious of anything hindering the flow, do not hurt My love by going away from Me in discouragement, for nothing can hurt love so much as that.

"Draw all the closer to Me; come, flee unto Me to hide thee even from thyself. Tell Me about the trouble. Trust Me to turn My hand upon thee and thoroughly remove the boulder that has choked thy riverbed, and take away all the sand that has silted up the channel.

"I will not leave thee until I have done what I have spoken to thee of. I will perfect what concerneth thee. Fear thou not, O child of My love, fear not."

Love, what is love?
Love is what inspired My life, and led Me to
My cross, and held Me on My cross.
Love is what will make it thy joy to lay
down thy life for thy brethren.
Lord, evermore give me this love.

I will say of the Lord, He is my refuge and my fortress: my God; in him will I trust.
PSALM 91:2

December 16

DOORKEEPER
Ruthe White

*See, I have placed before you
an open door that no one can shut.*
REVELATION 3:8 NIV

I am afraid, fearful of my own weaknesses, maybe even thinking what I have to give God is not quite good enough for His acceptance.

Sometimes I feel that the mental geniuses and the physically strong always walk ahead of me. They seem to pass through the open doors of opportunity, unaware of my long struggle in working, waiting for my turn; I need a chance to break loose from this cocoon of inferiority. Yesterday's disappointment will not stop me! What I was then is no excuse for what I am today. Instead of sitting down I will get up, and with every bit of energy I can muster I will as a not-so-saintly saint reach for my impossible dream.

With one deep breath I get up, struggling to stand on my own two feet. But I am standing! Steps are coming. . . . Wait. . .I see a door. . . . It is open. . .wide open. . .not closed, as I had thought. Someone is standing there. It is the Lord and I hear Him saying: "I know you well; you aren't strong, but you have tried to obey and have not denied my Name. Therefore I have opened a door to you that no man can shut" (see Revelation 3:8).

P.S. *"Forgive me, Lord, I forgot you are the DOORKEEPER AND THE DOOR!"*

LEFT ALONE
Mrs. Charles E. Cowman

Left alone! What different sensations those words conjure up to each of us.

To some they spell loneliness and desolation, to others rest and quiet. To be left alone without God would be too awful for words, but to be left alone with Him is a foretaste of heaven! If His followers spent more time alone with Him, we would have spiritual giants again.

The greatest miracles of Elijah and Elisha took place when they were alone with God. It was alone with God that Jacob became a prince. Moses was by himself at the wilderness bush (Exodus 3:1–5). Cornelius was praying by himself when the angel came to him (Acts 10:2). No one was with Peter on the housetop when he was instructed to go to the Gentiles (Acts 10:9). John the Baptist was alone in the wilderness (Luke 1:80), and John the Beloved was alone in Patmos, when nearest God (Revelation 1:9).

Covet to get alone with God. If we neglect it, we not only rob ourselves, but others, too, of blessing, since when we are blessed we are able to pass on blessing to others. It may mean less outside work; it must mean more depth and power, and the consequence, too, will be "they saw no man, save Jesus only" (Matthew 17:8).

To be alone with God in prayer cannot be overemphasized.

And Jacob was left alone;
and there wrestled a man with him
until the breaking of the day.
GENESIS 32:24

December 18

Is It a Good Buy?
Ruth Youngdahl Nelson

You fool! This very night your life will be demanded from you. Then who will get what you have prepared for yourself?
Luke 12:20 NIV

One would do well to read the entire parable with which Jesus concludes this decisive question. And we need to ponder the "bargains" that we have made.

A story about skylarks says that grandfather skylark takes the grandson high into the air to help train him. This little bird had only half an ear cocked to his grandfather's voice. His eyes were on a little man in the field below who was carrying an enticing sign. "Worms for sale: worms for skylark feathers." While his grandfather was absorbed in his rhetoric, the little bird scooped down to the man and asked how much. The reply was, "One worm for two skylark feathers." So the little bird made the transaction and was back at the grandfather's side. This was repeated each of the following days, until Saturday came. Then there was a bargain: five worms for ten skylark feathers.

The temptation to such a feast was too great for the little winged one, and he made the bargain. But when the ten feathers were plucked, he couldn't lift himself off the ground. He had sold his wings for worms.

Lord, help me to know that life has no bargains, that there is no shortcut to following You. Amen.

Good vs. Bad
Cheryl Biehl

For now, let me say that you can't do everything, but you can do what is best and most important for you. Few of us are tempted to allow bad things to keep us from achieving the best, but good things certainly can and do often consume our time, robbing us of what we want to do most.

In Philippians 1:9–11 (NIV), Paul tells the saints in Philippi of his prayer for them: "And this is my prayer: that your love may abound more and more in knowledge and depth of insight, so that you may be able to discern what is best and may be pure and blameless until the day of Christ, filled with the fruit of righteousness that comes through Jesus Christ—to the glory and praise of God."

Recall that there was a day when you looked down the continuum of seasons in your future and carefully chose the "best" for yourself as a Christian woman. You will be doing things because they are what you determined then were actually what you most wanted to do.

Other seasons in your future will afford you opportunities to achieve goals that you are currently postponing but not eliminating. Don't rob yourself of the joy of this season by wishing you were in a future or past one. Each season has its unique value; focus on present possibilities, and be content with today. Live each day to its fullest.

Shew me a token for good.
PSALM 86:17

GIVING GOD PLEASURE
Ruth Bell Graham

Know ye not, that to whom ye yield your-selves servants to obey, his servants ye are to whom ye obey; whether of sin unto death, or of obedience unto righteousness?
ROMANS 6:16

Grandmother's brother, Uncle Eddie McCue, lived on the old home place, "Belvidere," in the Shenandoah Valley of Virginia.

One day, while working the farm, he discarded his coat and told his collie dog, Chunk, to watch it.

That night, when Uncle Eddie got back to the house, he missed Chunk. No one had seen him. They called, but there was no response. Distressed, they ate supper, then continued searching. Bedtime came and still no Chunk. The next morning they looked outside hopefully. No sign of the old collie.

Time came for Uncle Eddie to return to the fields to work. There, in a distant field he saw something lying on the ground—his forgotten coat. And beside it lay Chunk, head and ears up, his plumed tail thumping the ground in the eager welcome.

It's the obedience training that gives us real joy. To stop, to sit, to lie down, to go away, to search, to stay, to heel. A disobedient dog is not only a headache; he can be a liability. Obedience makes a dog a joy.

Is it less so with God and His children?

ENDURING
Anna J. Lindgren

There was many a crisis time in my life, when eternal values hung in the balance; but not at such times did I meet the supreme test of character, or loyalty to Thee, my Lord. That test comes to me in the weary round of multitudinous and monotonous duties. It comes in the early morn, when my body cries louder for more sleep than my soul cries for Thee. "How hard it ofttimes is to see the dawn and gird up the soul for another day's high daring!" It comes—not so much when others have wronged me—as when I have wronged them, and my testimony has lost the ring of truth or is silenced.

First, I find clearly that Thou didst know who Thou wert. Thou didst know, and I, would I endure, must know who I am. I do know when I look upon the cross, and that is why I must never lose sight of it.

In the second place, I find that Thou didst know Thy mission. They tell me that Thou didst not, but they are wrong. They stupidly ignore that early in Thy earthly ministry the "must" of the cross was on Thy lips.

Then I find that Thou endured because of the joy set before Thee. "And the glory which thou gavest me I have given them; that they may be one, even as we are one" (John 17:22).

Thou therefore endure hardness, as a good soldier of Jesus Christ.
2 TIMOTHY 2:3

RACHEL
Gien Karssen

Rachel envied her sister; and said unto Jacob, Give me children, or else I die.
GENESIS 30:1

The human being is unable to change his own heart. Only God can transform it. Therefore He invites everyone to "Give Me your heart," to allow Him to work

Yet, in spite of His love, God often allows people to suffer in order to change their stubborn, self-willed hearts and bend them toward Him. He tests men and women to see if they are prepared to do His will.

In light of these facts, Rachel's heart was not exceptionally bad or unusually self-willed. Instead of surrendering her life to God, she chose to govern her own life. That wrong decision of self-rule led to egotism and multiplied her personal problems.

In spite of the seriousness and unhappiness of Rachel's person, a ray of hope still existed in her older son, Joseph. He was still young when his mother died, but he grew up to be an exceptional man of God.

Did Rachel's heart go out to God in the last phase of her life? Did the motherless boy, Joseph, become the product of his father's education? Or had Rachel changed enough through God's power that she was able to make an indelible impression upon him?

Whatever the answers, Rachel's pitiful and unfulfilled life could have been exciting and full of meaning if only her inner beauty had matched her lovely outward appearance.

GOING FORTH
Twila Paris with Robert Webber

"I Am Ready" is a song that expresses our going forth into the world to love and serve the Lord. This is one of those songs that just came to me out of my heart while I was responding to what God was doing in my life. Let me explain.

Like a lot of people, I'm not anxious to move out into the cruel and unknown world. But God was prompting me to move out. I wasn't sure that I had the gifts or talents to do what God was asking, so in my heart I was going through some resistance. But later, when I yielded to God, I knew that God would go with me.

A worship dismissal charges us to go forth into the world to be who God wants us to be and to do what God wants us to do. Our response to God's sending us should be to say, "Lord, I want to do what You're asking me to do, and I don't want to hold back anymore."

I need to hear myself say those words because I've had a tendency to hold my arms in close and protect myself. But I know the only protection is God. I know it's silly to hold back and be afraid of anything God wants of me. But refusing to do what God wants feeds the fear. It's the opposite of what you would expect. Doing God's will is a release.

The eternal God is thy refuge, and underneath are the everlasting arms: and he shall thrust out the enemy from before thee; and shall say, Destroy them.
DEUTERONOMY 33:27

By the Manger

Anna J. Lindgren

Let us now go even unto Bethlehem,
and see this thing which is come to pass,
which the Lord hath made known unto us.
LUKE 2:15

"Dark the night of sin had settled." To bring Light into that darkness God came to Bethlehem. God! How I have tried to comprehend that fact—tried in vain. I have listened to the voice of God, in the morning of time, as He spoke His creative words, "Let there be," and I have seen worlds flung into space, suns come into existence, the "Milky Way" span the measureless deep, and the countless orbs of light spring forth, at His bidding, and in dazed wonder I have cried out, "God!"

But when I come "even unto Bethlehem" with its lowing oxen, its straw, and its manger, and behold a helpless babe, my soul is too perplexed for words. I hear the angels' glory-song, and as I gaze upwards I catch a glimpse of a radiance that dazzles and a blinding light, and I see that the song that ripples down from heaven is sung by countless millions of adoring angels. What can I bring unto the One to whom all things belong! There is only one gift worthy of giving—that is mine to give—undying love, unbroken allegiance, ceaseless praise.

I want to stand by the manger long enough for all my foolish pride to die, all my vainglory to vanish, and my estimate of values to become adjusted to the humility that is God.

THE TRUE CHRISTMAS SPIRIT

Emilie Barnes

Markham wrote a poem based on a story by Tolstoy.

One night Conrad, a cobbler of shoes, dreamed that Christ would come to his shop on the following day. All morning he waited, but the only visitor was an old man who asked if he might sit down to rest. Conrad put the best pair of shoes in the shop on the old man's feet. Throughout the afternoon the only person he saw was an old woman struggling under a heavy load. Out of compassion he brought her in and gave her some of the food he had prepared for Christ. Just as evening was falling, a lost child entered Conrad's shop. Conrad carried the child home.

Finally, in disappointment, the old cobbler cried:

"Why is it, Lord, that Your feet delay?
Did You forget that this was the day?"
Then soft in the silence a voice he heard:
"Lift up your heart, for I kept My word.
Three times I came to your friendly door;
Three times My shadow was on your floor.
I was the beggar with the bruised feet;
I was the woman you gave to eat;
I was the child on the homeless street!"

May you find the joy of sharing with others in need. Then Christmas for you will not merely be a holiday, but a holy day.

Do to others what you would have them do to you, for this sums up the Law and the Prophets.
MATTHEW: 7:12 NIV

GOD'S BEST SECRET
Joni Eareckson Tada

I have learned, in whatsoever state I am, therewith to be content.
PHILIPPIANS 4:11

Webster defines "secret" as something beyond normal comprehension—something obscure, hidden from view, concealed from knowledge.

In light of that, it's curious that in Philippians, Paul says he has learned the "secret" of being content in any and every situation. Have you ever wondered what "secret" Paul was talking about?

Perhaps Paul's secret of learning to be content was simply learning to lean on God's grace.

What a secret, this working of grace in our lives!

A friend of mine named Susan recently experienced unbearable pain with the sudden, unexpected breakup of her marriage. I watched Susan go through months of agony, struggling against rejection and just plain nausea. But God's grace sustained her in a startling way. In fact, she commented to me that she believed the hardest thing to explain was how grace was at work in her life. To her, and to those of us who watched the tragedy, the sustaining, preserving, uplifting power of God's grace was truly a mystery. A wondrous secret none of us could understand.

Are you struggling today with discontentment, frustration, disappointment, or downright irritation? Take a moment right now to quiet your heart and listen to God's best secret—it's called grace, and it sounds like this:

Have hope. Take hold. He is sufficient.

THE PRINCIPLE OF RECOMPENSE

Jo Berry

The wicked worketh a deceitful work:
but to him that soweth righteousness
shall be a sure reward.
PROVERBS 11:18

Scripture teaches that for everything we do there is a consequence that is commensurate with the deed. This law of recompense, as stated in Proverbs 12:14 (NASB), says that, "The deeds of a man's hands will return to him." The apostle Paul, in Galatians 6:7 (NASB), explains it this way: "Whatever a man sows, this he will also reap." In science this dictum is called Newton's Third Law of Motion: "To every force and action, there is an equal and opposite reaction."

For some reason, many people approach this axiom from a negative point of view. They see it as a sort of, "If you aren't careful, you're going to get it," warning. And, depending on how they live their lives, that may be true.

An old proverb translates it as, "What goes around, comes around."

Exactly how does this "carousel theory" work? For example, if you chose to lose your temper, you will get turmoil in return because, "A hot-tempered man stirs up strife" (Proverbs 15:18 NASB). But, if you stay calm and are a peacemaker rather than an agitator, your life will be more harmonious because, "A gentle answer turns away wrath" (Proverbs 15:1 NASB). We can interpret these kinds of injunctions to mean that what we do boomerangs—it comes back to us in kind.

GROWING IN CHRIST
Hannah Whitall Smith

Consider the lilies how they grow.
LUKE 12:27

What we all need is to "consider the flowers of the field," and learn their secret. Grow, by all means, dear Christians; but grow, I beseech you, in God's way, which is the only effectual way. See to it that you are planted in grace, and then let the Divine Husbandman cultivate you in His own way and by His own means. Put yourselves out in the sunshine of His presence, and let the dew of heaven come down upon you, and see what will be the result. Leaves and flowers and fruit must surely come in their season; for your Husbandman is skilful, and He never fails in His harvesting. Only see to it that you oppose no hindrance to the shining of the Sun of Righteousness or the falling of the dew from heaven. The thinnest covering may serve to keep off the sunshine and the dew, and the plant may wither, even where these are most abundant. And so also the slightest barrier between your soul and Christ may cause you to dwindle and fade, as a plant in a cellar or under a bushel. Keep the sky clear. Open wide every avenue of your being to receive the blessed influences your Divine Husbandman may bring to bear upon you. Bask in the sunshine of His love. Drink of the waters of His goodness. Keep your face upturned to Him as the flowers do to the sun. Look, and your soul shall live and grow.

REACHING
Jill Briscoe

The Queen of Hearts started where she was with what she had. She was aware of her neighborhood and the troubled people that lived there. First, we need to reach out just where we are. It is an incredible thing to me that we can live such isolated lives, not even knowing the name of folks who live next door, in the name of respecting their privacy and independence. "It's none of my business," we say, shrugging our shoulders when we are told our neighbor has lost his job. God has made it His business to care, and what is His business is your business and my business. There may be real financial and material need right next door that we can tactfully alleviate.

One Christian I know heard the rumor that the husband of a young girl who lived on his street had just run out on her. "That's their concern, not mine," said the man. "I have enough trouble keeping my own marriage intact without worrying about anybody else's!" Little did he know that within three months, the young mother, not knowing what to do, had allowed herself to get into such a financial mess that she was selling her blood to the blood bank to help put food on the table! Start by looking at the need within reach; then reach out and meet it.

For if there be first a willing mind, it is accepted according to that a man hath, and not according to that he hath not.
2 CORINTHIANS 8:12

A NEW YEAR'S MEDITATION

Anna J. Lindgren

And a man shall be as an hiding place from the wind, and a covert from the tempest; as rivers of water in a dry place, as the shadow of a great rock in a weary land.
ISAIAH 32:2

The Millennium is ever nearing! Let me not forget it! Let the thought so take possession of me, this New Year's, that the Light of Eternity might fall over the commonplace, that my perspective may be truer and my horizon wider.

"Beneath the Cross of Jesus I fain would take my stand,
*   The shadow of a mighty Rock, within a weary land.*
*   Content to let the world go by, to know no gain nor loss,*
*   My sinful self my only shame, my glory all the Cross."*

My shame, as I look back, is that I gloried so little in the Cross. I gloried more in the knowledge I had and the sermons I preached.

Oh, my Lord, how many are they, back there, who failed to see the glory of the Cross because of an "unemphasized or wrongly emphasized word of mine"?

*   I need Thee with a deep, yearning need this year.*

CORRIE TEN BOOM'S TRADITION

Quin Sherrer and Laura Watson

When we moved to north Florida, we were part of a care group at Mike and Fran Ewing's home. A bonus was attending their New Year's Eve party each year. Because the Dutch evangelist Corrie ten Boom had used the Ewings' home as her "hiding place" for many years, her family's New Year's Eve tradition became theirs (and ours).

Just before midnight Mike opened his Bible, as Papa ten Boom had done, to read Psalm 91. When the clock struck midnight, we all hugged each other and cheered in the New Year. Always, from somewhere down the street, firecrackers exploded. The whole world had started a New Year.

Just as the first words the ten Booms heard in the New Year were from Psalm 91, so were ours.

Traditions, we either love them or fear them. But we all have them.

Any custom that has been repeated must have started with a good idea. The problem comes when we forget why we still dutifully perform the function.

So let's consider how we can build God-honoring traditions to make ours a household of blessing.

Yet I will rejoice in the Lord,
I will joy in the God of my salvation.
HABAKKUK 3:18

INDEX OF AUTHORS

ACKNOWLEDGMENTS

Barbour Publishing, Inc. expresses its appreciation to all those who generously gave permission to reprint and/or adapt copyrighted material. Diligent effort has been made to identify, locate, and contact copyright holders and to secure permission to use copyrighted material. If any permissions or acknowledgments have been inadvertently omitted or if such permissions were not received by the time of publication, the publisher would sincerely appreciate receiving complete information so that correct credit can be given in future editions.

"With Eyes Shut Tight" "Is Anybody Home?" "Mother," "Let Me See Your Face," by Doris Coffin Aldrich, from *Musings of a Mother* (Chicago, IL: Moody Bible Institute, 1949). Used by permission of Willard M. Aldrich.

"Give God Time," by Ann Kiemel Anderson, from *The Greatest Lesson I've Ever Learned*. ©Copyright 1991 by Bill Bright, Here's Life Publishers (now *New Life* Publications), Campus Crusade for Christ. All rights reserved. Used by permission.

"You'll Never Be Alone Again," "When Your Guilt Is Gone, You Have Peace," by Kay Arthur, from *Lord, Is It Warfare? Teach Me to Stand* (Portland, OR: Multnomah Books, 1991). Used by permission.

"God's Love," by Ney Bailey, from *The Greatest Lesson I've Ever Learned* (San Bernardino, CA: Here's Life Publishers, 1990). Used by permission of the author.

"Stand by Your God," "Offer Hospitality," "The True Christmas Spirit" by Emilie Barnes, from *15 Minutes Alone with God* (Eugene, OR: Harvest House Publishers, 1994). Used by permission.

"Keep Your Eye on the Rose," by Peggy Benson, from *Friends Through Thick & Thin* by Gloria Gaither, Sue Buchanan, Peggy Benson, and Joy MacKenzie. Copyright© 1998 by Gloria Gaither, Sue Buchanan, Peggy Benson, and Joy MacKenzie. Used by permission of Zondervan Publishing House, Grand Rapids, MI.

"Fear of the Lord," "The Principles of Trust," "Wising Up," "Wising Up About Money," "Cost of Good Living," "Gossip (Watch What You Say!)," "The Principle of Recompense," by Jo Berry, from *Proverbs for Easier Living*, copyright© 1980 Regal Books, Ventura, CA 93003. Used by permission.

"Shake Us To Wake Us," "Sarah's Beauty Regimen," by Lisa Bevere, from *Out of Control and Loving It!* (Lake Mary, FL: Creation House, 1996). Used by permission.

"Setting Goals for This Year," "Setting Time Aside Daily," "Coming Before the Holy God

"A Blessed New Year," "Conflicts Changed to Blessings," "Sorrow's Scars," "A Bountiful Blessing," "He Lives!" "Wings of Growth," "Contentment," "The Closure of Forget-Me-Nots," "Diamonds in the Rough," "Morning on the Mount," "Sailing by Faith," "Praying Patiently," "The Dove of Faith," "Pray and Believe," "Left Alone," by Mrs. Charles E. Cowman, from *Streams in the Desert* (Grand Rapids, MI: Zondervan Publishing House, 1925, 1959).

"Working Wonders," "Easter Week," "To Pray in the Name of Jesus," by Mrs. Charles E. Cowman, from *Streams in the Desert, Volume 2* (Grand Rapids, MI: Zondervan Publishing House, 1966).

"Into the Closet," "Little Things Mean a Lot," "Are You Listening?" "The Divine Ideal," by Linda Dillow, from *Creative Counterpart* (Nashville, TN: Thomas Nelson, Inc., Publishers, 1977). Used by permission.

"Let My Roots Sink Deep," "I Want to Leave My Mark for You," "I Don't Like My Job," "Through Life's Changes," "Comforter," "Depression," by Anita Corrine Donihue, from *When I'm on My Knees* (Uhrichsville, OH: Barbour Publishing, Inc., 1997).

"Angels," "I Won't Worry for the Future," "Say 'Yes' to God," "The Great Commission," "Praise You, Because of. . . ," "Take Comfort," by Anita Corine Donihue, from *When I'm Praising God* (Uhrichsville, OH: Barbour Publishing, Inc., 1999).

"The Coat," by Anita Corrine Donihue and Colleen Reece, from *A Teacher's Heart* (Uhrichsville, OH: Barbour Publishing, Inc., 1998).

"What Wonders!" "Blessed Are the Meek," "Blessed Are the Peacemakers," "Blessed Are the Pure in Heart," by Eileen Egan and Kathleen Egan, O.S.B., from *Blessed Are You: Mother Teresa and the Beatitudes* (Ann Arbor, MI: Servant Publications, 1992). Used by permission.

"The Desires of My Heart," "Wastelands," "Faith Is Holding Out Your Hand," "One Reason for Darkness," "Leave Her to Me," "All Things Serve Thee," "Volunteer Slaves," "Love of the World," by Elisabeth Elliot, from *A Lamp for My Feet*, copyright© 1985 by Elisabeth Elliot. Ann Arbor, MI: Servant Publications. Used by permission.

"Learning to Say No," by Colleen Townsend Evans, from *The Greatest Lesson I've Ever Learned.* ©Copyright 1991 by Bill Bright, Here's Life Publishers (now *New Life* Publications), Campus Crusade for Christ. All rights reserved. Used by permission.

"Finding Your Ministry," by Melinda Fish, adapted from *Restoring the Wounded Woman* (Grand Rapids, MI: Chosen Books, a division of Baker Book House, 1993). Used by permission.

"Tensions," "Contentment," "Solitude," "Principles Alone Are Not Enough," "Setting

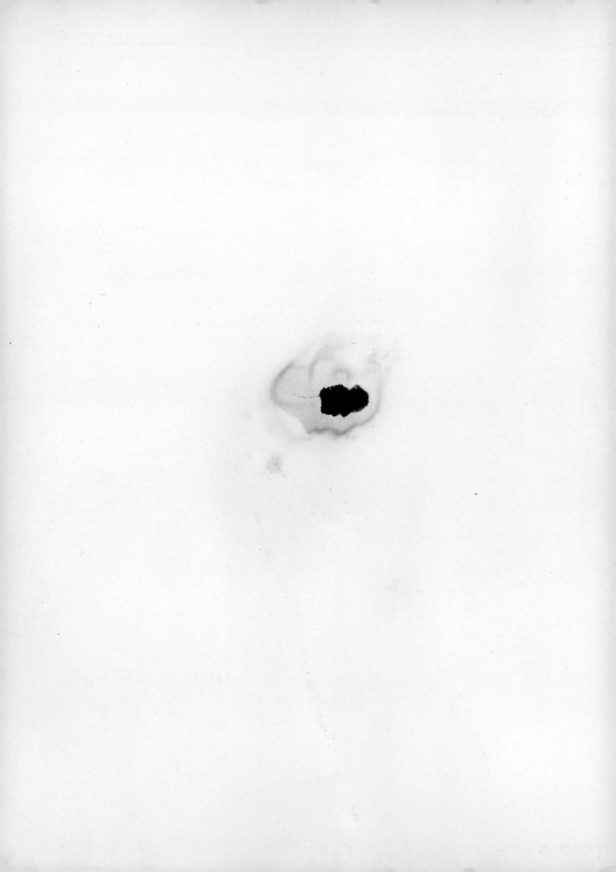